UNDERSTANDING
HUMOR IN JAPAN

Humor in Life and Letters Series

*A complete listing of the books in this series
can be found online at http://wsupress.wayne.edu*

GENERAL EDITOR

Sarah Blacher Cohen
State University of New York, Albany

ADVISORY EDITORS

Joseph Boskin
Boston University

Gerald Gardner
Author and lecturer

Alan Dundes
University of California, Berkeley

Jeffrey H. Goldstein
*Temple University and
London University*

William F. Fry, Jr.
Stanford University Medical School

Don L. F. Nilsen
Arizona State University

June Sochen
Northeastern Illinois University

UNDERSTANDING HUMOR IN JAPAN

Edited by
JESSICA MILNER DAVIS

WAYNE STATE UNIVERSITY PRESS   DETROIT

Published by Wayne State University Press, Detroit, Michigan, 48201.

No part of this book may be reproduced without formal permission.

Manufactured in the United States of America.

ISBN-13: 978-0-8143-3165-1   ISBN-10: 0-8143-3165-3

Library of Congress Cataloging-in-Publication Data

Understanding humor in Japan / edited by Jessica Milner Davis.
p. cm. — (Humor in life and letters series)
Includes bibliographical references and index.
ISBN 0-8143-3165-3 (pbk. : alk. paper)
1. Japanese wit and humor—History and criticism. 2. East and West.
I. Davis, Jessica Milner. II. Humor in life and letters.
PN6222.J3U57 2005
152.4′3′0952—dc22
2005007612

∞

Cover illustration: Reproduction of a red, white, and black *banzuke* (traditional poster program) for the regular comedy performance at the Ikebukuro Engeijō, a *yose* (variety hall) in Tokyo, September 11–20, 1988. Reproduced by kind permission of the management.

Key (translation and explanation by Marguerite Wells): The top band (reading left to right) gives the date, "11–20 September of the 63rd year of the Shōwa era" (1988).

The second band (reading down from the right) is the matinee program, beginning at 1 p.m. on Saturdays, Sundays, and public holidays only; it lists the performers' names. Most of the acts were *rakugo* (traditional comic narrative), but there were two double acts, probably *manzai* (stand-up comedy). The performers' names for the double acts are written in smaller characters and bracketed together. In this traditionally male theater world, one of the acts (Yukie and Hanako) is, interestingly, a double act by two women.

The third and fourth bands, again reading down from the right, give the bill for the evening performance, beginning at 5 p.m. Again, the acts (including a singer) are mostly one-handers, but some are double acts. The performers' names include Umpei, Nompei, Gimpei, Kampei, Shimpei, Kompei, Gempei, and just Pei. They belong to a school of *rakugo* that gives all its disciples stage names with the same final syllable.

The bottom band (reading left to right) gives the name, location, and telephone number of the yose: "Ikebukuro Engeijō, Third Floor, Umeda Building, in front of the west entrance to Ikebukuro Station, phone, Tokyo 971-4545." Opened in 1951, the Ikebukuro Engeijō closed down in 1990, reopening in September 1993 after being rebuilt.

CONTENTS

ILLUSTRATIONS

PREFACE

Although I have immersed myself principally in European comedy since selecting it as the topic for my doctoral dissertation more than thirty years ago,[1] I had long wanted to investigate styles of comedy and humor in Japan. The inspiration came from the fact that my early training in the history of world theater was provided by a fine scholar and man of the theater, C. Robert B. Quentin, who had some familiarity with traditional Japanese theater forms and was a student of Buddhism long before that was common or fashionable in the West. We students wrote *nō* versions of Hamlet, watched films of *bunraku* and *kabuki* performances, and wrestled with notions of *yūgen* and the translated writings of Kanami and Zeami. Naturally, when I began to study comparative versions of farce, I wanted to include *kyōgen*. But both time and language were a barrier.

My fine aspirations had to wait until I met Japanese scholars who shared my interests. Precisely because the traditions and realities of Japan are so different from those of the rest of the world, deep knowledge of both its language and it culture is essential if one is to venture on more than a toe-dipping exercise. Over the last few years such a group of scholars has come together, thanks to two organizations and their leaders: the Japan Society for Laughter and Humor Studies (JSLHS) and the International Society for Humor Studies (ISHS). The founding executive secretary of the ISHS, Don Nilsen, and its 2000 president, Alleen Nilsen, have always encouraged the society's efforts to be truly international, as has the editorial leadership of its scholarly publication, *Humor: The International Journal of Humor Research.* In 1996, when I served as the society's president and as co-chair of its eighth Conference (held in Sydney, Australia), I was inspired by colleagues from Japan, including Goh Abe and Kimie Ōshima, who presented fascinating papers on forms of Japanese humor both ancient and modern. The formation of the JSLHS in Osaka that same year, with Emeritus Professor Hiroshi Inoue as founding president, ensured that at each international conference thereafter (and at JSLHS meetings, of course) additional material has been presented. It was clear that there was much to be conveyed to the non-Japanese reader interested in humor; as a result, the present volume began to take shape.

It was, however, the generous offer of counsel and help from my now retired colleague Dr. Marguerite Wells that made the project of collecting and editing some of this material seem practicable. When we first met at the 1996 conference, we found that we were located in the same geographical corner of the world and shared the same interest in Japanese humor. Dr. Wells, an established scholar of Japanese culture and language, was about to publish a major book on the general subject of Japanese theories of humor,[2] and I had a broad background in studying humorous genres and types of comedy, with particular expertise in farce. She had trained in kyōgen acting and knew and loved the genre. We both knew several of our prospective colleagues, in Japan and elsewhere, and realized that there was a real need for a book that would be accessible to more than just the scholarly world (although it should satisfy those high standards among others).

Actually, if either of us had had the slightest idea of the technological minefields awaiting us as we exchanged e-mail texts around the globe and corrected *kanji* in multiple variations of font and program, we might never have volunteered for the project. But the result, I believe, has been worth it. Here is a book that provides both an accessible introduction to the subject for those unfamiliar with Japanese culture and an illuminating overview of the subject for those with extensive cultural knowledge. This is possible because it collects in one place a range of previously unpublished work and underpins each chapter with numerous concrete examples of the kind of humor being discussed, along with meticulous acknowledgment of sources. As many readers know, this kind of rigor is all too rare even in works intended for scholarly audiences on Japanese culture, let alone the more general reader.

It would never have been possible to conclude this work without Dr. Wells's guiding hand. Despite ill health, she provided an invaluable source of advice and expertise. Not the least of her contributions, drawn from many years' experience and scholarship in teaching and publishing in Japanese/English, was to assist in the preparation of the principles set out in the Editor's Note, which have guided me as editor of this volume. Indeed, for this whole book, Dr. Wells has been the *sine qua non*. Other colleagues and coauthors have also extended generous help, particularly Professors Abe and Kobayashi, in the vexed matter of checking references and obtaining permission to reproduce from rare sources held in Japan. This has made possible the illustrations, which go a little way at least to fleshing out the verbal wit being discussed. It is fatally easy in writing about humor to lose sight of the fact that even a joking exchange in everyday conversation is also a small comic performance, as many of these pictures show.

I also wish to express my deep appreciation to the editorial staff at Wayne State University Press, who were keen to include this volume in their Humor in Life and Letters Series. Again, it was a baptism of fire in terms of the technical challenges, but from the beginning, under the guiding hand of the series editor, Dr. Sarah Blacher Cohen, the Press appreciated the unique value of this academic but practical study. Refusing to be dismayed by the many difficulties, many staff members have shepherded the volume through its long gestation and brought it to life in its present form.

NOTES

1. Jessica Milner Davis, *The Mechanics of European Farce*, 3 vols., available electronically on the Australian Digital Theses (ADT) Program at http://adt.caul.edu.au/

2. Marguerite Wells, *Japanese Humour* (Basingstoke: Macmillan, 1997).

EDITOR'S NOTE

1. Japanese names are given in the Japanese order, family name first, then personal name. An exception is made for the names of the Japanese authors of chapters in this volume. These are given in European order, except where they appear as authors cited in references, in which case Japanese order is followed for consistency.
2. A modified version of the Hepburn system of romanization of Japanese words is used. Macrons are used to mark long vowels (e.g., "ō" for "ou").
3. Archaic Japanese spellings have been modernized, except where noted.
4. Recognizable words and place-names such as Osaka and Tokyo are given their common English spellings rather than their lengthened Japanese vowels (e.g., Ōsaka).
5. The Japanese word for "newspaper" is spelled in Japanese *shinbun*. In this book it is spelled *shimbun* so that the non-specialist reader will pronounce it correctly.
6. In pronouncing Japanese, it may be helpful for readers to note that there are five pure vowels in the spoken language (as in Italian) and that each vowel is given its full weight, as in the word *yose* (variety hall), pronounced *yore-say*.
7. All translations into English are original unless otherwise stated. In the case of classical poetry, the brevity of the Japanese forms may give rise on some occasions to unintended parallels with previously published English versions.
8. Every effort has been made to locate and acknowledge copyright ownership of the textual and illustrative material reproduced; where possible, full acknowledgments have been made in the text and/or notes.

Introduction

Jessica Milner Davis

This book presents a lively demonstration of why humor in Japan is often thought of as uncommon, obscure, incomprehensible, paradoxical, totally dissimilar to humor elsewhere, perhaps even nonexistent. In fact, the reverse is often true: funniness is frequent and well signaled, and it can be very much "in your face." It is not necessary to understand all the twists and turns of subtle Japanese *sha-re* (しゃれ；洒落 linguistic puns)[1] to appreciate the main point of their humor; and comedy, while paradoxical by nature, in Japan as elsewhere runs true to its own rules of logic. As for comparisons with humor elsewhere in the world, if one is watching Japanese television (with the sound off) while a pair of stand-up *manzaishi* comedians banter with each other, it is easy to wonder if the resulting spectacle is a program from Japan, North America, or Australia, so universal are these humorous semiotics. After editing the wise and readable chapters that make up this book, I can safely conclude that in Japan, as around the world, humor is an irrepressible force—if one knows where and when to look for it. However, I have learned that humor is not always permitted to appear in the same places and under the same conditions as in European cultures. These matters should be of major interest to all those who like to visit and do business in Japan as well as to those who take a scholarly interest in Japanese language and culture, and humor studies generally.

No matter how sensitive the non-Japanese speaker is to cultural differences, it is not always obvious where exactly to look for permission for humor's operations in Japan. Take for example the print media, specifically newspapers. Accustomed to a daily diet of cartoons (political and otherwise), gossip columns, humorous op-ed pieces, and letters to the editor that characterize general English-language newspapers (let alone specialist magazines), visitors to Japan may well puzzle over precisely which columns constitute the humorous component in the *Asahi Shimbun*. And they might be forgiven for missing the postage-stamp-sized columns to which it is allocated. Here there are indeed genuine differences in culture that need to be explored, as they are in chapter 11 by Hiroshi Inoue. The writer reflects persuasively a growing view that a larger role for humor in discussion of Japan's polity and economic problems would actually be healthy and healing for both the nation and its people.

In the electronic media, however, the case is very different, especially on television. What with drama, stand-ups, advertising, and talk shows and their idols (the *aidoru* アイドル of the younger generations), this most commercial of formats is saturated with laughter and joking in which the visual components are equal to the linguistic. In chapter 5, Heiyō Nagashima examines the link between the linguistic structures of the Japanese language and the nature of wordplay and its widespread use, for example in advertising and mnemonics generally. And for stand-up comedy, both live and on television, Joel Stocker explores in chapter 4 the deeply rooted folk tradition of *manzai* and how deliberate exposure to western forms of comedy onstage and in silent movies brought about a popular and commercial transformation, molding an ancient art to become part of Japan's deliberate process of modernization, particularly in prewar years.

Despite such overt similarities in entertainment between East and West, conversational norms are markedly different in English and Japanese, and these directly affect the employment of humor as a conversational strategy. Makiko Takekuro's analysis in chapter 6 of the linguistic differences in episodes of joke-telling between Japanese "real-life" films and those from the United States goes a long way toward explaining the pervasive sense of "otherness," of "that's not the way we do things," that haunts contact and communication between the two cultures. As in the case of newspaper humor, it is a question of understanding when and where joking is permissible. In chapter 7, Kimie Ōshima explores the age-old form of comic storytelling called *rakugo*, showing how it both exploits and depends upon the conventions of appropriate conversational exchange in Japanese culture. To visit the *rakugo* theater is to enter one of the most obvious of Japanese "laughter places" (笑いの場 *warai no ba*, described by Shōkichi Oda in chapter 1), a place where humor can be safely and openly indulged.

But even when the environmental parameters—the "when" and the "where" of laughter—do allow joking, the "what" and the "how" operate in a way that also differs markedly from English-language cultural conventions. Hiroshi Inoue's examination in chapter 2 of the merchant culture of Osaka (Japan's second principal city) and of the practical value of humor in enabling people to rise to life's everyday challenges shines further light on that subject. And yet, despite all differences, English-language performances of *rakugo* can have their non-Japanese audiences enthralled by laughter and by the universal wisdom of the narrator's comic insights into our common humanity. Ms. Ōshima's recent successful tours of English-language *rakugo* in both Australia and the United States demonstrate from the delight of her audiences that this mix of static mime and lively comic storytelling certainly has the power to cross cultural boundaries and provoke laughter.[2]

Behind these commonalities and differences lies a wariness toward laughter and being laughed at which, although in some senses universal (no one really enjoys being laughed at, except perhaps comedians paid for their art and suffering), operates with particular force in the "shame culture" of Japan. The interdiction on being held up to ridicule that was enshrined by samurai culture struck most forcibly those visitors from the West who made first contact with Japan and its people. It appears paradoxical: how can a people enjoy laughter so much in certain circumstances and disapprove of it so strongly in all others? This was not the puritanical blanket disapproval of all laughter and indulgence familiar to the European Protestant tradition—it was, and is, something much more complex. The introduction to these ancient cultural conventions provided by Shōkichi Oda in chapter 1 is a sensitive recitation of some of the most telling early stories of bewilderment and misunderstanding. Mr. Oda reveals what lies behind the pervasive link in high Japanese culture of the notions of beauty, laughter, and tears: "smiling on the outside, crying on the inside" (顔で笑って心で泣いて *kao de waratte, kokoro de naite*), as the old saying goes. For scholars and lovers of humor around the world reading this chapter, it might well seem that such moments of ambivalence are deeply related to our common efforts to grasp the nature of eternal truth.

Indeed, for Japanese people, the act of laughing could be said to be the act of successful preservation of the Japanese world: it was the Sun Goddess herself who restored light and life to the world after an eclipse by responding to laughter. The story is told in the *Kojiki*, Japan's oldest extant chronicle, which is known to have existed in A.D. 712 (the Nara period). It is described by Marguerite Wells in her study of Japanese humor as Japan's first comedy performance.[3] Amaterasu Ōmikami (ancestress of the Imperial family) hid herself in a cave, bringing on an eclipse and many disasters; but then one of the lesser goddesses intervened:

> AMË-NÖ-UZUME-NÖ-MIKÖTÖ bound up her sleeves with a cord of heavenly PI-KAGË vine, tied around her head a headband of the heavenly MA-SAKI vine, bound together bundles of SASA leaves to hold in her hands, and overturning a bucket before the heavenly rock-cave door, stamped resoundingly upon it. Then she became divinely possessed, exposed her breasts, and pushed her skirtband down to her genitals. Then TAKAMA-NÖ-PARA shook as the eight-hundred myriad deities laughed at once.[4]

Wells emphasizes that "the gods laugh repeatedly in the story as they go on to trick the goddess into emerging again into the world. The word used is *warau*, written *saku*, to blossom. Each time it is a case of humorous laughter."[5] The result of this trick, effectively a divinely performed "comical strip," was a creative rebirth. Comical striptease remains an important component of the varieties of nonrefined humor in Japan, and I will have more to say about it below.

The crucial ceremonial role played by laughter and humor in Japan is evidenced by the fact that yearly rituals directly relating to this tradition are current and even today are being actively transmitted from one generation to the next in some rural communities. In chapter 3, Goh Abe surveys such ritual survivals and conveys a sense of their continued spirit and meaning in these urbanized times. At a time when "laughter clubs" are springing up anew around the world in response to modern stresses and

4

anomie, and when medical evidence is growing for the value, in both physiological and emotional terms, of cheerful laughter, it is significant that the Japanese way of life has preserved this special place for laughter from time immemorial.

Of course, Japanese laughter is not confined by the cycle of the year, however important times of holiday enjoyment and time-out may be. Nor is laughter thought of as merely an expression of folk culture: humor and comedy span the full range of culture from high to low. From earliest human times, the literary and dramatic traditions have aspired to encapsulate delicate and witty laughter. In Japanese drama, ritual origins are as significant as they are in the European theater, and their tokens are well preserved in contemporary performance traditions of *nō*, *bunraku*, and *kabuki*, all of which remain popular if elite forms of drama. A range of styles of humor and laughter has always been integral to these forms, providing comic relief to their accounts of the high drama and moral dilemmas that bespeak the samurai culture in its golden age. For *nō* it is the *kyōgen* plays that correspond to the more familiar Greek satyr plays and the Old Comedy of classical Greece in the fifth century B.C. (Marguerite Wells and Jessica Milner Davis explore the history and nature of this comic tradition in chapter 9). The comic force of these playlets and the brilliance of their burlesque, *commedia dell'arte*–style acting mean that Japan possesses some of the world's best examples of farce. The stock comic types of the scheming servant and his fellow link directly to the roles of the *tsukkomi* (つっこみ the "sharp man") and the *boke* (ボケ the fool) in *manzai* and stand-up comedy. As comic creations they lose nothing in comparison with the scheming slaves of Roman comedy or the witty valets of Molière and Beaumarchais. Everywhere in the world of Japanese entertainment, humor flourishes and continues to be appreciated by young and old alike.

In terms of poetic and literary expression of humor, Japan has developed specialized forms for it and for the encouragement of smiling and laughter. As Heiyō Nagashima describes in chapter 5, these forms naturally respond to the richness and special linguistic characteristics of the Japanese language. With an influential inheritance of both written forms and some poetic structural models from Chinese traditions, and possessing not only their own mythology of divine insight through laughter but

5

also specialized linguistic and cultural forms, Japanese writers have evolved their own responses to poetic humor. Despite the conventionally low literary status of comedy, these forms have been and continue to be eagerly pursued, but they are not particularly well known. As several of this book's contributors point out, the whole world knows and loves the form of *haiku*, Japan's famous form of condensed three-line verse. However, very few outside Japan have any idea of the riches of the companion form of *senryū*. And yet this form is the poetic equivalent of the verbal puns (*sha-re*) that are so widely delighted in as a part of Japanese written and oral communication. The masterpieces of *senryū* cross socioeconomic boundaries to provide an outlet for wry reproof and ironic comment on the ways of the world, and they have done so for more than two centuries. As Hiroshi Inoue demonstrates in chapter 11, the *senryū* in the daily newspapers tell you more than all the diplomatic briefings and foreign affairs analyses ever will about what the ordinary Japanese person is thinking—and feeling—concerning public affairs. But one must understand the form and its delicate witticisms before that truth will out. In three concise but telling discussions of comic poetic form, Shōkichi Oda, Masashi Kobayashi, and Rokuo Tanaka (chapters 1, 10, and 8) provide an explication of the *senryū* and the *kyōka*, identify their historical precedents, and offer a wealth of entertaining examples and discussion of methodology.

And yet, for all their riches, the Japanese humor traditions have only ever given mild expression to a formal satiric critique of society's evils—its politics, fools, and upstarts. In part that is because subtlety of effect is not always consonant with the rough-and-ready ways of satire, which, to be successful, must make its purposes reasonably plain and unmistakable. As Marguerite Wells discusses, the genre's openly stated motivation of "rocking the boat in order to turn it about, if not over" sits uneasily with other conventions embodied in Japanese society and culture. These involve a tradition of formal state-sanctioned censorship of comic poetry (as Masashi Kobayashi explores in chapter 10), but even more significantly, they depend upon internal control and culturally self-imposed restraint, matters that are elaborated in chapters 1 and 12 by Oda and Wells. In chapter 6, Makiko Takekuro also points out the importance in all joke-telling of the fact that only particular kinds of interpersonal relations between the joker and others are considered appropriate in Japanese culture and language. From this flows the convention that, under normal circumstances, joking and humor occur only in the closer types of relationships. In the discussion in chapter 7 of *rakugo*'s narrative strategies, Kimie Ōshima tellingly observes (from personal experience) that it is customary to "rewrite" the story of a funny happening when retelling it so as to point it more directly to the narrator in self-deprecation, rather than allowing the inference that it happened to persons in a more distant relationship (who should be accorded proper respect).

Given all these considerations and the dynamics of culture and language, it is not surprising that Japanese writers of published comedy have traditionally sought the protection of various forms of disguise: novelists producing works that are symbolic *romans à clef*, needing a key to unlock their true interpretation (as described in Wells's chapter 12 on satire and constraint); or poetic authors seeking complete anonymity by using pen names that are themselves witty puns (often self-directed put-downs), both as defense and as permission to express comic criticisms. The discussion of this technique forms an important point in Rokuo Tanaka's chapter on early women poets, and it recurs in Hiroshi Inoue's up-to-date examples of topical comic comment in the newspapers. Behind the witty mask (essentially the same as the European jester's "fool's cap and bells"), there is a brief license to imply truth through humor, with the additional protection of recognized structural forms with stringent rules and techniques.

In European terms, the well-established hierarchy of comic styles, which dates back to the classical world, places satire and other serious-minded comic forms at the pinnacle, leaving "low comedy" to a lesser position. The difference is well summed up by the English critic L. J. Potts, who wrote that "comedy with the meaning left out . . . is as much as to say, with the comedy left out."[6] A similar low ranking of basic slapstick and knockabout comedy, disregarding "fun for fun's sake," has plagued the literary critical traditions of Japan, with much resultant misunderstanding of comic terminology and a devaluing of certain highly entertaining forms of comedy. One purpose of this book is to restore some better appreciation of the enormous vitality and skill to be found in the nonliterary forms of comedy in Japan. A

7

second is to advance a more precise understanding of the different styles of humor and comedy embodied in the forms under discussion. It may be helpful to discuss the question of terminology first.

Both Japanese and English terminology about comedy and humor are imprecise and somewhat ambivalent. In English, *comedy* implies some degree of dramatic enactment, often, but not necessarily, a formal stage play with a conventional happy ending (which may only ensue after some degree of suspense, as in romantic comedy, or of solemnity, as in existential or "black" comedy). In Japanese the comparable word indicates a specific form of theatrical performance, *kigeki* (喜劇), which can be qualified in various ways, for example, "new," or from a particular geographic location.[7] In chapter 9, Wells and Davis elaborate on the different types or styles of comedy (which can in English be applied by extension to the style or "flavor" of any humorous material).

The more general term in English is *humor*, which over the last two decades has come to be commonly applied to any material or behavior that produces in observers (whether intentionally or not) some degree of the laughing or smiling response.[8] Historically (and with a surviving specialist meaning), *humor* also has a much narrower sense whereby it describes a specific form of gentle, kindly "laughter with" some target. It is in this latter sense that it is used in Japanese, where *yūmoa* (ユーモア) means gentle, kindly laughter. Since this book is using the term principally in its broader sense, it is important to state for Japanese readers that throughout this book the word *humor* is therefore used largely in the sense in which the word *warai* (笑い laughter) is used in Japanese. When *warai* itself is used (as in chapter 3 by Goh Abe on ritual laughter), the focus is upon the act of laughing itself rather than on any humorous stimulus.[9]

Of course, the forms and styles of humor described in these pages are by no means an exhaustive collection of the riches available in Japan. Obscenity, for example, is not really addressed. It is an important factor in the humorous tradition of any culture, and Japan's humorous culture, unhampered by the Puritan tradition, is and has always been particularly robust in this respect. Unfortunately, the basic research on the subject is

8

still to be done, and, although the material for such research is vast, very little has yet been published, in either language, about Japanese obscenity.

To give an example: in the second half of the twentieth century (particularly the postwar years) there was a thriving theater of obscenity in theaters dedicated to live strip shows, where the actual strips were interspersed with titillating comedy sketches. Two of the biggest names in Japanese comedy at the beginning of the twenty-first century, Inoue Hisashi (also a novelist) and Beat Takeshi (whose television work is discussed by Joel Stocker in chapter 4), had their theatrical beginnings in the comedy of the strip theaters of the Asakusa district in Tokyo. The popularity of these two is such that their published scripts continue to appeal to certain audiences, although the strip theaters themselves are in terminal decline. Both film and the readily available resources of the Internet have undoubtedly had an impact. However, the fact remains that these shows dealt surprisingly routinely with onstage scatology, intertwined with purely sexual matters. In such sketches one is likely to find people urinating or defecating on each other, visual jokes about menstrual blood, and plots based on masturbation, voyeurism, incest, and sadism and masochism, as well as more mainstream theatrical devices such as humor derived from cross dressing, which may range from jokes about homosexuality to the "pantomime dames" who are widespread in Japanese comedy.[10]

Although in Japan humor about these topics can be freely enjoyed in "containers" of time or location, such as a specialist theater, one would not expect to hear references to scatological matters, humorous or otherwise, in everyday conversation. Purity and ritual defilement are central to the ancient Japanese religion of Shintō, and the subjects of scatological humor violate deeply held taboos on the treatment of blood and other forms of uncleanness. These matters relate to Wells's general discussion in chapter 12 about the intimate nexus between shame and such comic forms (or styles) as satire and farce.

Also, given the limitations of space and purpose, it has not been possible to deal with traditional dramatic forms such as *bunraku* puppet theater and *kabuki* drama. Here scripts and performance styles have largely been frozen in inherited formats that do include comic elements but render them subordinate to

9

larger theatrical purposes. However, numerous published studies provide extensive accounts of these theaters, even if they do not address directly the question of their comic style. Nor has it been possible for this volume to include much on joke books and collections of traditional stories, nor on caricature and *manga* cartoons (in contemporary times normally more violent and dramatic than comic, unlike in the western tradition). Work and writing on these areas of humor is very much in progress.

Despite these lacunae, there is an extensive literature *in Japanese* about the Japanese humorous tradition in general, and the contributors have noted and referred to many such sources. In English, apart from works on particular comic genres (that is, on the practice of Japanese humor in certain forms), works addressing the concept of humor generally in Japan are few and far between. Of course, the doyen of writers in English on Japanese literature, Donald Keene, has given some attention to humor in both literature and cultural history throughout his works, but not in any collected fashion. However, more recently, this has been the central concern of three academic books in English: Marguerite Wells's *Japanese Humour*, Joel Cohn's *Studies in the Comic Spirit in Modern Japanese Fiction*, and Howard Hibbett's *The Chrysanthemum and the Fish: Japanese Humor since the Age of the Shoguns.*

This volume owes much to Dr. Wells's pioneering academic survey, which carefully situates evolving Japanese concepts and theories about humor in their historical and international context. Although it deals primarily with theory, her book nevertheless ranges widely over various forms of humor, not confining itself to literary examples. Its scholarly structure, although lively, does not allow the kind of short, focused accounts of forms and genres that are our purpose here. However, for those who would like to read further on the issues and topics introduced here, it is the logical next step.

Joel Cohn's book focuses upon the strong tradition of the comic in the Japanese contemporary novel. He provides a dense and detailed literary critical analysis of the work of three authors writing in the twentieth century—Ibuse Masuji, Dazai Osamu, and Inoue Hisashi (of whom the last continues to write even into the present)—and seeks to draw a relationship between their differing stylistic and thematic approaches and the shaping pressures of contemporary Japanese society. While challenging for the nonscholar, his study provides an excellent account of the range of comic technique that is increasingly admissible and well regarded in Japanese creative fiction. Its existence balances to some extent the absence of a chapter on the contemporary novel in the present book.

Howard Hibbett's book is a welcome recent addition to the literature in English on the Japanese humorous tradition. It draws upon his erudition to give a brief survey of the history of humor in Japanese literature, performance, and social intercourse. While its principal focus is the famous Edo-period author Saikaku, the book also expatiates on the humor of the Edo and Meiji periods and addresses the late-twentieth-century revival of the Edo-period tradition of parody (which, it is important to note, is not the same thing as satire, a subject addressed at more length in the closing chapter of this book). Hibbett's title is a pun on the title of Ruth Benedict's pioneering book on Japanese culture, *The Chrysanthemum and the Sword*, where the chrysanthemum is the symbol of the Imperial house and the sword part of the Imperial regalia (see the discussion by Shōkichi Oda in chapter 1). This title was parodied in another book, *The Chrysanthemum and the Bat*, a book about baseball in Japan, and in true Japanese style, Hibbett has parodied the parody. The fish in his title is a reference to the *okoze*, the fish at the center of the Yama-no-kami Matsuri laughter ritual held in Mie Prefecture and discussed in chapter 3 by Goh Abe.

However, despite these significant landmarks, the present book effectively stands unique. It provides an accessible set of focused accounts of both literary and nonliterary forms of humor and the particular shapes they take in present-day Japanese culture. Where historical roots are important (as for example in the discussion of culture and manners, or hallowed poetic and dramatic forms), these are briefly delineated. Where distinctions from Western forms are marked, contrasts are drawn and discussed. The authors, writing either from within Japan or from well-established positions in Japanese scholarship, are fully conversant with humor as a topic for scholarly investigation, a strength that is rare enough among writers. Neither do they suffer the common illusion that humor is always and in every case a benign expression of social interaction: humor, like other human creations, can be used for good or for ill, and it is not surprising that a society as devoted to ideas of internal coherence and harmony as is Japan should have evolved detailed requirements governing its generation and appreciation. It is one of the chief purposes of this book to explore these ideas clearly and succinctly.

One of this book's strengths is its many practical applications for the classroom, whether as an introductory text on Japanese culture or a more focused study of specific comic genres. Both the high school class and more advanced classes will find chapters with suitable material for discussion and study. Students in high school or introductory-level classes are directed to chapters 1, 2, 3, 5, and 11 (by Shōkichi Oda, Hiroshi Inoue, Goh Abe, and Heiyō Nagashima), although these will also be of interest to the general or college-level reader. For more advanced work on specialist topics, readers are directed to chapters 4, 6, 7, 8, 9, and 10. Chapter 12, a highly original analysis by Marguerite Wells of the vexed question of satire in Japan, serves as a summation and integration of many of the themes introduced in earlier chapters.

Another strength of this book is that it offers the prospective student or visitor to Japan a range of practical insights into contemporary forms of Japanese entertainment and social intercourse, while acknowledging historic influences. From the teacher's point of view, each chapter provides a new topic for student reports and reflective investigation, with references demonstrating the solid foundations of conclusions being drawn. In all cases, the authors' careful attention to terminology and sources provides a reliable basis for additional research. But above all, and unlike other academic writing in this area, great care has also been taken to present primary materials not only in English translation but also in both the original Japanese and in romanization. This "triple text" format provides valuable material for classroom use, giving students direct access to the "joke work" and its linguistic and metaphoric implications and presenting novel and stimulating individual case studies, whether a comic strip, a short *senryū*, or a section of comic banter. It has been a labor of love on the part of authors, editor, and publishers to achieve such a presentation.

The forms of humor discussed in the following chapters, despite the few omissions discussed above, present a complete and accessible picture of how humor is used, perceived, and appreciated in contemporary Japanese culture. This is important, partly because Japan and its cultural conventions are in and of themselves important. The influence of this geographically small but artistically and economically powerful land is immense, and we should respond by attempting to understand its traditions and approach. The Japanese picture is also significant precisely because of the different ways in which this culture controls and uses humor. By comparing and contrasting such cultural approaches, a better insight into the nature of humor as a universal form of human behavior is possible. And if humor plays—as I believe it does—a useful part in our growing intercultural and international dialogues, then understanding our own humor by studying that of others must be a productive undertaking. Like the Sun Goddess, we should hearken to the sound of burlesque laughter and emerge from our caves to see what's going on.

Notes

1. For editorial policy on the transliteration of this and other terms, see the Editor's Note and note 1 to chapter 5.
2. The performing group *Eigo-Rakugo, or Japanese "Sit-Down" Comedy Performance in English*, toured to Sydney, Canberra, and Melbourne in 2001 and 2002 and to the United States in 2002.
3. Marguerite Wells, *Japanese Humour* (Basingstoke: Macmillan, 1997), 23–24.
4. *Kojiki*, trans. Donald L. Philippi (Princeton and Tokyo: Princeton University Press and University of Tokyo Press, 1969), 84.
5. Wells, *Japanese Humour*, 24.
6. L. J. Potts, *Comedy* (London: Hutchinson University Library, 1949), 137. A member of Queen's College Cambridge, Potts wrote this once-popular volume as a literary guide for students, writers, and actors of comedy on both sides of the Atlantic. It went into several editions, the latest in 1966.
7. For further discussion of *kigeki* and its types, see chapters 2 and 4.
8. It is so used by *Humor: The International Journal of Humor Research*, ed. Salvatore Attardo; see also the roughly parallel definition in Jan Bremmer and Hermann Roodenburg, eds., *A Cultural*

History of Humour (Cambridge, U.K.: Polity Press, 1997), 1 ff. (although their wording elides the issue of unintentional humor).

9. For further discussion on the terminology of humor, see the first section of chapter 9.

10. For example, the scripts of two such sketches can be found in Japanese in Beat Takeshi, *Asakusa Kid* (Tokyo: Ōta Publishing, 1988), 217–53.

1 Laughter and the Traditional Japanese Smile

Shōkichi Oda

Japanese Expression of Emotions

Public displays of emotion tend to be discouraged in Asian cultures, and the Japanese culture is no exception. This prohibition traditionally includes laughter and smiling. In fact, it is widely accepted by the Japanese themselves that they appear emotionless, because they control their emotions internally and do not express them externally.

Such "emotionless" looks can be observed at any Japanese sporting engagement. An excellent example would be a *sumō* wrestling match between two giant combatants, which is a centuries-old national sport with strong conventions about behavior. Compared with a Western-style wrestling match, the degree of control of expressed emotion is striking indeed. At the conclusion of a match one may notice how the *sumō* wrestlers, winner and loser alike, show no emotion on their faces when they bow to each other after the match before leaving the ring. The bows, incidentally, are a token of respect for each other's sportsmanship. The whole picture is far from the triumphant displays of a winner's pride and the despondent defeatism of the loser to be seen in the Western wrestling ring. The point is, this "emotionless" behavior is considered appropriate, even in these intensely emotional public events.

Japanese people, men in particular, have traditionally been expected not to show their emotions by maintaining calmness on their faces even when they suffer from some heavy psychological damage and are overwhelmed with grief. Japanese people are fond of the phrase "kao de waratte, kokoro de naite" (顔で笑って心で泣いて "smiling on the face, crying in the heart"). The aesthetic philosophy underlying this behavior lies at the heart of all Japanese classical art. It is summed up by the term *yūgen* (幽玄), which represents one of the major concepts of beauty in all Japanese literature and performance art. Its philosophy and practice were brought to perfection during the Heian period (794–1185). The original meaning of *yūgen* is "faint and dim,"[1] but it has long been used to express the ideal beauty to be found in traditional Japanese poetry and drama such as the classical *nō* plays. In *nō*, emotional expressions are compressed to the extreme in diction, music, and dramatic enactment. Paradoxically, concealed emotions come in this way to be all the more powerful in their revealed effect upon the audience.

To sum up, in Japan it has long been considered a virtue among upper-class men to refrain from laughing. In general, women traditionally try to laugh with their mouths only slightly open and to cover their mouths with one hand when laughing.

Controlling Laughter

There are several reasons why Japanese people try to repress laughter in particular as well as other emotional expressions. First, people are taught from childhood that it is shameful to be laughed at by others. Today such an idea may be rather obsolete, but people of my generation or older were admonished by our mothers when we did something silly with words such as, "People will laugh at you if they see you doing something stupid like that!" In those days it was considered truly shameful to be laughed at by others. Therefore, the rule "try not to be laughed at" became a precept for correcting the silly behavior of children and was taken to heart.

The American anthropologist Ruth Benedict, in her 1946 book *The Chrysanthemum and the Sword: Patterns of Japanese Culture*, examined in detail this Japanese notion of being laughed at as shameful. In her first contacts with Japanese culture at that time, this must have struck her as an important difference between that culture and her own, and she devoted quite a lot of attention to it. She pointed out that from the perspective of a person who is laughing at someone, the idea that to laugh at a person is to insult him or her appears as the flip side of the argument that "it is shameful to be laughed at."[2] Accordingly, for reasons of both civility *and* self-interest, all laughter in either direction has traditionally been regarded as best controlled; in my opinion, the Japanese moral precept "don't laugh at others" derives from this belief.

The second reason Japanese people try to repress laughing has to do with the classification of emotions. In traditional Japanese fashion, there is a hierarchy of emotions in which laughter is rated lower than other emotional expressions. For reasons that are not particularly obvious or rational, laughter is actually placed below anger or grief. Perhaps in part it is because laughter is often associated with forbidden subjects such as sexuality and excretion. In fact, sexuality and excretion as topics do generate a primitive form of laughter, and, perhaps as a consequence, laughter has come to be branded with a similar taboo.

The Japanese Smile

As human beings we have a natural instinct to laugh or smile when we find something funny or when we feel happy. Such emotional expression is quite natural and spontaneous. But this is not always the case with Japanese people. Their laughter is not necessarily connected to amusing or happy occasions. While it is surprising to learn this, many Japanese people are able to meet somebody with a smile on their lips even when lost in profound grief. In *Bushido: The Soul of Japan*,[3] Niitobe Inazō (1862–1933), a prominent educator who taught at Tokyo University, wrote that Japanese people were so adept at controlling their emotions that they could even receive visitors with smiles on their tearful faces.

Lafcadio Hearn, the early interpreter of Japan to people in the West, named this distinctive expression "the Japanese smile." Hearn not only introduced the concept overseas but helped the Japanese people realize that this was a distinctive cultural trait. Greek-born and Irish-raised, Hearn was initially sent to Japan in 1890 as a correspondent for a U.S. newspaper. He became an academic, taught English, married a Japanese woman, became a naturalized Japanese citizen, and died in Tokyo in 1904. During his time in Japan he contributed tremendously to interpreting Japanese culture to the rest of the world. An interesting episode is recounted in one of his major books, *Glimpses of Unfamiliar Japan*, in the chapter entitled "The Japanese Smile." It is a queer story recounted to Hearn by a foreign lady living at that time in Yokohama who told him her feelings about one of her Japanese servants, a nurse.[4]

This elderly nurse, coming back from her husband's funeral, showed her employer a vase containing someone's ashes. Saying "This is my husband," she laughed outright. The lady was infuriated and offended by the nurse's laughter, finding it unbelievable that someone could laugh on such a mournful occasion. Later on, the lady recounted the story to Hearn, asking, "Did you ever hear of such a disgusting creature?" Hearn commented: "[My] opinion is that she [the nurse] was obliged to gratify a wanton curiosity [of the lady]. Her smile or laugh would then have signified: 'Do not suffer your honourable feelings to be shocked upon my unworthy account; it is indeed very rude of me, even at your honourable request, to mention so contemptible a thing as my sorrow.'"[5]

The key to the mystery of the nurse's enigmatic smile is Japanese politeness. Smiles that look very rude to foreigners' eyes indicate the very reverse of rudeness or bad manners. They are smiles of exquisite consideration for others and indicate a desire not to place burdens upon their feelings. I share exactly those sentiments.

Social Permission for Smiling and Laughing

The fact that Japanese people restrain themselves from laughing does not mean that they dislike laughing. The truth, I believe, is that they love to laugh. It is just that our conventional wisdom says that we should not laugh indiscriminately or excessively; and so Japanese culture prescribes where to laugh and where not to laugh. People tend to avoid laughter on formal occasions, but in compensation they reserve places where they can laugh openly and to their heart's content. This depends on an unconscious sense of the appropriateness of the occasion. I have assigned a special term, *warai no ba* (笑いの場 "laughter places"), to places where laughing is socially permissible.[6] For example, if people drink together, the gathering place automatically turns into a permissible place for Japanese people to laugh openly and freely.

Another such opportunity occurs in the open air. Although the Japanese admire flowers in all four seasons, spring is the most popular time for viewing flowers. When we talk in Japan about flower viewing (花見 *hanami*), we are referring to the spring cherry blossoms (*hana* means "flowers," and *mi* means

18

"viewing"). On such occasions, families, friends, and relatives enjoy to the full drinking, eating, and laughing together under the beautiful cherry blossoms. Even the most reserved person laughs loudly and openly in such a group, as if he or she has been transformed into a totally different person. Pent-up laughter and emotions gush out in these circumstances.

Poetic Laughter in *Haiku* and *Senryū*

The distinction between when and where it is acceptable to laugh and when and where it is not can also be seen in traditional Japanese poetry. Two typical forms of classical Japanese poetry, *waka* (和歌) and *haiku* (俳句), reflect special rules about when and how to introduce humor.[7] Both *waka* and *haiku* are short forms of poetry with a fixed structure based on combinations of five and seven syllables. A *waka* is composed of five lines with a total of thirty-one syllables in a 5.7.5.7.7 sequence. The form dates back to before the seventh century, and today it is usually called *tanka* (短歌 short poem). The national anthem of Japan is itself a *waka*, composed by an anonymous poet about one thousand years ago. Its words well illustrate this 5.7.5.7.7 pattern, although it contains one additional syllable in the third line (this kind of variation is permissible):

君が代は	*Kimi ga yo wa*	5
千代に八千代に	*Chiyo ni yachiyo ni*	7
さざれ石の	*Sazareishi no*	5 + 1
巌となりて	*Iwao to narite*	7
苔のむすまで	*Koke no musu made*	7

The meaning of the anthem can be interpreted in different ways. Today the accepted interpretation is as follows, addressed to the Emperor: "I wish your life would last for a thousand, or even eight thousand years, or even forevermore, until a small rock grows into a huge one and moss grows on it."[8]

If the national anthem illustrates the normal *waka* form, an excellent example of the *haiku* is the famous one below,[9] composed by Matsuo Bashō (1644–94), well known both in Japan and around the world. Note that it has seventeen syllables in a 5.7.5 sequence, which corresponds to the first half of the *waka* structure. The result is a rich compression of both form and meaning:

古池や	*Furuike ya*	An old pond	5
蛙飛び込む	*Kawazu tobikomu*	A frog jumps in	7
水の音	*Mizu no oto*	The sound of water	5

Despite the quiet (and touching) comical note of this famous example, the chief aim and purpose of a *haiku* is the embodiment of *yūgen*[10] and solemnity: it is not the purpose of *haiku* to give free rein to laughter-provoking elements—that is the province of a parallel form known as *senryū* (川柳).[11] Both poetic forms have the same structure (seventeen syllables in a 5.7.5 sequence), but *senryū* is laced with wit and humor and even gentle satirical reflections on people, events, and human nature itself. While the *haiku* form is relatively well known outside Japan, *senryū* is not, and its antecedents require a little explanation.

Both *haiku* and *senryū* derive from the parent form of *waka* and are therefore like cousins. They developed in the following way. The first half (5.7.5) of the 5.7.5.7.7 sequence of a *waka* is called *kami no ku* (上の句 "upper lines"), and the second half (7.7) is called *shimo no ku* (下の句 "lower lines"). In a poetic compositional exchange called *renga* (連歌 "linked verses"), the *waka* came to be divided into its two parts, with one person providing the *kami no ku* and another the *shimo no ku*. When put together, all five lines completed a meaningful thirty-one-syllable poem. In the compositional process, a joking and competitive element was introduced whereby two persons would exchange witty and humorous observations, often incorporating mild satirical comment on events and personalities of the time. Since *renga* depended upon wordplay, these exchanges are often quite difficult to translate.

This style of witty, "chained," or linked verse became very popular in the twelfth century during the Heian period, following which the sequence gradually grew longer in the total number of lines, ending up sometimes with one hundred lines and involving three or more participants. Humor and laughter were lost on the way and were replaced by the notions of the elusive *yūgen* and solemnity of tone. But in the sixteenth century, at the end of the Muromachi period, *renga* made a comeback in a new form called *haikai-renga,* which involved a lot of humor. In fact, *haikai* (俳諧) essentially means "humor." *Haikai-renga* was increasingly welcomed as popular literature among the masses and settled into an established form of thirty-six lines, created by repetitions of the shortened sequences of 5.7.5 and 7.7.

The following is an example of a typical sequence in *haikai-renga.* A, B, and C signify the three participants, and 5.7.5 and 7.7 are the sequences that the participants are assigned to compose in the appropriate order:

1.	A	5.7.5
2.	B	7.7
3.	C	5.7.5
4.	A	7.7
5.	B	5.7.5
6.	C	7.7

This sequence would then be continued for another ten rounds.

Repetition of this pattern eventually completes a full thirty-six-line *haikai-renga.* The first line of verse is called *hokku* (発句 "opening verse"). *Haiku* as we know it today is the poetic form in which this opening verse became independent. The required linking was very complex. In the sequence shown above, the 7.7 of B would add itself to the 5.7.5 of A to form the full *waka* structure. However, following that, the 5.7.5 of C must combine with the same 7.7 of B to make a second *waka.* In this manner, each line is linked with the lines that precede and follow it, and each two consecutive lines form an independent *waka,* a true test of creativity and ingenuity!

In the eighteenth-century Edo period, a literary entertainment called *maekuzuke* (前句づけ)[12] appeared and soon gained popularity as an introductory stage of practicing *renga*-style composition that one would study before taking up *renga* seriously. In *maekuzuke* one person would provide the final 7.7 sequence, then another person had to complete the preceding 5.7.5 sequence. When put together, all five lines had to make up a coherent thirty-one-syllable verse. It is possible to compose a wide variety of *maekuzuke* poems using the same last two lines. For example:[13]

| 切りたくもあり | *Kiritaku mo ari* | 7 |
| 切りたくもなし | *Kiritaku mo nashi* | 7 |

These closing lines, provided first, mean "I want to cut, but at the same time I don't like cutting"—the expression of a dilemma. Once given these lines, the other participants must respond with versions of the first three lines. Here is one possibility:

盗人を	*Nusubito o*	5
捕らえてみれば	*Toraete mireba*	7
我が子なり	*Waga ko nari*	5

These lines mean "I caught a thief, but found he was my own son." So when put together, the result is a complete thirty-one-syllable poem meaning "I caught a thief, but found he was my own son—I want to cut him down but at the same time I just hate to do it, because he is my son!"

This is another possibility:

さやかなる	*Sayaka naru*	5
月を隠せる	*Tsuki o kakuseru*	7
花の枝	*Hana no eda*	5

These lines mean, "A cherry tree branch in full bloom is hiding a brightly shining moon." When put together with the given two last lines, we have another complete thirty-one-syllable poem with the same theme as the first example. This time, however, the poem comes to mean, "A cherry tree branch in full bloom is hiding the brightly shining moon—I want to cut the moon-hiding branch, but at the same time I hate to do so, because the branch with its blossoms is so beautiful."

A single-volume anthology titled *Haifū Yanagidaru*, published in 1765,[14] collected and celebrated outstanding *maeku-zuke* poems. As these witty and humorous poems developed a life of their own, the new, independent poetic form of *senryū* was born. It was named after Karai Senryū, the chief member of the selection committee for the anthology.[15]

Despite the similar origins of *haiku* and *senryū*, and despite their similar structure, the two are treated today as quite different forms of poetry. One of the major differences is the vocabulary considered appropriate to each. In *haiku* special words and phrases are used as references to the seasons, both to set the tone of the poems and to provide keys to their deeper meanings. These are called *kigo* (季語 season words).[16] Typical examples are *harusame* (春雨 spring rain), *yuri* (百合 lily), *akikaze* (秋風 autumn wind), and *yuki* (雪 snow). Another difference in terms of vocabulary is that in *haiku* relatively archaic, classical words and phrases are used, while in *senryū* modern Japanese language is used. In definitional terms, generally speaking a *haiku* is a short poem of serious tone whose favorite subjects are related to nature, while a *senryū* deals with humorous aspects to be found in human feelings and behavior. Although both must obey the same structural rules, the connection with laughter is considered appropriate only to *senryū*. This is a quite different approach from that of Western poetic conventions, which make no such distinction between the two forms.[17]

I would like to cite here two *senryū* that subtly illustrate the absurdity of human feelings. They were composed about 250 years ago during the Edo period.[18]

這えば立て	*Haeba tate*	5
立てば歩めの	*Tateba ayume no*	7
親心	*Oyagokoro*	5

The *senryū* can be translated as follows: "When a baby begins to crawl, we just wish he could stand up; and when he actually stands up, we wish he could walk: that's the kind of expectation all parents share!" How unreasonable is human nature!

Another wry observation gives a more biting sketch of a man showing off:

槍持ちを	*Yarimochi o*	5
はじめて連れて	*Hajimete tsurete*	7
ふり返り	*Furikaeri*	5

This poem tells of a samurai who has been promoted to the level where he is allowed to have his own attendant. Going out one day with the attendant for the first time, he cannot stop himself from glancing back over his shoulder again and again to see his attendant following a few steps behind. The truth is, he cannot conceal his delight in having an attendant after years and years of hard work.

It is said that as many as ten million people enjoy reading and composing *haiku* in Japan. The *senryū*-writing population is not as large, but several hundreds of specialized *senryū* societies publish newsletters regularly. *Senryū* lovers seem to feel that it is not enough just to appreciate humor and wit in their poems in isolation, but that this love of the form should bring them together. Various efforts have been made to promote the status of *senryū* as an independent poetic form. One example is the annual *senryū* contest sponsored by a life insurance company.[19] Office workers respond to this enthusiastically, entering more than fifty thousand *senryū* each year. Their many poems express a witty elegy for the condition of the white-collar worker in Japan (with a little exaggeration, of course) in a humorous and ironic way. A collection of outstanding poems from the contest is published in book form annually.[20]

The Japanese Smile Today

While this chapter has outlined the distinctiveness of the traditional Japanese approach to smiling and laughter, it is important to emphasize that this distinctiveness can be applied mostly to the people of pre–World War II Japan. Today the social practice of restraining smiling and laughter is disappearing, and Japanese youth laugh more freely than ever before. Also at risk of disappearing is the shame-sensitive society in which people feel it is shameful to be laughed at. And here a special mention should be made of young Japanese women, who have been more liberated from these restraints than anyone else. Getting jobs outside the domestic circle, they began to laugh more frequently and happily. They no longer follow the custom of covering their mouths with the palm of one hand when they laugh. It is perhaps thirty years too late for anyone to observe this distinctive hand gesture on the part of Japanese women. However, beneath these new and more liberated approaches to smiling and laughter, many other special and distinctive conventions about humor, both in daily life and in literature, can still be observed.

NOTES

I would like to acknowledge the generous help of Dr. Goh Abe in translating this chapter.

1. This term is essentially untranslatable in its aesthetic use: it stands for the quintessential quality that is achieved by all great Japanese art. For an argument that *yūgen* can most usefully be translated in contemporary English as "grace," see Marguerite Wells, *Japanese Humour* (Basingstoke: Macmillan, 1997), 29, 32.
2. Ruth Benedict, *The Chrysanthemum and the Sword: Patterns of Japanese Culture* (Boston: Houghton Mifflin, 1946), 253–96.
3. Inazo Nitobe [Niitobe Inazō], *Bushido: The Soul of Japan* (1899; New York: Putnam, 1905), 103–10.
4. Lafcadio Hearn, *Glimpses of Unfamiliar Japan* (1894; Rutland, Vt.: Tuttle, 1986), 656–83.
5. Ibid., 670–71.
6. Oda Shōkichi, *Warai to Yūmoa* (Tokyo: Chikuma Shobō, 1979), 252.
7. For more detailed discussion of these and other poetic forms, see chapters 8 and 10.
8. The national anthem is one of the *waka* collected in *Kokin-wakashū*, an anthology compiled in 905 in the Heian period. It appears in volume 7, among "Poems of Celebration," but with a variant version of the first five syllables, which read "Wagakimi wa" instead of "Kimi ga yo wa," as in today's public version. The translation is my own.
9. This famous *haiku* was composed in 1686; it is here quoted from Fukumoto Ichirō, *Haiku to Senryū* (Tokyo: Kōdansha, 1999), 135; the translation is my own.
10. See note 1 above.
11. See the complementary discussion of the evolution of *haiku* and *senryū* in chapter 10.
12. The history of this competitive form of versifying is outlined in chapter 10.
13. The following examples are both taken from Ebara Taizō, *Ebara Taizō: Chosakushū*, vol. 2 (Tokyo: Chūō Kōronsha, 1979), 454. This is a modern, revised edition of the original compilation, *Inutsukuba-shū*, selected by Yamasaki Sōkan, which appeared around 1530. The translations are my own.
14. The first anthology of *Haifū Yanagidaru* appeared in 1765 and be-

gan a series that lasted until 1838.

15. For a detailed discussion of this famous founder of the *senryū* verse form, see chapter 10.

16. See also discussions of these features in chapters 8 and 10.

17. A similar partitioning applies to the verse form *waka* or *tanka* and is discussed in chapter 8.

18. The first of these poems is quoted from the forty-fifth edition of the *Haifū Yanagidaru*, as cited by Hamada Giichirō, *Edo Senryū Jiten* (Tokyo: Tōkyōdō Shuppan, 1986), 74. The second appeared in the third edition of the *Haifū Yanagidaru* and is here quoted from Yamasawa Hideo, ed., *Haifū Yanagidaru*, vol. 1 (Tokyo: Iwanami Bunko, Iwanami Shoten, 1995), 134. Both translations are my own. R. H. Blyth, *Edo Satirical Verse Anthologies* (Tokyo: Hokuseido Press, 1961), gives an introduction to a selection of Edo-period *senryū* with accompanying translations into English.

19. The insurance company is Dai-ichi Mutual Life Insurance Co. and its competition, called "Sarariiman Senryū Kontesuto" ("Office Workers' *Senryū* Competition"), began in 1984. The best compositions have been published annually since 1990.

20. The 2000 volume (vol. 10) is entitled *Sarariiman Senryū Kessaku-sen* (*The Anthology of Masterpieces from the Office Workers' Senryū*); it was published by Kōdansha in December 2000.

Osaka's Culture of Laughter

Hiroshi Inoue

When we think about Japanese laughter, it seems evident that there are two different cultures of laughter in Japan. One is the culture of laughter accepted by the samurai (warrior) folk of Tokyo, and the other is the daily culture of laughter cultivated by the merchants of Osaka. Osaka is the second-largest city in Japan and has for a long time been a city of historical and economic importance. However, there are few books written in English on Osaka, compared to the many books written on Tokyo and Kyoto. Of course, there is a large variety of maps and shopping guides to Osaka, but little is written on Osaka's history and culture. Accordingly, it is very hard for English-speaking visitors to recognize the true Osaka, which includes the city's important culture of laughter.

The History of Osaka

The origins of Osaka date back to the fifth century, when it flourished as the political and economic center of Japan. In the seventh century the Naniwa-no-miya Palace was built, which is considered the oldest palace in Japan. Although the national government subsequently shifted to Nara and Kyoto, and later to Tokyo, Osaka has continued to act as the gateway of foreign culture and trade. It developed strongly after Toyotomi Hideyoshi completed Osaka Castle in 1582, and it became the generalissimo's home base, the center of the country's political power. Hideyoshi gathered some important merchants in Osaka and, as a means of maintaining his control, tried to develop Osaka as a business center. His successor, Tokugawa Ieyasu, continued Hideyoshi's business system, and the Tokugawa shogunate ensured Osaka's economic predominance nationally for 250 years, until the end of the Edo period in 1868. Osaka led Japan's economic development from the seventeenth through the nineteenth centuries and was called "Tenka no Daidokoro" (天下の台所 "Kitchen of the Realm").

A Culture of Laughter

Osaka has developed as a business city from the Edo period (1603–1867) up to the present, and the tendency to love laughter was born and flourished under these conditions. The various arts of laughter have been cultivated since the Edo era and have endured to this day, with Osaka always boasting more comedians and people who appreciate laughter than any other city in Japan. It is interesting to speculate on why the culture of laughter has developed especially in this city. In the Edo period samurai dominated the whole country, including, of course, Osaka. But there the samurai class was small compared to the number of ordinary citizens. Osaka's special place in the economy helped create this unique mix of population and accordingly the special local character. Other cities, including Tokyo, still tend to have the strict hierarchical structure characteristic of samurai culture, but Osaka has always had a more horizontal social structure.

In a horizontal society, harmonious laughter develops easily, since people do not care as much about differences in status. Thus the citizens of Osaka were likely to work with and be familiar with each other without paying much attention to their vertical status relations. Osaka, after all, is where the merchant mind-set predominates, and merchant culture views laughter as something that harmonizes human relations and makes people feel closer to each other. Because a merchant's foremost concern is developing favorable horizontal and egalitarian human relations—that is, regular and prospective customers—nothing is more important than the ability to get along with one's fellows. To do so requires skill at negotiation, verbal ingenuity, and a knack for lightening the atmosphere with a comic touch. Thus humor and laughter came to play a central role in daily merchant life, and the words, nuances, and intonation of the Osaka dialect itself developed in a way that helped to bring humor and levity to situations among people in Osaka.

Osaka's business culture appreciated and valued laughter because the merchants needed laughter in their public as well as private lives. They used laughter as an effective means of communication and, in addition, they knew that laughter has an abil-

28

ity to release human beings from their burdens. If we can laugh at ourselves—that is, at our unhappiness and depression—we will be able to feel as if we are being released from a burden. If we can laugh away our failures, we will recover ourselves much more quickly. Movements in the economy exert a great influence on the lives of merchants. When business is in a slump, it will cause many troubles, but even if their company goes bankrupt, merchants have no option but to struggle to stand up again. In order to do so, they know very well that laughing is invaluable in cheering themselves up.

Laughter in Daily Life: *Honne* and the Culture of Practicality

Such fundamental elements as attitude to life, ways of thinking, and personal values form the background to Osaka's love of laughter. Two commonly used words in Japanese are *honne* (本音) and *tatemae* (建前). *Honne* means the truth, or what a person really thinks, and *tatemae* means something akin to the official position of the group that person represents. Thus some people have characterized *honne* as the individual's voice and *tatemae* as the group's voice.[1] Very often, a Japanese individual will give precedence to the official or group *tatemae* position, but that does not mean that he or she has entirely abandoned his or her personal *honne*. Compared to the people of Tokyo, the people of Osaka tend to prefer talking in *honne* rather than in *tatemae*. In Osaka's local dialect, people like to say, "So what?" after listening to a superficial conversation. Since the people of Osaka love to talk in *honne*, they also use a lot of laughter as the "oil" in a conversation to smooth over any discord that might arise from using *honne*.

The popular stand-up comedy known as *manzai* (漫才 comic dialogue), in which a pair of comedians amuses an audience with their quick-fire banter, and which originated in Osaka, is usually performed by two artists taking the roles of *boke* (ボケ) and *tsukkomi* (つっこみ).[2] The *tsukkomi* always talks in *tatemae* and believes that the formal way of talking, using polite conversation, is important, while the *boke* reveals *honne*. The comic contradictions between the different roles of *tsukkomi* and *boke* are very appealing and extremely humorous for the audience. It is a commonplace that people laugh to themselves when they experience something they think is funny, but in cer-

29

tain regions in Japan, people only feel free to laugh out loud when they see that other people are laughing too. Thus it must be acknowledged that open laughter is not a universal phenomenon.[3] However, the people of Osaka feel free to laugh whenever they think something is funny—regardless of other people's feelings.

Because the people of Osaka prize laughter so highly, Osaka is also alive with an array of traditional performing arts, not only *manzai* but also *bunraku* (文楽), *rakugo* (落語), and general *kigeki* (喜劇). *Bunraku* is the Japanese puppet theater, with puppets two-thirds life size, each manipulated by two or three puppeteers, and with the occasional comic scene for relief. *Rakugo*[4] is traditional monologue storytelling in the local dialect (whereas *manzai* is two-person stand-up comedy). *Kigeki*, the general term for comedy, covers both youthful and innovative forms of entertainment (吉本新喜劇 *Yoshimoto Shinkigeki*) and the older, more traditional forms (松竹新喜劇 *Shōchiku Shinkigeki*).[5] Many of these acts are staged by the famous Yoshimoto Comedy Theater[6] in Osaka; others, such as the *bunraku* puppet theater, have their own specialized theaters.[7]

Negotiation and the Culture of Bargaining

Profit is of course the main concern of merchants: they want to earn as much money as possible. It is commonly accepted that you can get whatever you want if you are willing to pay a high enough price, and accordingly the people of Osaka value buying the highest quality for the lowest possible price: this is the heart of bargaining. Japanese housewives delight in seeing bargain sales as opportunities to demonstrate their budget-stretching skills.

Buying and selling involve a negotiation between the customer and the shopkeeper, but the result of these negotiations depends upon people's feelings, not just the amount of money involved, and feelings can sometimes get in the way of a successful outcome. For example, in the Edo era the common method of business was the terrifying one practiced by the samurai (or warrior class), whose ethics forbade them all negotiation, because if a samurai begged for a discount it would mean that he had compromised in "war" (that is, the dispute about the correct price) and thus lost honor. Nowadays, if there are shopkeepers who have threatening faces like samurai, nobody will buy at their

stores: it is accepted that it is very important to welcome customers with a smiling face. According to Matsushita Kōnosuke,
the former president of Panasonic, a smiling face is essential
if one wants to make a sale.[8] Starting with a smile, it becomes
possible to begin bargaining, meaning that the timing of a smile
is also very important: if you don't smile at all, you can never
start bargaining; in fact, the absence of a smile might provoke a
quarrel.

The Culture of Originality and Flexibility

To earn money, merchants must work hard and compete among
rivals. However, hard work alone is not enough; equally important are "wisdom and talent," according to an old saying. In
order to succeed, merchants have to create something original
using their own wisdom and ideas. Matsushita pointed out that
business is not only buying and selling but also creating original
products, and thus creativity is very important for merchants.
In order to create a new article or a new service, one's habits of
thought must be flexible enough first to imagine the new product. A person who is stubborn and who persists with fixed ideas
can run along in established ways as if along a railway track
quite easily but will have difficulty in seeing the world from a
different perspective or in thinking freely. What are needed are
people who are quick on the uptake. Laughter serves very well
to stimulate the brain and to release us from our fixed ways of
thinking, and thus it is important for relaxing thought patterns
and producing original ideas.

"The Doing Culture" and the Ideology of "A Comfortable Life"

The merchants and businesspeople of Osaka believe that people
need to live their lives with some pleasures included, since, like
all human beings, their life span is limited. They cannot imagine working hard without any enjoyment, and thus they pursue
a lifestyle in which they can feel relaxed. In Osaka people also
believe that they need to enjoy themselves by active participation, not merely by reflection. For example, it is possible to
enjoy flower arrangements by looking at a display of *ikebana*
and discussing its merits with others, perhaps even evaluating
or grading the displays. However, in Osaka people believe that

they can enjoy art more by doing it themselves. This is what I refer to as "the doing culture."

When people first try something new and adventurous they often find enjoyment in the process. Of course, one will feel even happier if others praise the results as successful. For example, one person might tell you, "Oh look! What a lovely flower arrangement you have done!" However, even if the other person criticizes what you have done, since you are the person who enjoyed doing it, the final evaluation is actually up to you. The people of Osaka do not hesitate to pursue their hobbies, knowing that they cannot enjoy life if they hesitate to try things out. In just this way, young people wanting to be professional comedians love to try to make other people laugh, because it is far more enjoyable to laugh with others than to laugh alone. Even children enjoy forming groups with their friends and acting out *manzai*. It is this enjoyment that encourages so many young people in Osaka to decide to become professional comedians. Spending an enjoyable life means for them spending a life with laughter.

Oral Culture and Local Dialect

The most frequent lesson given about speech in Japanese is that "silence is golden," hence the popular expression "To say nothing is a flower." This means it is a good idea to leave many things unsaid. Silence retains much appeal in Japan, even as a theme for advertisers. The well-known actor Mifune Toshirō, prototype of the strong, brooding male hero, was seen on television advertisements in 1972 exhorting all virile males to buy beer with the command: "Men, keep quiet, and drink Sapporo Beer!"

By contrast, Osaka is a talkative place: people never keep silent and love talking (in their local dialect, of course). They do not think that silence means to be reliable or trustworthy, and when they observe quiet people they tend to wonder what they are thinking. When you do business in Osaka, you too need to be talkative. Japanese business decisions are made with an emphasis on sincerity and trust: pressure for a quick decision is counterproductive. In the Japanese context, working out a business deal means more than simply hammering out the terms of a contract; it includes an effort to build mutual trust and long-term relations. For example, it is necessary to say good-bye with a smile and to say "Next time, please," even when the negotiations have completely broken down.

Naturally, these practices cannot be mastered by Western business negotiators overnight, and they require many specialized verbal expressions. Because the Japanese are always conscious of what other people in a group are thinking, the language has developed a large hedging vocabulary, allowing one to avoid directly answering either yes or no. Among the most common hedges are "I'll do what I can," "Let me get back to you on that later," "Let me sleep on it," and "I'll have to look into that." Sometimes these phrases can mean a tentative "yes," when the speaker is doing what is termed *nemawashi* (根回し), that is, needing to touch all bases and line up support. Sometimes it is a definite "no" that is phrased in a roundabout way to avoid hurting the other person's feelings.

Osaka dialect is especially rich in such expressions. In addition, the people of Osaka always tend to make their conversation funny by including jokes. According to Onoe Keisuke,[9] the Osaka dialect (大阪弁 *Ōsaka-ben*) contains "laughter," and it can certainly be said that one of the characteristics of communication in the Osaka dialect is laughing. As I have shown, the people of Osaka know the effectiveness of laughter in daily life. Laughing together makes good relationships, creates a good atmosphere, and allows one to enjoy the conversation. Laughter can even be created by pointing out the weakness or odd characteristics of one's own body. The people of Osaka know that laughing creates energy on which to live as well as helping one to recover from sorrow or a broken relationship. They have traditionally embraced a culture that intentionally uses laughter most effectively in their everyday lives.[10]

NOTES

1. Another way of describing these two concepts is to say that *honne* refers to the value system seen from the point of view of the individual, while *tatemae* describes it from the point of view of society, or the organization or group to which the individual belongs. Thus *tatemae* is apt to be formal, orderly, authoritarian, bureaucratic, and superficial, while *honne* leans toward diverting, challenging, making fun of, or avoiding *tatemae*, and consequently it is willing to create new values and views.

2. For a more detailed discussion of *manzai*, see chapter 4; for the roles of *boke* and *tsukkomi*, see also chapter 7.
3. Indeed, certain periods and classes of western society have had similar absolute prohibitions against laughter.
4. For a more detailed discussion of *rakugo*, see chapter 7.
5. Japanese theater always had comic relief, but the ancient Greek idea of a dichotomy between comedy and tragedy was a new and exciting idea in Meiji Japan. In the 1880s a new word, *kigeki*, was invented to mean "comedy in general." (Marguerite Wells explored the etymology of the word *kigeki* in "The Search for a Word," a paper delivered at the conference of the European Association for Japanese Studies, Budapest, 1997, unpublished, available from the author.) Then, in Osaka in 1904, an out-of-work *kabuki* actor (who later took the name of Soganoya Gorō) decided to start a new kind of theater to make people laugh. He called it the New Comedy, or *Shinkigeki*. Its descendants are *Shōchiku Shinkigeki* and *Yoshimoto Shinkigeki*, both of which have developed in Osaka and which are named for the production companies involved. *Shōchiku Shinkigeki* (owned by a film company) is older and more traditional than *Yoshimoto Shinkigeki* (the comedy of the Osakan theatrical empire; see note 6 below). The former is liked by older people, while the latter is likely to be supported by the younger generation.
6. The Yoshimoto Comedy Theater is managed by the Yoshimoto Kōgyō Co. Ltd. The company may be contacted at 11-6 Namba, Sennichimae, Chuo-ku, Osaka, 542-0075, Japan. For an account of the key role played by this extraordinary company in the development of comedy in twentieth-century Osaka and Japan generally, see chapter 4.
7. The National Bunraku Puppet Theater may be contacted at 1-12-10, Nipponbashi 1, Chuo-ku, Osaka, 542-0075, Japan.
8. Matsushita Kōnosuke is the founder of Panasonic (otherwise known as Matsushita Electric). The reference is to his book *Shōbai Kokoroechō* (Tokyo: PHP Research Institute, 1973).
9. Onoe Keisuke is associate professor in the Faculty of Literature, Tokyo University. The reference is to his *Ōsaka Kotobagaku* (Tokyo: Sōgensha, 1999).
10. It is thus no accident that in July 2000 Osaka played host to the twelfth Conference of the International Society for Humor Studies (ISHS). As president of the Japan Society for Laughter and Humor Studies (which was founded in 1994 and now embraces some one thousand members and enjoys support from nine corporations), I was honored to act as chair of the organizing committee

and chair of the conference itself (with Goh Abe as co-chair). The JSLHS aims to deepen understanding and to promote the cultural development of laughter and humor through comprehensive research into those subjects. There are no special qualifications for membership other than payment of an annual fee, and I invite interested persons to contact the society at 201 Showa Building, 4-7-12 Nishi-Temma, Kita-ku, Osaka 530-0047, Japan, or e-mail warai@xage.ne.jp.

3 A Ritual Performance of Laughter in Southern Japan

Goh Abe

Humor and laughter have for centuries been essential parts of folk festivals around the world. Gaijatra, a traditional festival in Nepal, is one such good example. Among the many Nepalese festivals, Gaijatra, the festival of holy cows, is the one most closely related to the Nepalese tradition of political and social satire. Humor and laughter are essential parts of the festival. During the festival, a parade takes place in which families who lost one or more of their members during the past year send along their cows and a group of people who act as their representatives. Those who cannot afford living cows may ask their representatives to wear colorful clothes and baskets covered with painted paper as masks, so as to disguise themselves as the needed cows. This parade is intended to inspire the deceased to speed their way to heaven. People in general also masquerade and dress up in the oddest clothes possible. Some wear rags while others wear straw and hay to make themselves look funny. Some even paint their faces like devils. Another interesting thing done during the festival is to drag along the ground heavy iron wheels or broken pieces of metal cans and drums. This is particularly true in the district of Patan.[1]

This Nepalese festival dates back to medieval times, when King Malla was the ruler of Kathmandu. One day his son died due to a smallpox epidemic. The queen was torn apart with such great grief that the king ordered those among his people who were suffering from the loss of their own sons to come to the palace to show the queen their pain and grief, hoping that the queen could share her pain with those sufferers and thus be consoled. Then the king announced that those who had funny items or those who could perform entertaining acts should also come forward, hoping they would further ease the queen's sorrow. Some came with funny-looking, colorful clothes and made-up faces, while others decorated themselves like cows and brought drawings of cows' faces (in Nepal, cows had long been considered a vehicle to take the soul of the dead to heaven). Next, hermits came to demonstrate that life is an empty dream, while others exhibited sexual symbols and made garlands of chilies. In the end, the queen (as well as the other mourners) came to understand the harsh realities of life and was able to come to terms with her son's death. The funny cartoons, comical performances, and joking conversations had made the queen laugh, and her grief was finally gone.[2]

With this background tale as its core, the tradition of Gaijatra developed into a weeklong festival. During the festivities, people try to ease the souls of the dead so that they can open the gates to heaven, leaving earthly cares behind. In the nineteenth century (the Rana period in Nepal) different cultural groups began to use humor to entertain political authorities during the Gaijatra festival. Then, humor was gradually turned into a tool for the people in Nepal to openly satirize the political and social issues of the day. Regardless of how effective the tool was, such defiant and critical acts were permissible to the people only during the festival.[3]

In contrast with Nepal, Japan has seven major traditional festivals that feature ritual performances of laughter (笑い warai). In this chapter I will describe and analyze the organization and function of one of the seven festivals, known in Japan as Warai-kō. The dates, sites, and regional locations of the seven major festivals are listed in figure 3.1.[4] It is interesting to note that all seven festivals are carried out in and around Shintō shrines, with implications that will be discussed later. The geographical locations of the festivals are marked on the map of Japan in figure 3.2.

As an example of the nature of the activities of these festivals, I will briefly outline festival no. 4, Warai Matsuri. Participants in the ritual laughter march along the road to Niu Shrine, telling the spectators of their procession to laugh. They say aloud in a cheerful manner, "Laugh! Laugh! The world will be a place of ease!" and the spectators respond in the same manner. The participants carry in their hands twelve different kinds of autumn crops skewered on sticks and branches. The skewered crops are the token of their gratitude to the gods for the year's

	Festival Name	Festival Site	Location	Festival Date
1	Waraizome shiki 笑初式	Kodai Shrine	Mita City Hyōgo Prefecture	January 7
2	Yama-no-kami Matsuri 山の神祭り	Yanahama District	Owase City, Mie Prefecture	February 7
3	Suishōjin Shinji 酔笑人神事	Atsuta Shrine	Atsuta Ward, Nagoya City, Aichi Prefecture	May 4
4	Warai Matsuri 笑祭	Niu Shrine	Kawanabe Town, Wakayama Prefecture	October 10
5	Owarai Shinji お笑い神事	Shimotoda Hachiman Shrine	Nishiwaki City, Hyōgo Prefecture	October 10
6	Warai-kō 笑い講	Daido-Omata district	Hōfu City, Yamaguchi Prefecture	First Sunday in December
7	Shimenawagake Shinji 注連縄掛神事	Hiraoka Shrine	Higashi-Osaka City, Osaka Prefecture	December 25

Fig. 3.1 The seven principal *warai* festivals in Japan

good harvest. Arriving at the shrine, the participants solemnly offer those crops before the Shintō altar, and then they complete the ritual by roaring with laughter, all together in unison. This festival has its origin in a legend according to which a goddess named Niutsu Hime no Mikoto secluded herself in the shrine, refusing to come out. The worried villagers tried to lure her out of it with laughter. It worked! Since then people in the area have believed in the power of laughter.[5]

Another example is festival no. 2, Yama-no-kami Matsuri, held in Yanahama District at Owase City, Wakayama. Its ritual is performed for the purpose of pleasing a mountain goddess by showing her several *okoze* (虎魚), or stonefish, a very ugly fish. According to folklore, there once lived in a mountain in

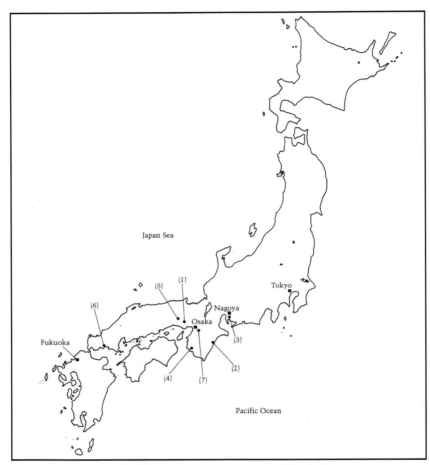

Fig. 3.2 Locations of the seven major *warai* festivals

that district a mountain goddess who was desperately unhappy because of her terrible looks. One day villagers offered her an *okoze* in order to cheer her up. Taking one look at its hideous features, the goddess instantly realized that there existed a creature uglier than her. More than pleased, she laughed a big laugh of relief. This is the origin of the festival.[6]

Knowledge of this ritual has been handed down from generation to generation, producing variations in different regions. Today it is performed mostly in its simplified form. In Yanahama, people put an *okoze* in their inside breast pockets and gather at a traditional site in the mountain to show their *okoze* by turns (just a small part of it at a time), saying such things as "Isn't my *okoze* marvelously ugly?" and laughing at each other's specimen. This is meant to entertain and please the mountain goddess and to entreat her not to harm them, specifically, to bring no misfortune and disaster. It can be said that the laughter of the participants symbolizes that of the mountain goddess. In this manner, performances of ritual laughter at Japanese festivals are closely related to Japanese folk religion and the Shintō gods.[7]

As Hiroshi Inoue explains,[8] Japanese people have traditionally believed in two kinds of gods: one who brings happiness and another who brings misfortune and disaster. The Japanese word *kami* (神) is usually translated as "god" in English, but strictly speaking these two words are not identical in many respects. For an explanation of *kami* I would like to cite some passages from a study of Japanese religions by Byron Earhart, who insists that there is no exact English equivalent for *kami:*

> *Kami* is much more inclusive than the English word "god." The notion of *kami* is elusive because of the great number of *kami* and their various forms. Early Japanese writings relate that many *kami* participated in the creation of the world and in a mythological age of specialized divinities not too different from the mythological world believed in by the ancient Greeks and Romans. In addition to the *kami* of mythology, in ancient times as well as at present, natural objects, animals, and even human beings have been identified as *kami.*[9]

Earhart continues by quoting one of the greatest Shintō scholars, Motoori Norinaga (1730–1801):

> Generally speaking, the word *"kami"* denotes, in the first place, the deities of heaven and earth that appear in the ancient texts and also the spirits enshrined in the shrines; furthermore, among all kinds of beings—including not only human beings but also such objects as birds, beasts, trees, grass, seas, mountains, and so forth—any being whatsoever which possesses some eminent quality out of the ordinary, and is awe-inspiring, is called *kami.*[10]

41

Earhart adds:

> If they were considered powerful enough, "evil and mysterious things" also rated as *kami,* because the primary consideration was the power to inspire and not "goodness or meritorious deeds." The identity of *kami* is so elastic that perhaps the best general term for understanding *kami* is the notion of the sacred.[11]

Thus people need to turn a god who brings them misfortune and disaster into another god who brings them happiness and safety. For that purpose they employ ritual performances of laughter. People dedicate their laughter to gods to please them, and in return the entertained gods will hear their wishes. In this respect, people's laughter is a symbolic expression of the gods' pleasure.

Festival no. 6, Warai-kō, is held annually on the first Sunday of December in Daido-Omata District in Hōfu City, Yamaguchi. On December 6, 1998, I conducted a field survey of the festival from which this detailed report is taken. The district's ritual performance of laughter, Warai-kō, has about eight hundred years of history, with its origin dating back to 1199 in the Kamakura period in Japanese history.

As I have noted, the *warai* of Warai-kō means "laughter." *Kō* (講) is a kind of mutual aid society in which local people help each other when crises occur—drought, flood, and famine, to name just a few of the disasters that plague country people. *Kō* has also functioned as an entertainment association where people organize and carry out fun events. As a whole, it has been intended to work in the best interests of the local people. *Kō* associations still exist, mostly in southern Japan.[12]

In Daido-Omata, Warai-kō consists of twenty-one members whose memberships are hereditary rights. Members take turns hosting an annual Warai-kō event, which means that each member's turn comes around every twenty-one years. The host offers rooms in his house (usually a traditional two-room-style drawing room with an alcove in one corner) for the event and presides over the ritual. When I visited in 1998 it was Matsutomi Ichirō's turn to host the ritual, but his membership had been handed over to his son due to his old age (eighty-two). Thus his son

Name	Age/Sex	Hosting Years
1. Hayashi Torazō	(53) M	'78 '99
2. Matsumura Shigeo	(54) M	'79 '00
3. Yamamoto Shigemitsu	(55) M	'80 '01
4. Sadayori Jirō	(56) M	'81 '02
5. Yoshitake Jirō	(57) M	'82 '03
6. Suenaga Takeo	(58) M	'83 '04
7. Tanaka Yukinari	(59) M	'84 '05
8. Tanaka Yoshihiro	(60) M	'85 '06
9. Uchida Den	(61) M	'86 '07
10. Yoshimura Ayako	(62) F	'87 '08
11. Nishimura Naritaka	(63) M	'88 '09
12. Tokunaga Yoshikazu	(64) M	'89 '10
13. Harada Fukuji	(65) M	'90 '11
14. Nakagawa Shin'ichi	(66) M	'91 '12
15. Kazunishi Kyōji	(67) M	'92 '13
16. Tamura Shōichi	(68) M	'93 '14
17. Yamane Tadao	(69) M	'94 '15
18. Takahashi Katsumi	(70) M	'95 '16
19. Kumano Takeshi	(71) M	'96 '17
20. Ishikawa Shōzō	(72) M	'97 '18
21. Matsutomi Ichirō	(73) M	'98 '19

Fig. 3.3 *Warai-kō* members in 1979 (Tanaka Yukinari, *Daidō Gei no Mukashi* [*Street Performances of the Olden Days*] [Hōfu City: Kōbunsha, 1980], 8; reprinted with permission).

acted as host, and Matsutomi Sr. played only a symbolic role in the ritual. Figure 3.3 lists the twenty-one Warai-kō members and their years of hosting the ritual from 1979 on.

Figure 3.4 shows the seating arrangements for the members participating in the 1979 Warai-kō. The same organization is followed each time the ritual is carried out. Members are seated around an open rectangle with plenty of room for food

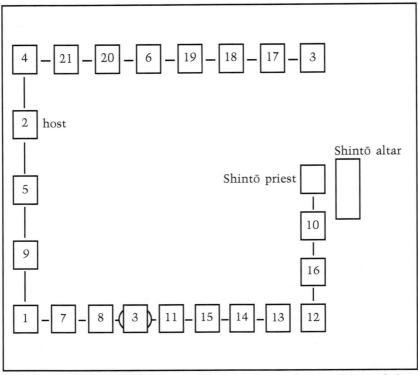

Figure 3.4 Seating arrangement for 1979 *Warai-kō* ritual (Tanaka Yukinari, *Daidō Gei no Mukashi* [*Street Performances of the Olden Days*] [Hōfu City: Kōbunsha, 1980], 5; reprinted with permission).

trays and other items to be placed in front them. At the head is the Shintō priest and a small altar. Pride of place is given to the year's host.

On the festival day, flags are set up either in the yard of the host's house or on the roadside nearby to indicate the site of the ritual, as is shown in figure 3.5, taken from my field visit to the 1998 ritual. Members come to the host's house in twos and threes and are expected to be there at around nine or ten in the morning. Upon their arrival, they take seats in the traditionally fixed seating order (see figure 3.6, also from my field trip). With all members in place, the ritual is ready to be performed. First,

Fig. 3.5 Outside the house of the host for the 1998 *Warai-kō* ritual
(photo by Abe Goh)

Fig. 3.6 Seated participants preparing for the 1998 ritual (note the
television crews in the background) (photo by Abe Goh)

meals are served by waiters. Participants eat specially prepared foods and drink sake and beer. And they chat and chat. When their stomachs are full and they have consumed quite an amount of alcohol, one of the Shintō priests announces the beginning of the ritual and selects one of the members and commands him or her to laugh. The member accordingly tries to make the right sounds, with the right feelings and expression.

Three kinds of symbolic laughter must be included: (1) those that give thanks for and celebrate the year's good harvest; (2) those that pray for the next year's good harvest; and (3) those that laugh away worries accumulated during the year. (It is important to note that the festival takes place at the end of the year.)[13] The members take turns, and two members may laugh in pairs at a time (see figures 3.7, a joint laugh, and 3.8, a solo effort). One of the members acts as a judge to evaluate the laughs. The judge strikes the bottom of a big pail loudly several times, in a showy manner, if the laugh is satisfactorily joyful and loud, coming from the bottom of the members' hearts, but strikes only once, in a disappointed manner, if the laugh is poor and banal. At the climax of the ritual, all the people present—Warai-kō members and Shintō priests alike—laugh the last big laugh together. This act symbolizes the end of the festival, and a figure of the local shrine god, a token of responsibility, is handed to the next host.

From the moment the Daido-Omata Warai-kō ritual began, I found myself fascinated by the amusingly funny world of ritual laughter. Meals, drinks, and conversations constituted, so to speak, a warm-up stage. Participants tried to relax their minds and their face muscles. In spite of their efforts, however, the first couple of laughs were clumsy and awkward. But soon the laughs began to gain momentum, becoming more and more loud and radical, as well as more wholehearted. It was a moment of relief and catharsis. Exposed to such powerful laughs, even a bystander like myself felt wrapped up in an inexplicable sense of relief and comfort. It was certainly a precious experience. But I soon wondered if the ritual had been handed down from generation to generation intact in its original form. The answer is obviously no, because the world around us has changed drastically over the centuries. Along with it, common practices must have gone through many twists and turns. Then how did it change?

Fig. 3.7 A pair of 1998 participants laugh in unison, holding symbolic branches (photo by Abe Goh)

Fig. 3.8 Trying for the right public laugh is a serious business for this participant (photo by Abe Goh)

It is not difficult to imagine how hard life might have been in Japan in the twelfth century, at the end of which the kō was first organized. The ordinary people had neither the knowledge nor the means to cope with various obstacles in their daily lives. They were constantly affected by natural disasters, diseases, harsh rules imposed by the governing classes, warfare, and other afflictions. A mutual aid society, was, therefore, an indispensable tool for their survival. Kō members united against their common enemies, and their concerted efforts occasionally proved successful, but mostly people were still at the mercy of cruel reality. In such vulnerable conditions, they needed to vent their pent-up stress and therefore employed laughter. They began to laugh away their worries, and this practice developed into Warai-kō. I went to the local library in Daido-Omata to get further information on Warai-kō. To my disappointment, there were few historical documents available.[14]

After the festival on December 6, 1998, I was on my way to a restaurant in the suburbs in a car driven by a city employee who works for the city's tourism promotion section. Soon I noticed a very interesting signboard by the roadside set up by the city to attract tourists. The sign said in Japanese, "This place has been known for the world's weirdest festival." I instantly understood that it was part of the city planning scheme to revitalize the district as a tourist destination. They needed a thrilling catchphrase for a commercial use of the festival. But it was more than a mere catchphrase. It was a clear indication that the festival could be interpreted differently in each historical period with values in constant flux. As James Clifford has observed, cultural traditions are reinvented in each historical period:

> Twentieth-century identities no longer presuppose continuous cultures or traditions. Everywhere individuals and groups improvise local performances from (re)collected pasts, drawing on foreign media, symbols, and languages. . . . The roots of tradition are cut and retied, collective symbols appropriated from external influences . . . culture and identity are inventive and mobile. They need not take root in ancestral plots; they live by pollination, by (historical) transplanting.[15]

I still remember the remarks that Mr. Yamamoto, the judge

at the 1998 Warai-kō, made at the festival. "We've enjoyed a good harvest this year," he said, "thanks to the good laugh we had last year. Another good harvest has been promised for next year, because our laughter this year turned out to be another incredible one." I felt relieved to know that the original spirit of Warai-kō had not been lost yet.

NOTES

I want to express my gratitude to the participants of the 1998 Warai-kō festival, who welcomed me as an outside observer; to Inoue Hiroshi and Oda Shōkichi, who provided me with valuable information regarding the festival; and to Mrs. Fumi Umeda, who typed up this manuscript.

1. Abe Goh, "Political and Social Satirical Cartoons in Nepal," in *Bungakuronsō: A Collection of Treatises on Languages and Literature*, vol. 15 (Kagawa: Tokushima Bunri University, 1998), 53; also see Ram Kumar Panday, *Nepalese Humour* (Kathmandu: Muskan Prakashan, 2000), 36–39. This chapter is based on a paper I presented in July 1999 at the eleventh ISHS Conference at Holy Names College, Oakland, California.
2. Dhurba Deep, *The Nepal Festival* (Kathmandu: Variety Printers, 1992), 57–60.
3. Abe, "Political and Social Satirical Cartoons," 54–56.
4. Figure 3.1 is the work of the author, based on information Oda Shōkichi shared with me and on an article by Togazawa Hidetoshi and Takano Satoshi in the *Mainichi Shimbun*, "Warai no Kagaku," January 3, 1997.
5. Haga Hideo, "Matsuri no Naka no Warai," *Gengo Seikatsu* 325 (1979): 45.
6. Iijima Yoshiharu, *Warai to Ishō* (Tokyo: Kaimeisha, 1985), 63.
7. Inokuchi Shōji, "Nihon no Warai Gyōji," *Gengo* 23, no. 12 (1994): 34–35.
8. Inoue Hiroshi, *Warai no Ningen Kankei* (Tokyo: Kōdansha, 1984), 19–20.
9. Byron Earhart, *Japanese Religion: Unity and Diversity*, 3rd ed. (Belmont, Calif.: Wadsworth, 1982), 8.
10. Matsumoto Shigeru, *Motoori Norinaga, 1730–1801* (Cambridge: Harvard University Press, 1970), 84.
11. Earhart, *Japanese Religion*, 8.
12. Haga, "Matsuri no Naka no Warai," 44.
13. Tanaka Yukinari, *Daidō Gei no Mukashi* (Hōfu City: Kōbunsha, 1980), 4.

14. The collections of historical material available for Hōfu City are listed in "Additional Sources" below.
15. James Clifford, *The Predicament of Culture: Twentieth-Century Ethnography: Literature and Art* (Cambridge: Harvard University Press, 1998), 14–15; see also Roy Wagner, *The Invention of Culture*, rev. ed. (Chicago: University of Chicago Press, 1980).

ADDITIONAL SOURCES

Anon. "Omata no Waraikō" ("The Warai-kō at Omata"). In *Hōfu Shi Shi: Shiryō 1—Shizen, Minzoku, Chimei* (*A History of Hōfu City: Documents Vol. 1—Nature, Folklore, Place-Names*), ed. Hōfu Shi Shi Hensan I'inkai (Committee for Compiling the History of Hōfu City), 407–8. Hōfu: Hōfu City Authority and Ōmura Printing Company, 1994.

Anon. "Omata no Waraikō" ("The Warai-kō at Omata"). In *Zoku Hōfu Shi Shi* (*A History of Hōfu City Continued*), ed. Misonoo Ōsuke, 707–9. Hōfu City: Zōten Hōfu Shi Shi Kankōkai (Association to Publish a Further Volume of the History of Hōfu City) and Ōmura Printing Company, 1960.

Anon. "Waraikō." In *Hōfu no Minzoku Geinō o Tazunete* (*Visits to Folk Performances of Hōfu*), ed. Hashiguchi Teruo, 6. Pamphlet produced by the Twentieth Anniversary Project Group of Hofu. Hōfu City: Hōfu no Bunka o Takameru Kai (Association for Promoting Hōfu Culture), 1989.

Furusato Daidō o Horiokosu Kai (Study Group for Rediscovering Daidō—our Old Home Village), ed. *Furusato Daidō* (*Daidō—Old Home Village*). Vol. 3. Yamaguchi: Kobunsha, 1982. Vol. 8. Yamaguchi: Colony, 1993.

Hashimoto Hiroyuki. "Warawanai Hito ga Arimasu ka—[Owarai Geinin] no Genzō" ("Is there Anyone Who Doesn't Laugh?—A Prototype Image [of a Professional Humorist]"). *Nihon no Bigaku* (*Japanese Aesthetics*) 20 (1993): 155–77.

Panday, Ram Kumar. *The Himalayan Heritage of Humour.* Paper presented at the eighth ISHS Conference, University of New South Wales, Sydney, Australia, July 2000.

Yoshikoshi Emiko. "Warai no Kaishaku—Atsuta Jingū Suishōjinji o Rei to Shite" ("The Interpretation of Laughter—Taking the Atsuta Shrine Suishōjin Ritual as an Example"). *Geinō* (*Performance*) 33, no. 6 (1991): 22–30.

4 *Manzai*: Team Comedy in Japan's Entertainment Industry

Joel F. Stocker

In July 2000, at the annual conference of the International Society for Humor Studies, I presented an account of the little-known history and nature of *manzai* immediately following a *rakugo* comic narrative performance.[1] I noted at the time that, although *manzai* had become more popular than its rival form of comedy in the variety halls of Kansai and Kanto by the late 1920s, and although it continues to be the genre in which most of Japan's comic entertainers are trained, *rakugo*'s status as an oral art has steadily improved while that of *manzai* has remained quite low. This state of affairs can be explained, first, by the fact that today's *manzai*, which is characterized by the friendly antagonism of its *boke* (ボケ fool) and *tsukkomi* (つっこみ wit) roles, is usually portrayed as a reflection of the special qualities of the urban commoners of Osaka, who are said to "sound like *manzai* comedians" (and vice versa).[2] At best, this widespread view has given *manzai* a patina of folk nostalgia and proletarian nobility. Second, and somewhat contrary to the first point, *manzai* is known to be dominated by a commercial entertainment giant, Yoshimoto Kōgyō Inc., a fact that has given the genre an even more practical, worldly, and vulgar face. Third, *manzai* comedians and their promoters have always been responsive to changes in market demand and commercial strategies, and this adaptability and the resultant unruly development of the genre are perhaps further reasons why *manzai* has been relatively ignored and devalued as an oral art. But is it an oral art? Is it Osakan? Does it originate from the common people or from media companies? To answer these and other questions, in this chapter I will discuss the dynamic history and the current state of *manzai* within the Japanese entertainment industry.

The Early Years

Manzai began in the Middle Ages as a rite performed at New Year's by pairs of traveling entertainers who combined auspicious (芽出度い；目出度い *medetai*) rituals with laughable (可笑しい *okashii*) acts. According to Maeda Isamu, who has written the most thorough account of the history of *manzai*, a *manzai* of the Imperial palace (宮中) existed by the late Heian period (794–1185). However, it is the history of the "strolling art" of folk *manzai* (民間万歳 *minkan manzai*), apparently existent by the Muromachi period (1392–1573), that may extend to today's *manzai*. This door-to-door or "gate" (門付け *kadozuke*) *manzai* was ordinarily performed by a pair of men: one, a serious fellow called the *tayū* (太夫), was outfitted in a ceremonial hat (烏帽子 *eboshi*), a coat imprinted with large seals (羽織 *haori*), and a hand fan (扇子 *sensu*), and would sing blessings and dance in a dignified manner in return for a handful of rice or a bit of money; the other, a buffoonish fellow called the *saizō* (才蔵), wearing a similar hat and coat with a rice bag over his shoulder, would beat a hand drum (鼓 *tsuzumi*). In closing, the *saizō* would cheekily interject a certain amount of humor into the proceedings and the *tayū* would verbally rebuke him and whack him on the head with his fan. Along with the more weighty blessings, this laughter at the beginning of the year was thought to bring good fortune. Figure 4.1 provides an example of a late-twentieth-century revival of the traditional *manzai* presentation for the New Year's festivities.[3]

In time, many regional varieties of *manzai* appeared, and *manzai* also came to be performed at other times of the year as an attraction (見世物 *misemono*). For instance, in the early part of the eighteenth century, the *manzai* stage performers at Ikutama Shrine in Osaka, who dressed in black-crested everyday *kimonos* (着流し *kinagashi*), were quite well known.[4] In the latter half of the eighteenth century, *manzai* was performed on makeshift stages in entertainment districts such as Sakaichō in Edo and Gion in Kyoto. *Manzai* did not become popular onstage as a commercial entertainment until the end of the nineteenth century, when, after a period of decline in the late Edo period, it emerged as a pastiche of amateur and semi-amateur entertainment. It was gradually professionalized on small stages in

Fig. 4.1 Poster from a 1994 classic *manzai* festival in Aichi Prefecture (Reproduced from copy in author's possession)

amusement quarters in the Kansai area of Osaka. During this period, many genres of song, chant, and dance were performed in neighborhoods as a pastime, in the streets on festive occasions, and on entertainment stages; these often found their way into *manzai* acts, whose rules were the most flexible of all the variety acts (色物 *iromono*).

By 1900 there were approximately sixty-five *yose* (寄席 variety halls) in Osaka, which made that city preeminent in the development of many of Japan's popular entertainments. These *yose* featured verbal arts (話芸 *wagei*) such as *rakugo*, *kōdan* recitation (講談), *rōkyoku* (浪曲), *naniwa-bushi* accompanied by a *shamisen* (a traditional Japanese stringed instrument), and, to some extent, *manzai*, as well as physical arts (体伎 *taigi*) such as magic (手品 *tejina*), acrobatics and stunts (曲芸 *kyokugei*), and plate spinning (皿回し *sara mawashi*).[5] By 1912, the beginning of the Taishō period, many types of songs had become popular (folk songs, romantic songs, narrative ballads) and *manzai* performers were still primarily singers and chanters, but now with a broader range of (especially contemporary) material and modes of expression.[6]

The person considered the founder of modern *manzai*, Tamagoya Entatsu,[7] was originally a singer of *gōshū ondo* (江州音頭),[8] a regional style of folk singing accompanied by *bon* dancing, that was already a popular pastime and *yose* act by the 1890s. Each song would go on for about an hour, so Tamagoya Entatsu apparently spiced it up with the comic banter of Nagoya-*manzai* (learned during his previous travels as a singing egg seller) to create an act that, for the first time, emphasized the laughable (おかしみ *okashimi*) over the auspicious (目出度さ *medetasa*).[9] Another key figure in the development of stage *manzai* is Sunagawa Sutemaru, who first performed onstage in Osaka around 1899 at the age of ten. He also was a singer of *gōshū ondo*. Sutemaru played an important role in "cleaning up" *manzai*, and he is also well known for managing to preserve his style of *manzai* and remain independent from the controlling Osaka comedy production corporation, Yoshimoto. At the beginning of the Taishō era a show proprietor invited him to perform in the city of Kobe when it was still a developing port area. The proprietor's aim was to get the ban on *manzai* lifted in that area. Monitored by the police, *manzai*'s scandalous content and the dubious venues at which it had appeared in the red-light districts in Kobe had led to a ban of the ribald genre there from about the time of the Russo-Japanese War (1904–5).[10] The proprietor asked the police who had jurisdiction over his theater to watch Sutemaru perform *manzai*. Sutemaru's relatively refined performance won the day, the ban was lifted, and he and his troupe of twenty entertainers were allowed to perform on a regular basis.

Sutemaru created a "high-class *manzai*" (高級万歳 *kōkyū manzai*),[11] in part by adopting the formal dress (and equipment) of a famous *naniwa-bushi* performer. He donned a seal-imprinted *kimono* and a formal coat (*haori*) and skirt (袴 *hakama*) and toted a *tsuzumi* drum, while his partner (相方 *aikata*) played a

Fig. 4.2 Sunagawa Sutemaru and Nakamura Haruyo (Mita Jun'ichi, *Shōwa Kamigata Shōgeishi* [Tokyo: Gakugei Shorin, 1993], 92)

shamisen. In this way, as part of a dignified-looking double act that mixed joking with song and dance, he set himself apart from run-of-the-mill acts, who wore the *kinagashi* (casual *kimono* with no *hakama* or *haori*) in the fashion of Ikutama Shrine *manzai.* Living until 1971, Sutemaru became a valuable source of information about the commercial beginnings of *manzai,* serving as a model for what the genre was like in the early years.[12] This high-class *manzai,* well illustrated by figure 4.2 (which depicts the founder himself with his third and last partner),[13] had by the late 1920s become a style representative of Kansai-area *manzai* performers; these were popular in Tokyo as well (along with Osaka dialect).[14]

A recording exists of a performance of one of Sutemaru's signature routines, "Owarai Konjiki Yasha," with Nakamura Haruyo, which shows how stage *manzai* of the early years (he first performed this routine in the 1920s) incorporated a colorful assortment of performance arts and stories from the past.

Here a short dialogue is built around the romantic characters of a late-nineteenth-century newspaper serialization of a novel, later turned into a popular *shinpa* (新派 new school) drama. The well-known male and female protagonists were called Kan'ichi and Omiya. The following is an excerpt from the *manzai* performance between Sutemaru (S) and Haruyo (H):

S:	あんたなんですって	*Anta nan desutte*	Who'd you say you are?
H:	わたしか	*Watashi ka*	Who, me?
S:	はい	*Hai*	Yes.
H:	お宮	*Omiya*	Omiya.
S:	「お宮」？	*"Omiya"*	"Omiya"?
H:	おおっ	*Ô(tt)*	Ah-uh.
S:	ほう、お寺 みたいやか	*Hō, otera mitai ya ka*	[Chuckling] Haha, like an *otera* [temple]!?
	（観客が爆笑する）	[*Kankyaku ga bakushō suru*]	[Audience laughs loudly]
H:	「お寺」？ （観客の笑い声に かき消される）	*"O-tera"* [*Kankyaku no warai goe ni kakikesareru*]	"O-tera"?! [Her voice is lost in audience laughter]
H:	「お寺」あほ いうな、バカもの！	*"Otera" aho yū na bakamono*	Don't call me an "otera" you idiot!
S:	今年のお宮は 出来が悪い お宮としらんが、 顔にいっぱいしわ がある	*Kotoshi no Omiya wa deki ga warui Omiya to shiran ga, kao ni ippai shiwa ga aru*	This year's Omiya are poorly made. I'm not sure if you're an Omiya, but your face is sure wrinkled.[15]

Sutemaru sets up both a visual and an auditory contrast between a delicate and temporary shrine (*omiya*, phonetically the woman's name) and a temple (*otera*, weather-beaten and permanent), observing that his partner, a physically imposing figure with a booming voice, looks more like an *otera* (temple) than an *omiya*.[16] The double joke of course is that she is certainly *not* the traditional Omiya from the love story *Konjiki Yasha*, who, as the audience knows very well, is a romantic figure bringing to mind images of striking beauty. In short, Sutemaru exploits the coincidence of his partner's given name as presented in this

56

comedy routine with the heroine of that story, building a series of verbal and visual jokes upon shared knowledge with the audience.[17]

The Yoshimoto Brand and *Shabekuri Manzai*

By the late 1920s, even as the genre's popularity was on the rise, producers of *manzai* began to struggle with its old-fashioned aspects—the old clothing, songs, and instruments. Things new, Western, and modern (household appliances, coffee at jazz cafés, rapidly changing clothing styles, movie halls, and so forth) were being pursued by contemporary urban Japanese. At the same time, as Xavier Bensky notes, "the social class of those who sought out entertainment in the *yose* gradually shifted from the merchant class of the harbour area, that had supported Osakan *rakugo*, to the salaried and working class."[18] In 1930, Yokoyama Entatsu and Achako, a newly formed *manzai* double act introduced under the imprimatur of the Yoshimoto Corporation in Osaka, began to perform *shabekuri manzai*, a new style of *manzai* based on the dialogue (喋くり；しゃべくり *shabekuri*), attire, and antics well adapted to the fast pace of modern life in urban Japan. This duo's *shabekuri* style soon became the most common form of *manzai* in Japan. They engaged in a friendly, complementary antagonism, formally divided between the two of them: the *tsukkomi* played the *kashikoyaku*, the role (役 *yaku*) of the smart one (賢い *kashikoi*), and the *boke* played what in Osaka dialect is called the *aho no yaku* (アホの役), or more generally the role of the fool (愚かな *oroka na*). Although dialogue had been one feature of *manzai* in the past, it had never before been the sole focus of a *manzai* double act. And, moreover, the actors stood onstage in Western suits, looking and acting very similar to characters out of film comedies from England and America. In an era when suits were just beginning to catch on and the older forms of *manzai* had no doubt begun to look out of step with the flashy, novel entertainments of the modern age, Entatsu and Achako shed the *kimono*, the drum, the fan, and the instruments and singing of their predecessors (see figure 4.3, which illustrates their appearance in the 1930s).

Yoshimoto executives decisively shaped and promoted this new *manzai*. Credit is usually given to Hayashi Shōnosuke, brother of the company co-founder Yoshimoto Sei and a central

Fig. 4.3 Entatsu (*right*) and Achako in the 1930s (copyright Yoshimoto Kōgyō. Image from *Yoshimoto Hachijūnen no Ayumi* [Osaka:
Yoshimoto Kōgyō Ltd., 1992], not for sale)

figure at Yoshimoto by the mid-1920s (after the death of Sei's
husband and co-founder Kichibei, in 1924), for telling Entatsu
and Achako to wear Western suits and instructing Entatsu to
wear "glasses like Lloyd's" and "a mustache like Chaplin's."[19]
Hayashi saw the potential for a revamped *manzai* in replacing
the waning *rakugo*, which had previously been dominant in the
yose, and in dealing with the rise of film as the number one form
of entertainment in the urban areas traditionally dominated by
performance stages. He went so far as to take the commercially
risky step of pulling Achako out of an already popular *manzai*
duo in order to pair him with Entatsu in the new formula. The
Yoshimoto company also took the unprecedented step in 1930
of reducing its basic *yose* admission price to 10 *sen*.[20] The 10-*sen*
yose was perhaps successful in part because of the worldwide
economic depression from the late 1920s, when many unem-
ployed people were in the urban areas looking for work and saw
the cheap comic entertainment as a way to pass the time, forget
their troubles, or vent their frustrations. The lower-priced ad-

mission was put into effect after Yoshimoto's market consolidation of the *yose* and their entertainers, which also created the conditions by which the company could put entertainers on stable monthly salaries—the trade-off being that many had to perform three or four shows every day within what journalists referred to as Yoshimoto's "entertainment kingdom" (演芸王国 *engei ōkoku*).

Another key step in Yoshimoto's promotion of *shabekuri manzai* was the public announcement at New Year's in 1933 that they would use new characters (漫 *man,* as in *manga,* and 才 *zai,* meaning skill or talent) for *manzai* to give it a modern image, a policy based on a proposal by their advertising director, Hashimoto Tetsuhiko.[21] Furthermore, they hired the first *manzai* scriptwriter, Akita Minoru, who even set up a short-lived *manzai* school in an attempt to meet the new demand for *manzai* teams onstage and in the media. Akita subsequently helped to transform *manzai* into a salable, mass-mediated, commercial genre in the era of radio and film (he also wrote a number of film scripts). He fine-tuned his scripts to the current events and the everyday features of life in Japan's rapidly expanding urban society. For example, instead of the personal pronouns *omae* (お前 you) and *ore* (俺 me, I), his scripts featured the equivalent but slightly more formal *kimi* (君) and *boku* (僕), which are used, for example, between employees in the workplace.

Shabekuri manzai caught on through stage performances, radio shows, films,[22] script books, phonograph records, newspaper and magazine articles, and eventually television shows and videotape (now even over the Internet). Entatsu and Achako are remembered for the novelty and unprecedented mass-circulated popularity of their style of *manzai;* in fact, their fame is due in part to the fact that the record of their performances has been preserved by the various media in which they worked. Similar to Abbott and Costello in the United States, the two rose to national fame after a national radio broadcast live in 1934 (via a Yoshimoto-operated theater in Osaka) a routine that was soon to become their most famous one, on the timely topic of a recent "Sōkeisen" baseball game.[23] In this dialogue, Entatsu, the *boke,* introduces the main theme, which is the university baseball game featuring Waseda versus Keiō, in the fall of 1933 (it was famous or infamous for the "apple incident," in which a fan threw an apple at a player, who threw it back, with a scuffle ensuing). The pair's reliance on dialogue worked well with the aural medium of radio and with the use of a microphone. The content of their routine even mirrored the radio setting, since they imitated the style of baseball commentary done by radio announcers. The following segment of (one version of) the routine illustrates how the *boke*, Entatsu (E), misconstrues what is said, while the *tsukkomi*, Achako (A), tries to clarify both the name of the event (which is a combination of the characters for the names of the two schools) and who is competing:

E: 早慶戦、 / 何といっても絶対 / のもんですな — *Sōkeisen, nan to itte mo zettai no mon desu na* — The Sōkeisen . . . it's, whatever's said about it, something else.

A: まったく、 / 文字通り天下の / 早慶戦ですな — *Mattaku, mojidōri tenka no Sōkeisen desu na* — Indeed, it's THE Sōkeisen.

E: しかし、あれ、相手は / どこでしたかいな？ — *Shikashi, are, aite wa doko deshita kai na?* — But who's the opponent?

A: えっ、相手？ / いえ、早慶戦の話を / してるんですがな — *E(tt), aite? Ie, Sōkeisen no hanashi o shiterun desu ga na* — Huh . . . opponent? No, we're discussing the Sōkeisen.

E: 早慶戦は分かって / ますけど、その相手 / ですがな。つまり / 早慶対 / どこそことか。。。 — *Sōkeisen wa wakatte-masu kedo, sono aite desu ga na. Tsumari, Sōkei tai dokosoko to ka . . .* — I understand—"the Sōkeisen." But what about their opponent? In other words, Sōkei versus someone or other . . .

A: 頼りない人 / やな。早慶戦はやね、 / 早稲田と慶応が試合を / するから、「早慶戦」 / というんやないか — *Tayorinai hito ya na. Sōkeisen wa ya ne, Waseda to Keiō ga shiai o suru kara, Sōkeisen to iun ya nai ka* — You're impossible. The Sōkeisen is called the Sōkeisen, ya see, because Waseda and Keiō are matched up.

E: それは / わかってるよ。それが / わからずに何を見に / 行くのや — *Sore wa wakatteru yo. Sore ga wakarazu ni nani o mi ni iku no ya* — I understand that. Without understanding that, what would I go to watch?

A: そんなら、 / 早慶対どこそこや、 / なんて情けないこと — *Sonnara, Sōkei tai dokosoko ya, nante nasakenai koto* — Then don't say stupid things like "Sōkei versus

をいうな	*o iu na*	someone or other."
E: ちょっと洒落 をいうてみたんです	*Chotto share o iute mitan desu*	I was trying to do a little play on words.
A: そんな洒落 は通らん	*Sonna share wa tōran*	That doesn't pass as a play on words.
E: 洒落が わからんのやから、 本当に君は扱いにくい	*Share ga wakaran no ya kara, hontō ni kimi wa atsukainikui*	You're really a hard one to deal with because you don't get wordplays.[24]

The conversation is structured for a battle of words and worldviews in which the *tsukkomi* attempts to "correct" the *boke*'s errant interpretations, oftentimes using one hand to tap or strike him on the shoulder, back, or head. The *boke*'s ideas seem to run freely with the perspectives of his own unique, absurd world, while the *tsukkomi* tries to apply a line of reasoning or common sense to the dialogue. The *boke* constructs what appear to be foolish or absurd interpretations of "reality" or of what the *tsukkomi* has opened for discussion; he twists these things into an entirely different logic, often wandering off into what appears to be a completely different matter. The implicit rules of the genre are that the *tsukkomi* nods and says filler words (相槌言葉 *aizuchi kotoba*) in response to the *boke*'s relatively normal-sounding statements, but, more importantly, he also "digs into" (突っ込む *tsukkomu*) the *boke*—to criticize, to correct, and to point out the illogic or stupidity of the *boke*'s crazy, silly, off-the-wall, or ignorant remarks, gestures, and movements. Thus the *tsukkomi* tends to be the one who frames the overall routine and its progress, acting as the commonsense voice of social order in the face of the trickster-like *boke*'s chaotic utterances and behavior which upset that order.

In this dialogue-based stand-up *manzai* comedy, the normal routine will consist of a conversational theme or a series of unrelated or tangentially related anecdotes, broadly held together by being portrayed as "real" personal experiences, by *manzai* performers who are basically performing "themselves," with their distinct team's stage personalities changing little from one routine to another or from show to show. Although separate narratives or stories may occasionally be told as part of this "dialogue" structure, this aspect is more typical of another type of *manzai*, especially popular since the 1980s, called skit *manzai* (コント マンザイ *konto manzai*). Skit *manzai* commonly contains the same style of dialogue that typifies *shabekuri manzai* (the *tsukkomi/boke* repartee), but when performing a *konto*, *manzai* comedians generally also use some form of costuming and props, enact characters distinct to the skit, and enter directly into the performance with no introductory explanation. This way, they create a special "once-off" situation.

The importance of the "personal experience" aspect of *manzai* is illustrated by the career of one contemporary team who, like most, have followed in the footsteps of Entatsu and Achako. Nakata Kausu and Nakata Botan formed their duo in 1969 when they were teenagers.[25] The names "Kausu" and "Botan" refer to "Cuff(s) and Button (or cufflink)," which suggests both complementarity and oneness (since together they could be a "cuff-button"). Although *botan* is the normal Japanese word for *button*, *kausu* is a variant of *kafusu*, the usual Japanese word for *cuffs*. Kausu, who always stands on the right, is the *boke*. Early on their target audience was junior high and high school girls, a distinct and newly emerging group to whom contemporary *manzai* entertainers had not yet thought of tailoring their acts. The duo became one of the first "idol" *manzai* teams when they grew their hair long and changed out of the flashy, expensive silk suits that were de rigueur at the time. They replaced these with the blue jeans and T-shirts becoming fashionable in the newly developed American used-clothing district called American Village (*Amerika Mura*) in downtown Osaka. This area was a focal point for Japanese youth culture in the Kansai region. The team's gags deliberately incorporated slang expressions used by girls and young women. However, when one of them got married the young female fans lost interest and the duo faced the challenge of trying to appeal to a broader audience, including adults.

They then struggled for many years, reaching a low point in 1988, when Botan was arrested on suspicion of gambling (playing craps). After the Yoshimoto Corporation suspended Botan for three months, Kausu turned this apparent setback into a win by employing the incident in their routines. On a talk show featuring the life story of the duo, Kausu said that, for a *manzai* comedian, "one's faults are one's greatest asset" onstage, because they humanize the performers and provide the public with en-

Fig. 4.4 Kausu (*right*) and Botan on their television show *Kamigata Manzai Ōkoku* (produced from a noncommercial videotape [Kansai TV, spring 2000])

tertaining firsthand accounts of their "life story."[26] In his view, it does not matter how fabricated or embroidered that may be as long as the story is well done and has the odor of reality. Kausu also commented that "what *manzai* shows us is how well [two] unrelated fellows get along. . . . Our *manzai* would turn into a fist fight if we didn't really share the same feelings. I suppose over half of it [our antagonism] is for real."[27] This duo eventually became quite popular again after the early 1980s' nationwide "*manzai* boom," becoming a fixture in the Osaka entertainment business. In 1991 they won the top award at the Kamigata Manzai Taishō contest, proving the durability of their approach. Their appearance has consistently featured two working-class Osakan men going through the ups (as young idols) and downs (as criminals, bad husbands, poor drunks, and so forth) of life (see figure 4.4).

The opening of a fast, short routine (46 seconds) performed by Kausu (K) and Botan (B) on their television show, *Kamigata Manzai Ōkoku*,[28] illustrates their style of *manzai*. This routine was recorded in front of a live audience of mainly elderly people at a performance hall for a later television broadcast.

K: はい、どうも ようこそお越し いただきました！	*Hai dōmo* *yōkoso okoshi* *itadakimashita.*	Yes, thank you very much for coming.
B: ありがとう ございます。ほんまに ね。。。ほんまに	*Arigatō* *gozaimasu, honma ni* *ne . . . honma ni*	Thank you, really, truly . . .
K: そこからここまで 出てくる間に、 客席をパッと見て どんな話しが合うのか をあたまの中で考えて いるんでっせ。	*Soko kara koko* *made dete kuru aida ni* *kyakuseki o patto mite* *donna hanashi ga au no ka* *o atama no naka de* *kangaete irun desse.*	In the moment it takes to get from there to here [the mike], we glance at the audience and think over what kind of conver- sation will be appropriate.
B: そうでっせ。 私たちが出てきて 好きなことだけを 喋って帰っているわけ ではおまへんねんで。	*Sō desse.* *Watashitachi ga dete kite* *suki na koto dake o* *shabette kaette iru wake* *de wa omahen nende.*	That's right. Don't think that we just appear, say whatever we please and then leave.
K: お客様の 雰囲気に合わしたネタ せんやあかんね。	*Okyakusama no* *fun'iki ni awashita neta* *sen'ya akan ne.*	Ya hafta do a routine that matches the feel of the audience.
B: そう、そう、そう。 一番大事なんのは 客席に合わすという ことやろうね。	*Sō sō sō.* *Ichiban daiji nan no wa* *kyakuseki ni awasu to iu* *koto yarō ne.*	Yes, yes, yes. The most important thing is to adjust to the audience.
K: パッと客席を 見て頭良さそうなお客 さんが多いと思う時は 政治経済の漫才を せんやならんの。	*Patto kyakuseki o* *mite atama yosasō na* *okyakusan ga ōi to omou* *toki wa seiji-keizai no* *manzai o sen'ya naran no.*	When we think there's a lot of audience members who appear to be smart, we've gotta do *manzai* about politics/economics.
B: ほんまに。	*Honma ni.*	You bet.
K: ね。	*Nē*	Yup.
B: ちょっと堅い 目の話しをね。	*Chotto katai* *me no hanashi o ne*	Talk that's a little serious. . . .

K: ご婦人の方が 多い時は、家庭生活 の話しが 喜ばれますし。	*Gofujin no kata ga ōi toki wa, katei seikatsu no hanashi ga yorokobaremasu shī*	When there are a lot of wives, they enjoy talk about household matters.
B: ええ、気使うなあ。	*Ee, ki tsukau nā*	You're so considerate.
K: 当たり前やない かい、プロやんけ。	*Atarimae ya nai kai, puro yanke*	Of course: I'm a pro.
B: まあ、今日の お客さんやったら、どう いうお話しがええかなあ？	*Mā, kyō no okyakusan yattara, dō iu ohanashi ga ē ka nā!*	Well then, what topic of conversation would be good for today's audience?
K: 今日のお客さん は、年輩のお方が 多ございますから、	*Kyō no okyakusan wa, nenpai no kata ga ō gozaimasu kara*	Since there's a lot of elderly folks today . . .
B: そうですね。	*Sō desu ne*	Yes, there are . . .
K: 失敗のない墓石 の選び方で行こうと （観客が笑う）	*Shippai no nai hakaishi no erabikata de ikō to [Kyaku ga warau]*	The sure-fire choice would be gravestones. [Audience laughs]
B: ちょっと待って	*Chotto matte . . .*	Wait a minute . . .

Manzai comedians who perform *manzai* onstage throughout their careers (usually because they have failed to create or sustain a career in Tokyo as general television personalities) must play to diverse audiences, the elderly as well as the young, tourists as well as local people of all ages. Here the performers have made their necessary professional concern with the composition of the audience an integral part of their routine. *Manzaishi* (漫才師 *manzai* comedians) almost always address the crowd in this personalized way, acknowledging their particular existence, and in the case of television, using the live audience as surrogates for a wider audience of viewers.

The genre of *shabekuri manzai* ushered in by Entatsu and Achako has changed surprisingly little since 1930, retaining its core of humorous dialogic tensions between the twin roles of the fool and the wit. What has changed in the last few decades, however, is how *manzai* comedians have increasingly become multimedia entertainers. Dialogue-based *manzai* is still popular in Japan, supported by young audiences who are inundated with the media but who seek the satisfaction of live participation.

65

But these days, watching almost any Japanese television show, you are likely to see entertainers who are (or once were) *manzai-shi*. Many of the most famous entertainers—for example, Beat Takeshi (his real name is Kitano Takeshi), Shimano Shinsuke, Matsumoto Hitoshi and Hamada Masatoshi (known as "Down-Town"; see below), or Okamura Takashi and Yabe Hiroshi ("Ninety-Nine")—were once *manzai* comedians. Now they do most of their entertaining in other capacities, as hosts on radio and television variety and talk shows and even as pop singers, drama actors, and politicians. Star appeal has become more important than *manzai* entertainers' training or background, and the demands of the entertainment world both reshape content and limit the amount of time entertainers have to devote to developing their craft.[29] For Yoshimoto's *manzai-* and *rakugo-*trained entertainers, as for other comedy theater people, there is little time or incentive for development. They must work continuously to perform where the money is, on the thousands of television and radio programs broadcast every year and also at dozens of theaters and other venues throughout the year.[30]

Manzai since the New Star Creation School

In the early 1980s there was a shift in *manzai* training from long-term apprenticeship to one-year vocational schooling and the creation of "no-brand" *manzai*. Within ten years, a majority of the young *manzai* entertainers in Japan were being trained at Yoshimoto's New Star Creation (NSC) school and were no longer associated with a specific *manzai* master. Instead, they gave substance to the ubiquitous brand image of Yoshimoto, the corporation where a few lucky graduates would get contracts and high-profile careers. The school also ushered in an era in which new opportunities for participation and interaction opened up for the large numbers of fans of *manzai* and individual *manzai* teams: it gave them a chance to visit and see the inner workings of the star-maker Yoshimoto, perhaps to perform *manzai* themselves, and possibly to become a star. Such innovations were accompanied by parallel moves in television programming, for which *manzai* routines proved highly suitable, not only in their own format but as part of the ubiquitous talk and variety shows.[31]

In 1983, the first year of graduation from the Osaka NSC, the graduating duo called DownTown, formed by Matsumoto Hitoshi and Hamada Masatoshi, emerged. They have become among the most sought-after multimedia, multigenre entertainers in Japan. Together with other successful NSC graduates, they have inspired many young people to enter Yoshimoto's school. After becoming popular at a local Osaka theater for NSC graduates in the late 1980s, DownTown quickly moved on to the larger Tokyo Media Center and then quit performing regular *manzai* altogether. They have continued to work together mostly as an entertainment duo in the format illustrated in figure 4.5. Matsumoto (shown on the left in a "free talk" section of their show) continues to play a *manzai boke* role to his partner's *tsukkomi* on the many television shows in which they appear together.

The following is an excerpt from *Not a Task for Kids* (*Gaki no Tsukai ya Arahen de*), the long-running and popular television show they host, which began on late-night television in Tokyo in the early 1990s. Here Matsumoto (M) and Hamada (H) are talking about Matsumoto's new "monk" (坊主 *bōzu*) hairstyle, which received a great deal of media attention in 1998, shortly after which he released a book titled *Matsumoto Bōzu*.[32] Now, he argues, he will suit action to his name:

M: 色んなこと
に対して「だめだよ」
と言えるように
なりましたよ。
昔は何にでも
オラァーと叫ん
でましたが、今
は何にでも
「ダメだよ」と 軽く
言ってます、よ。

Ironna koto ni taishite
"dame da yo"
to ieru yō ni
narimashita yo.
Mukashi wa nan ni demo
orā to
sakendemashita ga,
ima wa nan ni demo
"dame da yo" to
karuku ittemasu yo.

I've gotten so that
I can say "No"
to many things.
In the past I'd
blow up,
but
now it's just
a light "No."

H: 何を言ってるの？
人に何か言われた
時でも？ 文句を
つけられた時でも？

Nani o itteru no.
Hito ni nanika iwareta
toki demo? Monku o
tsukerareta toki demo?

What are you trying to say?
Even when someone
says something about you
in complaint?

M: なんかちょっと
仏の心が目覚めて
きましたね

Nan ka chotto
hotoke no kokoro ga
mezamete kimashita ne.

The spirit of the Buddha
has sort of awakened
within me.

67

H: あらららら。前の 頭の時には 「まっちゃんちょっと こわい」という イメージがあったけどね	*Ararara. Mae no atama no toki ni wa "Matchan chotto kowai" to iu imēji ga atta kedo ne.*	Ohhh. Your past look gave you the image of "Matchan's kind of scary."
M: でもね、 今はこんな にかわいいです からいいこと しますよ。。 「一日一善」、ね	*Demo ne, ima wa mō konna ni kawaī desu kara ii koto shimasu yo: "Ichinichi ichizen" ne.*	But now that I've become this cute. . . . I'm going to do good: "one good deed a day."[33]

This excerpt comes from the duo's style of "free talk," which makes up the majority of this weekly show. It is used to discuss an array of mainly personal topics and observations in a manner similar to, but looser than, their old *manzai* routines. Thus the rigid exchange of blows between the two characters is relaxed to a friendlier style. Following the "free talk," they read postcards that contain comments and questions from fans. On *Hey! Hey! Hey!*, a music show they host, Matsumoto takes every irreverent opportunity to dig into the band members or the music idols who appear, acting up to the audience's expectations. Hamada pounces verbally on the show's guests, who inevitably come across as (often innocent) *boke* fools. If the pop music idols who appear as guests try to answer back and redress the situation, Matsumoto will step in with his polished *boke* act to confound them even further. On many Japanese television shows with *manzai* performers acting as hosts or guests, the television personalities (タレント *tarento*) and, especially, media idols (アイドル *aidoru*) who appear with them are fated to become the satisfying targets of *manzai*-style *boke* and *tsukkomi* humor in this way.

Conclusion

A number of historical precedents to the urban, western-dressed, dialogue-centered specialization of *shabekuri manzai* have been suggested in accounts of the history of *manzai*: the humorous exchanges of door-to-door New Year's *manzai* mentioned here; the repartee (掛け合い *kakeai*) of *karukuchi* (軽口), which derived from the prologues for stage *niwaka*; even *onna dōraku*

Fig. 4.5 The *manzai* duo DownTown engaging in "free talk" in *Not a Task for Kids* (Produced from a noncommercial videotape [Nihon TV, 1998])

(女道楽), a genre in which two women would intersperse songs and dance with joking; and so on.[34] Despite these precursors from the Kyoto-Osaka area, *shabekuri manzai* appears to have been seen in a very different light in the early 1930s: it was an almost complete refiguring of the genre of *manzai*, which nonetheless maintained a grounding in Osakan culture. For instance, some people considered Entatsu's appearance to be insulting because most people still wore traditional Japanese clothing at the time.[35] Also, there was the novelty of the faster-paced dialogue that took up the events surrounding the average person's everyday life in a rapidly changing, urban, industrial, commercial Japanese society. Moreover, *manzai* had not been very popular up to the early 1920s. It was largely a variety act whose practitioners hailed from a variety of places and traveled all over the country (especially in western Japan) with performance troupes (劇団 *gekidan*) that did a bit of everything, from drama to hit film songs. Yoshimoto had contracts with the following variety acts in the early 1920s: three or four *karukuchi* acts, three to six *onna-dōraku* acts, and only one or two *manzai* acts. What most likely occurred at the beginning of the Showa period (1925, prior to the advent of *shabekuri manzai*) was that all these other acts began to appear more and more in the new *manzai*-centered *yose* of Osaka and were gradually absorbed into the genre,[36] while other *manzai* performers still struggled in smaller, seedier venues in Kobe, Osaka, Kyoto, and Tokyo as well as in the countryside.

In answer to the questions I put forth in a rhetorical spirit at the beginning of this chapter, it is difficult to narrowly define *manzai* as a genre or as a specific type of oral art up to 1930. Moreover, it is hard to say that it was then specifically and closely associated with Osakan culture until Yoshimoto, headquartered in Osaka, popularized it in the late 1920s by gathering *manzai* performers in Osaka, training them there and in Kobe and Kyoto, then sending them to Tokyo and elsewhere.[37] The dominance of the relatively well-defined *shabekuri manzai* since 1930 has been propelled further by a mass-mediated Osaka dialect and by the easily understood images of Osaka presented in much of the *manzai* produced by Osaka-trained performers managed by Yoshimoto.

Mahadev Apte noted in 1985 that in the United States "it appears that the mass media have made humor ubiquitous and diverse . . . humor appears to have pervaded every walk of life. Comedy shows dominate television programs."[38] The same is clearly now true for Japan, and *manzai* is an integral part of that invasion. The *manzai* of today, like that of the past, is difficult to appraise on its own as an oral performance art. Influences such as the impact of the large corporate comedy schools and the concomitant decline of intimate master-apprentice training, the forces of Japan's media entertainment world which both drive and entice performers into becoming generic media entertainers, the sheer number and ubiquity of television programming on which *manzai*-like interactions and amateur competitions can be found, all these make it impossible to be definitive about the genre (even after the advent of *shabekuri manzai*). And this is so even without taking into account the ephemeral nature of *manzai* routines themselves (usually not written down, then changed "on the fly," and soon discarded). Yet *manzai* remains a fascinating topic precisely because of these variegated linkages—the complex, productive interplay of *manzai*, practitioners, producers, and fans within the Japanese media culture. It is very clear how prevalent and how thoroughly invested are *manzai* and its performers in Japan's entertainment world, as well as how popular are the performances themselves, and the corporate offerings (theater and television shows, brand goods, schools) through which audiences take part as viewers, fans, consumers, guests, and amateurs of *manzai* in Japan's major urban media industries. Its very popularity, its hybrid nature as a genre and as a social phenomenon, should not condemn *manzai* to the sidelines of art and scholarship. Despite, perhaps even because of, its protean adaptabilities, *manzai* has thrived in the modern world of Japan and, hopefully, has found its place within English-language Japanese studies as well.

NOTES

1. International Society for Humor Studies (twelfth) Conference, Osaka, Japan, July 25, 2000. For an account of *rakugo*, see chapter 7.
2. For an account of Osaka's merchant culture and the city's status in comparison with other, more aristocratic cities of Japan, see chapter 2.
3. The Tōzai Koten Manzai Taikai, held in Nagoya City in 1994, was sponsored by the Aichi Prefectural Government. The meeting featured regional varieties of classic (both New Year's and early variety act) *manzai*, among which Aichi's Nagoya-*manzai* is quite famous.
4. For a more detailed account of the development of *manzai* as an entertainment, see Maeda Isamu, ed., *Kamigata Engei Jiten* (Tokyo: Tōkyōdō Shuppan, 1966), 111–17.
5. Tanaka Hatohei, "Kamigata Engei no Nagare," *Sōzō Suru Shimin* 40 (1994): 36.
6. See, for instance, Muneo Jay Yoshikawa, "Popular Performing Arts: Manzai and Rakugo," in *Handbook of Japanese Popular Culture*, ed. Richard Gid Powers, Hidetoshi Kato, and Bruce Stronach (New York: Greenwood Press, 1989), 79.
7. He was known as Tamagoya Sutemaru prior to a name change sometime after starting his stage career.
8. Gōshū is the old name for the area that today is Shiga Prefecture, near Lake Biwa.
9. On these points see Mita Jun'ichi, *Shōwa Kamigata Shōgeishi* (Tokyo: Gakugei Shorin, 1993), 87–89; also Taho Akira, "Taishō Bunka no Shakaiteki Kōsei: Kindai 'Manzai' no Seiritsu o Jirei

ni," in *Jinbu Ronsō*, vol. 28 (Osaka: Osaka City University, 2000), 22–23.

10. As Mita explains, "For the [Japanese] authorities, in many ways taking foreign countries as their model, and conscious of being watched by them, *manzai* was, if one were to exaggerate, an embarrassment to the nation and, worse yet, a national disgrace." *Shōwa Kamigata Shōgeishi*, 89; my translation.

11. At some point in the 1910s, Tamagoya Entatsu renamed his Nagoya-*manzai* act Kansai-*manzai* in order to compete with Sunagawa Sutemaru's "high-class *manzai*"; see entry for *Manzai* in Maeda, *Kamigata Engei Jiten*, 588.

12. Mita, *Shōwa Kamigata Shōgeishi*, 86.

13. This illustration (from Mita, *Shōwa Kamigata Shōgeishi*, 92) has been reprinted in good faith, every effort having been made to find the copyright holder. If the copyright information becomes known, correspondence with the proper party will be pursued.

14. Yet Horie Seiji says that "if one were to ask [in 1929] if its [*manzai*'s] quality had, along with its popularity, 'modernised' and become 'cultural,' befitting the era, one regrettably would have to say that it certainly had not." *Yoshimoto Kōgyō no Kenkyū* (Tokyo: Asahi Bunko, 1994), 86; my translation.

15. "Owarai Konjiki Yasha," recorded by the author from an unidentified radio program on display at the Osaka Prefectural Wahha Kamigata Engei Shiryōkan (NHK Osaka Broadcasting Bureau, n.d.). The routine probably aired in the 1960s.

16. *Otera* would be an odd name, but the structural similarity of *Otera* and *Omiya* makes it plausible enough for the routine, and can also be taken as an enjoyable form of soundplay, regardless of specific meaning.

17. Such referentiality is typical of comedy and crosstalk. For example, the repertoire of Sannin Yakko, a *manzai* trio formed in 1950, included the routine "Okaru Kanpei," which draws on the *Kanedehon Chūshingura*, a mid-eighteenth-century puppet theater (*jōruri*) play cycle (later turned into a *kabuki* play). Today, comparable references and importations are usually derived from television shows and advertisements.

18. Xavier Bensky, "*Manzai*: Metamorphoses of a Japanese Comic Performance Genre" (unpublished master's thesis, McGill University, 1998), 56.

19. Nanba Toshizō, *Shōsetsu Yoshimoto Kōgyō* (Tokyo: Bungei Shunjū, 1991), 81–82. Many of these assertions can be found elsewhere; for instance, Horie, *Yoshimoto Kōgyō no Kenkyū*, 96. In addition to the films of Harold Lloyd and Charlie Chaplin, the silent film

duo Stan Laurel and Oliver Hardy appear to have influenced the reshaping of *manzai* in terms of both body movements and clothing. Another factor to consider in the emergence of *shabekuri manzai* is that Entatsu is known to have traveled to the United States for a number of years as the head of a theatrical troupe after the Great Kantō Earthquake of 1923, and he presumably ran across vaudevillian double acts. This remains speculation, since, as far as I know, no record of his trip exists.

20. The going rate at the time was between 30 and 60 *sen,* and a movie was about 40 *sen* (100 *sen* is equal to 1 *yen;* these prices are not adjusted for today's values). Soon after, "10-*sen* stores" appeared within department stores.

21. It was originally written as 萬歳 or 万歳 and, from the start of the Shōwa era (1926), also as 万才 and then as 漫才 from 1933. In the 1980s, マンザイ in katakana and "MANZAI" in roman characters were at times used to denote the shift to a new youth- and media-oriented *manzai.*

22. There is some irony in the fact that Entatsu and Achako broke up their *manzai* act in 1934 but then became even more famous by appearing together in films, the nemesis of *yose manzai,* while many of their film scenes featured *manzai*-like episodes of dialogue.

23. Bud Abbott and Lou Costello, who teamed up in 1936, were one of the few American comedy teams to successfully take their act from the burlesque stage to radio, to Broadway, to film, and lastly to television. Although they became popular in the world of burlesque, it was not until they appeared on the Kate Smith Radio Hour (performing their now-classic routine "Who's on First?") that they were launched on the way to stardom and Hollywood.

24. From the "Sōkeisen" transcript in Horie, *Yoshimoto Kōgyō no Kenkyū,* 131–33.

25. They apprenticed under Nakata Daimaru of the famous duo Nakata Daimaru and Nakata Racket.

26. *NiteInNite: Namba 1 Bankan* (Asahi Broadcasting Corp., coproduced by Yoshimoto *Kōgyō,* fall 2000). My translation is used in this and subsequent quotations from the interview.

27. From the same talk-show episode.

28. Ibid.

29. For example, routines are kept brief in order to fit television show schedules: usually three minutes, certainly less than fifteen, rather than the fifteen to twenty of a full stage routine, which includes more interaction with the live audience. The shortness also accommodates the great increase in the number of aspiring

manzai performers, who often face each other in competitions onstage, sometimes televised. In these, from five to forty *manzai* teams commonly perform, one after the other, necessitating routines only a few minutes long. Those allowed to perform longer routines on television are generally veteran performers with large audiences, both live and television, on special *manzai* programs aired around New Year's. In this way, *manzai* performers still herald the new year in the spirit of the ancient "gate *manzai*" discussed above.

30. By my estimate, in 2000 Yoshimoto entertainers appeared on roughly ten thousand television shows (about eighty per week in Kansai, seventy per week in Kantō), and many of their theater appearances also made it onto television.

31. Examples of television shows that feature or test aspiring *manzai* comedians are NHK's *On Air Battle* (*On Eea Batoru*), Nihon TV's *Warai no Jikan* (ended in October 2000), Mainichi Broadcasting's *Shirōto no Meijinkai*, Yomiuri TV's *Owarai Network*, NHK's *Warai ga Ichiban*, and a host of local Osaka late-night programs.

32. Matsumoto Hitoshi, *Matsumoto Bōzu* (Tokyo: Rocking On (Rokkingu On), [January] 1999).

33. *Not a Task for Kids* (*Gaki no Tsukai ya Arahen de*), Nihon TV, 1998.

34. For a summary see Maeda, *Kamigata Engei Jiten*, 589. Maeda makes the case for the centrality of *karukuchi* in the development of *manzai* as an entertainment in the Kansai region (128).

35. The duo soon became so popular that they actually contributed to the rapid changeover to Western clothing in urban Japan, as noted by Kizugawa Kei in *Kamigata no Warai: Manzai to Rakugo* (Tokyo: Kōdansha, 1984), 67. Yoshimoto Kōgyō inaugurated a company policy in 1934 that all employees should wear Western-style clothing.

36. Maeda, *Kamigata Engei Jiten*, 589.

37. Performers who were not from the area learned to perform in Osaka dialect for local crowds and came to be seen as Osakans, as attested by the autobiography of a famous *manzai* entertainer, Miyako Chōchō, *Miyako Chōchō: Onna no Isshō*, Nihon Keizai Shimbun, retrieved November 12, 2000, from the World Wide Web at <http://www1.sphere.ne.jp/pilehead/osaka/kirinuki/miyakohonbun.htm>.

38. Mahadev L. Apte, *Humor and Laughter: An Anthropological Approach* (Ithaca, N.Y.: Cornell University Press, 1985), 264.

5 Sha-re: A Widely Accepted Form of Japanese Wordplay

Heiyō Nagashima

The most frequently used technique to provoke laughter in Japan is called *sha-re* (しゃれ；洒落).[1] It is effectively what is called "punning" in the West, not only in terms of its rules and its social acceptability but also in the nature of the response expected. Linguistics scholar Nakamura Akira has defined the form as "a rhetorical manipulation of a language that makes the indicative function of utterance complicated, introducing words whose pronunciations are homonyms, or very similar, but whose meanings differ."[2] The definition holds good for both Eastern and Western puns.

In order to study *sha-re,* I collected more than one hundred commercial messages from Japanese television advertisements broadcast between January and March 1999.[3] Given the fact that more than one thousand different commercial messages and announcements were aired during this period, it is astonishing that such a large number, 10 percent, were cast as or made use of puns. Certainly the finding alone justifies the choice of subject material. In addition, there were some special advantages to using this source of *sha-re* for study: first, that spoken *sha-re* were used rather than written ones, which are sometimes ambiguous in their successful punning; and second, that the major purpose of any *sha-re* is one it shares with the purposes of these television messages, that is, to make a strong impression on a selected target audience. Thus the context and the verbal construct share a common intention.

In speculating about why *sha-re* are so widely used and appreciated in Japan, it seems to me that the phonetic characteristics of the Japanese language provide a good explanation. According to the noted linguist Kindaichi Haruhiko, there are only 111 phonemes in Japanese.[4] The next smaller number is found in the Hawaiian language, which has substantially fewer at forty-five phonemes; this is held to be the absolute minimum required. In Japanese the 111 phonemes give rise to at least 450,000 words, which inevitably supply plenty of phonetic homonyms. *Sha-re* allows that circumstance to be exploited for pleasure and laughter. It is interesting to note that, despite this, my own observations and inquiries among Hawaiian speakers have not yet provided much evidence of puns occurring in that language.

There may be other reasons for the popularity of *sha-re* in Japan. From ancient times the Japanese people have believed that words possessed spirit and soul, a power that could overwhelm mere human power from time to time. While this belief in the magical power of words has been part of the thought system of all races and cultures through the ages, many others have over time put aside this idea or else restricted it to the realm of magical purposes such as spells, curses, and the powers for good or ill of witches and wizards. In Japanese culture, some part of this respect for the power of words has continued as part of daily life, especially in relation to the everyday use of the *tanka,* or short poetic form. The form of the *tanka* dates back to the fifth century and remains unchanged today. It consists of just thirty-one syllables in five lines, with a certain number of syllables in each line.[5] Such a condensed and rigid prescription encourages poets to make use of homonyms so as to capture the full scope of their thoughts and feelings within the limited framework. From this deliberate ambiguity arises the idea of *kakekotoba* (掛詞), a "pivot word" or pun that allows the reader or speaker to infer that two separate meanings or sentences exist at the same time collapsed into one. This effect is synonymous with Japanese linguistic practice and is highly prized.[6]

In addition, in Japanese aesthetic values, escaping from everyday, commonsense conventions and social standards has its own beauty and virtue. In the Edo period this became the elegant and sophisticated ideal of court society and refined manners. Paradoxically, what could be admired and praised were not only appropriate manners but also the bizarre and unusual, acknowledging the limitless creative powers of human beings. Such behaviors were referred to as *sha-re,* a word that embraced from that time the earlier expression *shūku* (秀句), or clever expressions, and so came to be applied to sophisticated and witty phrases. Strictly speaking, then, *sha-re* includes not only the linguistic activities that are its current common meaning but also fashion and way of life. Today, however, linguistic *sha-re* are totally accepted as a proper, even admirable, form of self-expression.

How do sentences including *sha-re* differ from those without it? In a symposium on studying *sha-re* conducted by the Japan Society for Humor and Laughter Studies, Nomura Masaaki said:

> It is hard to answer this question clearly. *Sha-re* only performs its function under the complicated conditions that a speaker uses words or sentences which include homonyms for the hearer, and that the hearer understands the implied as well as the literal meanings of the words or sentences. There is no indicative marker telling us that this sentence carries *sha-re* within it. However, some part at least of the spoken sentence will draw attention to deliberate artifice by a kind of uneasiness, either in the pronunciation, the intonation, the grammar or the syntax. Whether the *sha-re* is recognized or not depends totally on the circumstances of the hearer.[7]

Upon hearing this explanation, I understood at once that although in Japanese we use *sha-re* in everyday conversation all the time, only the complicated manipulation of sounds and meaning signal that the device is being used. The definition of *sha-re* is thus determined by the hearer's ability to perceive it. To provoke this perception, the complex manipulations by the speaker are often deliberately allowed to create misunderstanding so that laughter will be evoked both by the confusion and by the correct understanding of the confusion (that is, by perceiving the ambiguous and multiple meanings).

The comic playwright and author Inoue Hisashi tells us there are three easy steps to creating a sentence with *sha-re*:

1. Select one syllable, word, or phrase and call to mind all the homonyms for it that you can.

2. Select from that list a pair of words or sentences that convey independently different meanings.

3. Insert the *sha-re* into the conversation at an appropriate time.[8]

For most Japanese, the first two steps above are simple, but acting on the third presents some difficulty, and not just in finding the right time. The speaker of *sha-re* needs to possess not only a sense of humor delighting in these ambiguities but also the nerve to challenge others with the pun and then manage the resultant situation between the speaker and the hearer.

Although *sha-re*, despite these challenges, are widely used in everyday life in Japan, set narrative jokes are seldom encountered this way. They are, however, the essence of *rakugo*,[9] and references to popular *rakugo* stories are certainly common in daily conversation; but new jokes are not borrowed from it and repeated to others as in Western conversational exchanges. Perhaps one reason for this is the Japanese speakers' attitude toward their conversational partners: as they converse, the speaker wonders if an obvious joke might humiliate or embarrass the hearer if that person were not to grasp the point of it when told. Jokes and their appreciation often depend upon one's capability to understand them and one's personality and circumstances in life.

In contrast, when *sha-re* is used there is no such risk of embarrassment because the rules are clear. The hearer is free to respond with any of the following reactions:

1. Just laugh at it.
2. Respond with a further *sha-re*.
3. Just ignore it.

Thus, without risk, *sha-re* provide all the benefits of jokes: they entertain cheerfully and strengthen the sense of shared togetherness. Both men and women enjoy *sha-re*, although until the present period women have tended to make less use of them, because of the prevailing Japanese belief that women should not draw attention to themselves.

Some of the benefits of *sha-re* are indeed that they do draw attention to themselves, do communicate strong messages to the hearer, and are memorable. These characteristics undoubtedly contribute to their frequent use in television commercials, many of which depend upon puns, as my collection of examples and analysis of them showed. Although it is difficult to communicate completely their combined visual and verbal effects, I offer the following examples.

1. The first is an advertisement for a pen. Whereas signatures are used in English, in Japan family seals are used. This advertisement from the pen-making company Shachihata is to promote a pen with a family seal on its end. The video clip shows a man holding a pen, with a contemporary office as background, and saying the words "tsuite iru" (ついている) six times in different ways. There are at least a dozen verbs in Japanese that produce *tsuite iru* as their present continuous form. Three of them that make good sense in this context and therefore spring to the viewer's mind are:

付いている   It is attached (that is, the seal is attached to the end of the pen)

ツイている   I'm in luck

突いている   I have put my seal (to the document)

The pleasing coincidence of simultaneous meanings creates a memorable promotion for the object on sale.

2. Two advertisements for life insurance, produced by the insurance company Nihon Seimei, provoke laughter by parodying the famous words of two heroes in Japanese history, each of whom is known for having reorganized Japan in his time. In the first case the hero is Oda Nobunaga (1543–82), who began the unification of Japan after centuries of civil war between warlords and provinces. His image is instantly recognizable when portrayed by the actor onscreen, and brings to mind his most famous saying: 日本統一じゃ ("Nippon tōitsu ja," "I will unify Japan!"). In the advertisement, however, the actor makes him say, in very determined and authoritative tones, 保険統一じゃ ("Hoken tōitsu ja," "I will unify my insurance policies!"). The result is not only funny but also an effective plug for a client-oriented insurance company offering versatile combinations of policies.

The second advertisement in this series personifies Sakamoto Ryōma (1835–67), who was a warrior of the Tosa clan. He advocated the modernization of Japan and was assassinated by conservative forces, dying a martyr to the cause of progress.

79

One of his most famous sayings was 世の中変えなあかんぜよ ("Yononaka kaena akan ze yo," "We must change our country"). The actor parodies this by proclaiming in noble tones, 保険変えなあかんぜよ ("Hoken kaena akan ze yo," "We must change our insurance"). The message is, of course, that this would be a change for the better, if Sakamoto advocates it. The voices of both men have been convincingly re-created for broadcast by computer on the basis of historical materials, although no one can say for sure what their voices were like.

3. An advertisement for the fruit juice brand Takara exploits the verbal rhythm of the name of a popular performer, Fujiwara Norika, who is famous for her alluring ways and sexy poses and for the power of her pheromones to lure men to her. Holding out the bottle of juice, she calls out her own name and then asks enticingly, "Would you like to drink it fresh made?" Thus:

| ふじわらのりか | *Fujiwara Norika* | [her name] |
| できたてのむか | *Dekitate nomu ka?* | Will you drink it just made? |

Although these two utterances are quite different in meaning and grammatical structure, they share a verbal rhythm and a sensory, erotic appeal that combines them in a punning way.

4. A number of television ads employ *sha-re* based on numbers. Japanese people derive a good deal of entertainment from an amusing mnemonic system for remembering long numbers, particularly telephone numbers. It works by reading off the first syllable of the name for each number to form a word. This same mnemonic system is exploited in a television ad promoting a business called ArtNature, which has a toll-free number in which the last four digits—2323—are the important variables; these give a nicely onomatopoeic word:

フサフサ   *fu-sa fu-sa*   bushy/abundant/full head of hair

The company's business? Selling wigs!

5. Even in advertisements that do little more than feature the product and name it, puns can be useful, both in English and in Japanese. Names often directly incorporate *sha-re*-type puns. For example, a similar but even more complex structure

applies to the name for a Toshiba refrigerator called Toridashi Yasai (とりだしやさい). This machine has a particularly wide, shallow box for storing vegetables that makes it easy to take the vegetables out. Although Toridashi yasai is not very good grammar, it means "taken out vegetables" and can be understood as referring to several meanings: *yasai* (vegetables), which sounds very much like the verbal suffix *yasui* ("easy to"), which relates closely to the adjective *yasashii* ("easy"). The pun is thus a triple one (although only one of the three possible meanings is good grammar):

Toridashi yasai	taken out vegetables
Toridashi yasui	easy to take out (good grammar)
Toridashi yasashii	take out—easy

Another such portmanteau naming is that used in an advertisement for another refrigerator (in this case made by Hitachi), which is shown accompanied by the spoken words "Hayai zo, umai zo" (はやい蔵、うまい蔵). This product has a system for cooling the food very quickly and preserving its taste. The wording plays on the facts that *hayai* means quick; *umai* means delicious, *zo* (with a long "o" sound) means a storage box and occurs in the word for refrigerator (*reizōko*); and *zo* (with a short "o" sound) is a grammatical particle used by men at the end of sentences to make a forceful exclamation.

Thus *hayai zo* means "It's quick!!!" or "Quickstore" or "Quickfridge," and *umai zo* means "It's good!!!" (in the sense of delicious), or "Goodstore," or "Goodfridge." Accordingly, the words associated with the refrigerator are both "It's quick. It's good" and "It's quickstore fridge!!! It's goodstore fridge!!!"

6. Puns can also mix up English and Japanese to comic effect. The Suntory distilling company has an advertisement in which a well-known former sumo wrestler, Konishiki, sings a little song while featuring a bottle of the relevant alcohol. The song plays upon the word *suki* (好き), meaning "to like" or "to love":

I *suki*	I love
You *suki*	You love
I and you make "we"	"I" plus "you" = "we"
We *suki*—whiskey	We love whiskey ("We" + "*suki*" = whiskey)

In Japanese, "whiskey" is pronounced "uisukii," which sounds almost the same as "we suki," the only difference being the long "I" at the end of "whiskey." The cleverness of this pun is to bring both cognitive and phonetic combinations into play, associating both with the strength, virility, and international status of the sumo wrestler.

Another advertisement, this one for IBM, shows a person doing business on a computer, with a voice-over that puns on "e" in "e-mail," "e-business," and so on. Although the "e" stands for "electronic," it is pronounced as a long "i" ("*ii*") in Japanese. Thus:

> *ii* means e- (as in e-mail), but
> *ii* also means "good" in Japanese
> Therefore, "e-business" is "good business"

So both by definition and by wordplay, the message means that Internet business must be good. The simplicity of this wordplay makes it easy to promote the concept by the punning techniques of *sha-re*.

Conclusion

These examples show just a few of the myriad uses of *sha-re* on Japanese television. It may be that English advertising is also increasingly picking up this intense Japanese delight in punning and wordplay. Certainly in Japan, *sha-re* techniques will continue to live on and to adapt their own style and presentation to our changing times.

NOTES

1. The correct romanization of this Japanese word would be *share*; in order to avoid prompting the English pronunciation of "share," as in "share price," the editor has chosen to render the word as *sha-re* throughout.
2. Nakamura Akira, *Nihongo Rhetoric no Taikei* (Tokyo: Iwanami, 1991), 11; my translation.
3. The television stations selected were ABC (Asahi Broadcasting), MBS (Mainichi Broadcasting System), KTV (Kansai-TV), and YTV

(Yomiuri-TV). For further discussion of methods for studying *sha-re*, see also Nagashima Heiyō, ed., "Sha-re-, Dajare-gaku Koto Hajime," report of a symposium between panelists Oda Shōkichi, Nomura Masaaki, W. Young, and Nagashima Heiyō, in *Warai-gaku Kenkyū*, no. 6 (Osaka: JSLHS, 1999), 55–67.

4. Kindaichi Haruhiko, *Nihongo*, rev. ed., vol. 1 (Tokyo: Iwanami, 1988), 104–34.

5. *Tanka, waka*, and other poetic forms are discussed at length in chapters 1, 8, and 10.

6. See chapter 8 for a more detailed discussion of this construct.

7. Nagashima, "Sha-re-, Dajare-gaku Koto Hajime," 60; my translation.

8. Inoue Hisashi, "Jiguchi Ochi ni Tsuite no Mono," in *Go*, Great Essays of Japan, no. 70 (Tokyo: Sakuhinsha, 1988), 237–44.

9. See chapter 7 for a detailed account of this form of narrated "sit-down" comedy.

ADDITIONAL REFERENCES

Nomura Masaaki. *Rakugo no Rhetoric*. Select Books of Heibonsha, no. 165. Tokyo, 1996. See esp. chapter 5, "*Sha-re*," 221–82.

Oda Shōkichi. *Nihon no Yūmoa*. Tokyo: Chikuma Shobō, 1986.

6 Conversational Jokes in Japanese and English

Makiko Takekuro

It is often said that there are potential differences between Japanese conversation and English conversation when it comes to perceiving and using jokes, or even that the Japanese lack a sense of humor altogether. What makes people say this? Do Japanese people indeed exchange jokes? If so, when, and with whom? How are jokes used in Japanese? How does this differ from English usage in joking—for example, in American English?

In order to answer these questions it is necessary to distinguish typical Japanese joking from similar American English joking. By comparing what I call conversational jokes in the two languages, it may be possible to discover some fundamental differences in communicative strategies between Japanese and American English.

The Theoretical Framework

In their universal framework of linguistic politeness, Brown and Levinson (1987) consider joking as one linguistic politeness strategy used to put the hearer at ease and to lessen "a face-threatening act."[1] Jokes can mitigate aggression and promote a sense of intimacy among participants, thereby aiding in the cultivation of a smooth relationship. Despite the importance of jokes in polite interaction, no contemporary empirical evidence about conversational jokes has been reported from a cross-cultural perspective, and this chapter attempts to remedy that significant failure. First it is important to analyze jokes in Japanese conversation and distinguish them from their equivalent in American English conversation. Through comparative analysis it may be possible to discover the preferred rhetoric for conversational jokes in each language and to discuss the relationship between conversational jokes and sociolinguistic practices in Japanese and American English.[2]

Conversational Jokes and Their Definition

According to most definitions in the literature, jokes are similar to humor in that both have an amusing line and make participants laugh. What makes jokes different from general humor, however, is the punch line and its consequences. For this study I will adopt the definition of Francis Landy, who suggests that jokes, because of the punch line, provoke loud laughter, whereas humor may not bring more than a smile to the lips.[3] In addition, I consider conversational jokes and formal joke-telling as quite distinct from each other. Conversational jokes can be regarded as impulsive speech behaviors and as what participants spontaneously create to exchange in the course of interaction. As for joke-telling itself, it is "a highly conventionalized and socially bound speech behavior"[4] accompanied by such structural clichés as "Have you heard this one?," "I heard the joke about . . . ," or "A funny thing happened. . . ." In order to examine in what situations, and with whom, participants spontaneously exchange informal jokes in everyday conversation, I decided to focus on impromptu conversational jokes, which I define as follows: *impulsive speech behaviors in which participants spontaneously create something humorous, ironic, and witty in order to provoke amused laughter.*[5] Accordingly, in my selection of data I have avoided formal, set jokes and joke-telling sessions.

Method Chosen for the Study

The materials chosen for this study include three Japanese movies, six Japanese television dramas, six American movies, and two hours of conversation among friends in both Japanese and English.[6] The advantage of using data from both scripted materials and actual discourse data lies in the possibility of observing a more diverse range of social contexts. It also allows for a comparison between the "real-life" and the fictional jokes and their characteristics. In choosing the scripted movie and television material, I paid attention to the following points:

1. Whether each source covered interactions, both formal and informal, with family members, friends, partners, colleagues, new people, and strangers.
2. Whether materials in Japanese and English were roughly

equal in terms of levels or degrees of formality, of gender, and of educational background of the participants.

3. Whether stories portrayed events that were likely to happen in ordinary life.

Bearing these points in mind, I excluded movies and television shows designed to be completely comical and those that are too unrealistic or too futuristic to be part of ordinary life. My intention was to select material generally accepted as illustrating normal conventions for acceptable social behavior. I then proceeded to collect from the scripted and live conversations the number of occasions on which the participants made conversational utterances and the number of occasions on which they exchanged conversational jokes, according to my definition, compared to the total number of utterances and the total elapsed time of the scripts.

Quantitative Analysis

My first finding was that Japanese movies were typically low in total utterances compared to English-language movies (compare Japanese movies' 577 utterances in 110 minutes, 538 in 115 minutes, and 432 in 100 minutes with English movies' 988 utterances in 111 minutes, 1012 in 114 minutes, and 735 in 92 minutes). Internal analysis of the Japanese sources showed that despite a greater amount of conversational exchange in the television dramas, there were no marked differences between movies and dramas in terms of the proportion of joking exchanges to utterances, just more of both in a shorter period of time. To obtain a matched set of total running times from both Japanese- and English-language sources, I reduced the number of Japanese sources by eliminating three instances (one movie and two dramas) of matching lengths and internal characteristics. This gave a final Japanese sample of 687 minutes' running time provided by two movies and four dramas that compared well with an English total of 691 minutes from six movies (see figure 6.1).

Then I compared the total number of conversational jokes collected from the English movies with that from the Japanese movies and television shows. I also compared the characteristics of the participants between whom such jokes can be used

JAPANESE			ENGLISH		
Title	Min.	Jokes/ Utterances (%)	Title	Min.	Jokes/ Utterances (%)
Ai to iu Na no Moto ni	135	4/1327 (0.30%)	*Thelma and Louise*	128	9/1033 (0.87%)
Itsu ka Doko ka de	110	1/577 (0.17%)	*Working Girl*	114	5/1012 (0.49%)
Kita no Kuni kara	133	2/302 (0.66%)	*Steel Magnolias*	118	28/1256 (2.23%)
Haru yo Koi	104	2/765 (0.26%)	*Sixteen Candles*	92	5/735 (0.68%)
Natsuko no Sake	115	2/538 (0.37%)	*Wall Street*	128	8/1122 (0.71%)
Fuzoroi no Ringotachi	90	3/1008 (0.30%)	*Baby Boom*	111	6/988 (0.61%)
Subtotal/ Average	**687**	**14 (0.34%)**	**Subtotal/ Average**	**691**	**61 (0.93%)**
Daikon no Hana	130	5/1507 (0.33%)			
Heya to Waishatsu to Watashi	100	1/432 (0.23%)			
Haha no Tabidachi	105	5/785 (0.64%)			
Total/ Average	**1022**	**25 (0.36%)**	**Total/ Average**	**691**	**61 (0.93%)**

Fig. 6.1 Title, length of source material, and ratio of jokes to utterances in English and Japanese examples

in English and in Japanese. The totals for elapsed time, number of conversational jokes and utterances, and the resulting percentages are tabulated in figure 6.1. They show very clearly that for a set period of time, far fewer jokes are collected from Japanese sources than from English sources. During nearly the same length of time I found sixty-one English instances and only fourteen Japanese instances. When these numbers of conversational jokes are tabulated in the two subtotals/averages in figure 6.1, they reveal that jokes occurred roughly four times as frequently in English sources as in Japanese sources.

As indicated in the subtotal averages, English jokes amounted to 0.93 percent of whole utterances in a period of 691 minutes, while Japanese jokes amounted to only 0.34 percent of 687 minutes. Further, in terms of the relative percentage of jokes to all utterances during that period, English jokes outnumbered Japanese jokes by a ratio of nearly three to one. Even considering the additional Japanese data, the gap narrowed only slightly in the total average calculation.

Next I analyzed the relationship between the frequency of jokes and the degree of formality in the relationship between the participants. I divided the participants into six groups and examined each scene in which the jokes were exchanged, noting whether the interlocutors were friends, partners, family members, business partners, new people joining a group, or strangers.[7] Taking into consideration the degree of formality inherent in the context of the conversations, I classified each situation as either formal or informal.[8]

The data recorded in figure 6.2 point to at least two pieces of evidence for marked cross-linguistic differences in the appearance of jokes in Japanese and English. First, the appearance of Japanese jokes depended on how close the participants are. In the scripted sources examined, Japanese jokes were mostly exchanged among friends, partners, and family members rather than between business partners, new people, or strangers. The difference is striking, with the ratio being twenty-four to one. On the other hand, English jokes were used in the presence of *all* participants regardless of degree of intimacy. Although the majority of English jokes were told to "close" participants, as with Japanese jokes, nearly 45 percent of the total number of English

Participants	JAPANESE		ENGLISH	
	Informal	Formal	Informal	Formal
Friends	16	0	26	0
Partners/Spouses	2	0	2	0
Family members	6	0	6	0
Business acquaintances	1	0	6	13
New people	0	0	2	3
Strangers	0	0	1	2
Totals	**25**	**0**	**43**	**18**

Fig. 6.2 Number of jokes in relation to participants and formality

jokes (twenty-seven out of sixty-one) were uttered between business acquaintances, new people, and strangers.

The second difference concerns the fact that Japanese jokes are much more sensitive to the degree of contextual formality than English jokes. I found no jokes at all in formal Japanese situations, but English jokes occur in both formal and informal situations, with totals of forty-three and eighteen, respectively. Furthermore, nineteen English jokes appeared when participants were with business acquaintances in both formal and informal situations, while only one Japanese joke involving a business acquaintance was found, and that was in an informal situation.

The data suggest that Japanese conversation has more limiting conditions for jokes than English conversation does. Japanese jokes are limited to situations in which participants know each other well and the degree of formality is low. The data suggest that it is the norm in Japanese conversation not to tell jokes to business acquaintances, new people, and strangers, even in informal situations. On the contrary, a general trend of jokes in English conversation appears to be that jokes are generally acceptable, regardless of the participants and the degree of formality. Although these observations are drawn from fiction and drama, it should be borne in mind that a key criterion for my selection of the source material was its applicability to everyday life.

Qualitative Analysis

When representative examples of jokes in Japanese and English are examined and analyzed, important qualitative differences emerge. For the purposes of this section I included material drawn from actual conversations by Japanese speakers as well as the material already considered. By focusing on how jokes draw on a point of view in both languages, it is possible to describe some important rhetorical differences in the quality of conversational jokes.

First, Japanese jokes pay careful attention to words and phrases previously used in the same conversation. The following example, taken from the popular 1995 television series *Daikon no Hana* (Radish Flower), is typical of the Japanese jokes collected.[9] This series features the lives and crises of middle-aged women, two of whom—Mitsue (M) and Hiroko (H)—work at the same office and share confidences. In this exchange they are talking about their daughters-in-law:

M: うちは家にいると 息子の嫁に いじめられるとよ
Uchi wa ie ni iru to musuko no yome ni ijimerareru to yo.
When I stay at home, my son's wife bullies me.

H: いじめとるやろか
Ijimetoru yaro ka
(You) bully *her*, don't you?

Step 1: Mitsue thinks she is bullied at home where the extended family lives.

Step 2: Mitsue, complaining that her daughter-in-law bullies her, does not seem to realize how frightening a mother-in-law she is.

Step 3: Her friend, Hiroko, tells her the reality of the situation: that she actually scares her daughter-in-law.

In this example, the joke in Hiroko's speech originates from the root of the verb mentioned in Mitsue's speech. Hiroko refers back to this previous phrase, *ijimerareru* ("to be bullied"), changing the voice from passive to active: *ijimetoru* ("to bully"). The wordplay of this joke and its punch line indicate that the joke is exchanged within the same discourse-context as the previous words. That is to say, the uttering and the comprehending of the joke exchange do not take place outside the word-level context, since what was said literally on the word level in the previous exchange becomes itself the source of the joke. This pattern, which is very common in the Japanese jokes studied, suggests that the discourse-context of jokes in Japanese does not expand with the joke.

The next example, taken from actual conversation, reinforces the importance of such wordplay in Japanese jokes. Two young people—Chie (C) and Tsuyoshi (T)—are talking about a friend who lives overseas on a tropical island. He is bored and has nothing to do because all the shops close at 4 P.M.:

C: そんな常夏の 国でおまえ 冬時間かよって	*Sonna tokonatsu no* *kuni de omae* *fuyujikan ka yo tte*	In an everlasting summer land is it like they use "winter time"?
T: そんなん自分の 時計を二時間 遅らせてさ 一人で なんちゃって サマータイム やりゃあいいじゃん	*Sonnan jibun no* *tokei o nijikan* *okurasete sa hitori de* **nanchatte** **samaa taimu** *yaryaa iijan*	Then his watch should be two hours behind; [so] he, alone, can have **a sort of** **"summer time."**

Step 1: It surprises Chie that in a tropical place everything closes at 4 P.M., and she thinks it is as if they were using "winter time," when days end early.

Step 2: Tsuyoshi thinks that their friend, in order to fully enjoy that kind of a day, should wind his watch back so that he can gain two extra hours of daylight and enjoy a pretend "summer time" all by himself.

In linguistic terms, Chie first juxtaposes *tokonatsu* ("everlasting summer") and *fuyujikan* ("winter time"). Picking up on Chie's word *fuyujikan* as opposite the concept of summer time, Tsuyoshi mentions *nanchatte samaa taimu* ("as if it were summer time"). In this example, too, the punch lines of Tsuyoshi's joke are inspired by Chie's previous phrase *fuyujikan*, and the joke is exchanged on the word level.

These examples indicate that Japanese jokes are sensitive to words, phrases, and the literal meaning of what has been uttered in the previous context. This tendency can be seen in the use of repeated words and phonemes and in the addition of different or multiple meanings to the previous words by changing just one part of the utterance. Since the words themselves are the principal source of the jokes in Japanese, the point of view of the participants remains within the same discourse-context.

On the other hand, the most prevalent type of the English jokes in my data (half of them) involves imaginative descriptions, as is illustrated in an example from the popular movie *Working Girl* (1988). Here, a colleague offers Tess an envelope of money the day she is dismissed from her job:

Colleague: So what are you gonna do now, huh?
Tess: Oh, you know. Play some golf. Redecorate the country house.

Step 1: Tess, being dismissed, needs the money to find a job and a place to live.
Step 2: She talks about her dream of expensive retirement in the country, but she knows (and they all know) it cannot come true.

In this example, when the colleague asks Tess about her future plans, Tess deliberately contrasts her ideal lifestyle—playing golf and having a house in the country—with the devastating reality of her life. Instead of seriously answering the question, Tess gives a seemingly unrealistic reply. Here, by means of her imaginative description, she introduces into the discourse-context new information on golf and a country house as sources for a joke. It is this reply that creates the punch line of the joke. Her imaginative description brings in new information from outside the existing discourse-context and broadens the scope of the context.

The English example illustrates that this kind of joke draws on a point of view outside the discourse-context, which makes the context of the jokes expand to "outer space." I frequently found similar patterns in the English-language material, suggesting that the imaginative description by which the source of the joke can be incorporated from outside the discourse-context plays a central role in producing impressive punch lines in English conversation.

I believe that these differences in Japanese and English jokes are the result of rhetorical differences in the two languages. The above analysis indicates that Japanese jokes use "word-bounded rhetoric," while the English jokes prefer "far-fetched rhetoric." The way of drawing the point of view in the jokes reinforces this difference. Japanese jokes keep the point of view inside the discourse-context and relate the point of view to the other speakers' utterances by altering or adding other meanings to those already in play on the utterance level. Word-bounded rhetoric in Japanese jokes does not expand the point of view outward but instead remains inside the discourse-context. On the other hand, English jokes anchor the point of view outside the discourse-context and introduce the sources of jokes as new material. In other words, far-fetched rhetoric makes it possible to position the point of view outside and to bring new information into the discourse-context.

The differing rhetorics of Japanese and English jokes conform to the different communicative styles respected in the sociolinguistic practices of each language. It is commonly observed that speakers of Japanese think highly of harmonious communicative styles,[10] and indeed word-bounded rhetoric serves to reflect a sensitivity to the creation of harmony with other participants in conversation. In spoken English, in contrast, self-assertion and individual expression play an important role, and the same is true for English jokes. Individual speakers use far-fetched rhetoric to elicit a source of jokes from outside the discourse-context in order to impress their own sense of humor on the conversational exchange. Thus, the way the point of view is drawn differently in Japanese and English jokes displays a preference in each case for a different rhetoric, which relates to the distinctive sociolinguistic practices in each respective language and culture.

Conversational Jokes and Variations in Sociocultural Norms

In North America, especially in the business environment, starting a conversation with a series of jokes has recently become almost the norm[11]—quite unlike the conventions in Japan. My quantitative analysis of the use of jokes in both formal and business occasions accords with this norm, as I found a far greater number of jokes in formal business scenes in my English sources than in my Japanese ones. In Japanese society, jokes are the least-expected verbal behavior on formal occasions, but in the United States, sociocultural norms actually encourage people to exchange jokes on these occasions. This suggests that English jokes may be intended to shorten the psychological distance between the teller and listeners, while the use of Japanese jokes in conversation indicates the speaker's sharp awareness of time and place, including space between the participants. Thus the Japanese see jokes as inappropriate in formal situations and consequently do not appreciate them, because the sociocultural norm is that people are expected to behave according to the situation. Consciousness of one's situation then becomes the most influential factor in deciding when to tell jokes in Japanese conversation.

These differences in sociocultural norms observed in conversational jokes also relate to perceptions of interpersonal relations. The Japanese construal of self is characterized as having distinctive domains of interpersonal relationships, such as *uchi* (内 in-group), *soto* (外 out-group), and *yoso* (余所 out-group of out-group).[12] Around the private self is an interpersonal space called *uchi*, which comprises family members, close acquaintances, and partners. The space surrounding *uchi*, called *soto*, includes colleagues, business acquaintances, and neighbors. The space called *yoso* includes strangers and those with whom one is hardly in contact. Compared to the Japanese construal of self, that of the west does not make clear distinctions between domains of interpersonal relationships.

It seems clear that this difference in the construal of self is reflected in different attitudes toward jokes between speakers of Japanese and speakers of English. English-language speakers do not have very clear separations between groups such as neighbors, acquaintances, friends, and family, and they certainly do not divide them rigidly according to the concept of personal space (*uchi*, *soto*, and *yoso*) as Japanese speakers do. Thus it is easier for English speakers to overcome awkwardness in interpersonal relations and to exchange jokes with anyone, regardless of space divisions. And indeed, my English data show that jokes occur with all possible participants in all domains of interpersonal relations. On the other hand, the clear distinction between

95

uchi and *soto* must influence Japanese sociocultural norms, and since formal linguistic forms should almost always be used in the domains of *soto* and *yoso*, jokes would not be allowed there. This is certainly supported by my data, which show that almost all jokes in Japanese were observed in *uchi* and that none appeared in *soto* and *yoso* domains. Evidently this clear separation of *uchi* from *soto* and *yoso* in the Japanese construal of the self plays a crucial role in determining when and where jokes are permissible. Thus Japanese and American perceptions of interpersonal relations directly influence the use of conversational jokes in both languages.

Considering again the cross-cultural communicative settings for jokes, those settings that are mostly formal and where participants come from the areas of *soto* and *yoso* will obviously create difficulties for Japanese people in telling jokes. Criticizing them for disapproving of jokes in such settings ignores the sociocultural norms upon which they unconsciously depend in the course of communication. By recognizing the sociocultural background norms operating in Japanese society, we are able to understand why Japanese consider jokes inappropriate in some settings and hence do not tell jokes in those settings. As a result, the frequency of conversational jokes in Japanese, as well as their participants and the situations in which they are told, differ from those in English in accordance with the distinct sociocultural norms and perceptions of interpersonal relations in the two languages and cultures.

This study, as far as I am aware, is the first empirical cross-cultural study to address the nature of conversational jokes in the two languages, and further investigations from interdisciplinary approaches are certainly needed if we are to arrive at a full understanding of the relationship between conversational jokes and sociocultural backgrounds. However, it is clear that cultural differences in conversational jokes in English and Japanese are grounded in differing and habitual sociolinguistic practices in the two languages.

NOTES

This study began as a paper entitled "Conversational Jokes as a Politeness Strategy: Observations from English and Japanese," which was published in an internal publication of the Japan Women's University,

Tokyo, *Journal of the Graduate School of Humanities* 4 (1997): 75–90. Extensive revisions and new data are included here.

1. Penelope Brown and S. C. Levinson, *Politeness: Some Universals in Language Usage* (Cambridge, U.K.: Cambridge University Press, 1987), 124.
2. From here on, when I say "English" I refer to "American English."
3. Quoted in Chaim Bermant, *What's the Joke? A Study of Jewish Humour through the Ages* (London: Weidenfeld & Nicholson, 1986), 5.
4. Diana Boxer, "From Bonding to Biting: Conversational Joking and Identity Display," *Journal of Pragmatics* 27 (1997): 277.
5. Hereafter, the term "jokes" is equivalent to the term "conversational jokes."
6. For English data, the movies chosen for this study include *Thelma and Louise* (1991), *Working Girl* (1988), *Steel Magnolias* (1989), *Sixteen Candles* (1984), *Wall Street* (1987), and *Baby Boom* (1987). The Japanese examples are taken from the movies *Itsu ka Doko ka de* (*Sometime, Somewhere*, 1992), *Heya to Waishatsu to Watashi* (*Room, Shirt and Me*, 1993), and *Natsuko no Sake* (*Natsuko's Sake*, 1994); and from the popular television drama series *Ai to Iu Na no Moto ni* (*In the Name of Love*, 1992), *Haru yo Koi* (*Come, Spring*, 1995), *Daikon no Hana* (*Radish Flower*, 1995), *Fuzoroi no Ringotachi* (*Irregular Apples*, 1983), *Haha no Tabidachi* (*Mother's Departure*, 1995), and *Kita no Kuni kara* (*From the Northern Province: Homecoming*, 1989). I viewed and recorded the data noncommercially in 1995, when all these movies and shows were still current, either as new releases or in repeat or video release.
7. On this distinction of participants see Miyake Kazuko, "Nihonjin no Gengo Kōdō Patān—Uchi, Soto, Yoso Ishiki—," in *Tsukuba Daigaku Ryūgakusei Center Nihongokyōiku Ronshū* (*Proceedings of Japanese Language Education at the Foreign Students Center, Tsukuba University*), vol. 9 (Tokyo: Tsukuba University, 1994), 29–39. See also the discussion later in this chapter.
8. In distinguishing the degree of formality, the context rather than the nature of the participants was judged the most important factor, so that conversations among business acquaintances, new people, and strangers, as well as speeches at a stockholders' meeting or a conference, were considered formal, while conversations between strangers and new people on the street or in a shop were considered informal.

9. The actual jokes in the conversational exchange (that is, the utterances that give rise to laughter, as in my definition above) are given in bold and are followed by steps explaining why laughter is produced as an appropriate response.
10. See, for example, Diana Boxer, *Complaining and Commiserating: A Speech Act View of Solidarity in Spoken American English* (New York: Peter Lang, 1993); Senko Maynard, "On Back-channel Behavior in Japanese and English Casual Conversation," *Linguistics* 24 (1986): 1070–1108; and Yamada Haru, *American and Japanese Business Discourse: A Comparison of Interactional Styles* (Norwood, N.J.: Ablex, 1992).
11. Ronald Scollon and Suzanne W. Scollon, *Intercultural Communication* (Oxford: Blackwell, 1995), 26.
12. These distinctions are discussed at length in T. Sugiyama Lebra, *Japanese Patterns of Behavior* (Honolulu: University of Hawaii Press, 1976), and in Patricia Wetzel, "Are 'Powerless' Communication Strategies the Japanese Norm?" *Language in Society* 17 (1988): 555–68.

7 *Rakugo* and Humor in Japanese Interpersonal Communication

Kimie Ōshima

Rakugo (落語) can best be described as Japanese "sit-down" comedy or comic storytelling.[1] Just as western countries have stand-up comedy, Japan has sit-down comedy, or comedy performed sitting down. An obvious difference from the west is that the performer sits on his knees when he performs; this takes some training, as a performance lasts at least twenty minutes. The performer also wears traditional formal Japanese clothes (着物 *kimono*) and sometimes a pair of long, wide pants (袴 *hakama*) and/or a formal jacket (羽織 *haori*). For props or accessories the performer usually has a fan (扇子 *sensu*) and a hand towel or handkerchief (手拭い *tenugui*). These items help him express and act out the story: for example, the fan can "be" chopsticks, scissors, cigarettes, or a pipe; the towel could "be" a book, handkerchief, bills, or banknotes. The performer, dressed in his *kimono*, sits on a small cushion and acts out the whole story by himself (see figure 7.1).

The roots of *rakugo* can be traced back to the end of the seventeenth century. It developed from brief stories told among common people, and some *rakugo* stories originated in the preaching and teaching of Buddhist priests.[2] Because many common people did not read in the seventeenth and eighteenth centuries, oral sermons were essential for the priests. To capture people's attention, the priests created humorous stories illustrating the thoughts and theories of Buddhism. Thus some of the original *rakugo* stories were intended to teach, using laughter to give people moral instruction. The style of performance or presentation of *rakugo* was crystallized in the late eighteenth century and has not changed. Early on, local entertainers discovered they could actually make a living as professional storytellers if they rented a large room (寄席 *yose*) in a house and sat on the floor on a small cushion as their stage for performing *rakugo*

Fig. 7.1 Katsura Bunji, an early *rakugo* performer, performing his narrative by candlelight (from Katsura Bunji, Jippensha Ikku, et al., *Ōyose Hanashi no Shiriuma*, vol. 1, f. 1 (a), Tempō era, 1830–1844, reproduced by kind permission of Osaka Prefectural Nakanoshima Library)

(see figures 7.2 and 7.3). As the custom developed, it became entertainment for common people, and the *yose* became centers for social gatherings. Traditionally, there were no female *rakugo* performers, and even now there are only a few. In Japanese culture, performance activities have normally been considered the province of men.

As *rakugo* became popular, a tradition for learning the art and the narratives became established. Pupils who want to become *rakugo* performers are called *deshi* (弟子) and learn by apprenticeship. Someone who wants to become a pupil of a favorite *rakugo* performer goes to the performer and simply asks to be accepted as a student. If the professional *rakugo* performer finds the prospective pupil to be talented and chooses to teach him, he becomes a *deshi* of that *rakugo* performer.

Fig. 7.2 Interior of a *yose* in the Tempō era, between 1830 and 1844. *Rakugo* is the main item on the *yose* bill of fare, but the picture lists a number of other items, including *karukuchi* (a comedy-patter genre that eventually merged with *manzai*) and *sumō* wrestling. (From Katsura Bunji, Jippensha Ikku, et al., *Ōyose Hanashi no Shiriuma*, vol. 2., f. 52(a), Tempō era, 1830–1844, reproduced by kind permission of Osaka Prefectural Nakanoshima Library)

Fig. 7.3 A view of the Ikebukuro Engeijō (a traditional *yose* in Tokyo), where performances of *rakugo, manzai*, and other variety acts (most of them comedy) could be seen on one bill. It closed down in 1990 but was reopened in 1993 after reconstruction. Today it continues its fine comic tradition. (Photo by Marguerite Wells, 1988)

The master trains the student verbally by imitation and repetition. First the master tells a story, perhaps a short one from his repertoire; then the student imitates it as best he can. After much practice, the pupil can add to the story or modify the style and introduce some original touches. All training is verbal, and no written texts are used. It should be remembered that when *rakugo* started, many people could not read and therefore the tradition was passed down orally. Recently, it has become acceptable to use audio- and videotape, but written text is still not used in training or performance, except for published scripts on sale to the public.

The *deshi*'s duties include carrying out tasks for the master, even housework such as cleaning, cooking, and laundry, driving the master to a *yose*, and looking after the younger *deshi*. The apprentice learns how to tell stories, dance, and play instruments like the Japanese three-stringed banjo, the drums, and the Japanese flute. In many cases, *rakugo* performers-in-training live with their master in the master's house, and therefore their work conditions last twenty-four hours a day.

The master is primarily responsible for teaching the student everything needed to be a *rakugo* performer, including skills, manners, and attitudes, and he will also provide opportunities for pupils to perform onstage. Training is usually completed within two to three years, and, with the master's permission, a *deshi* becomes a full-fledged *rakugo* performer. The first few years after a *deshi* graduates as a *rakugo* performer and leaves his master's roof is usually the most difficult time in his career. He must try to get onstage without the master's help and also strive to increase his repertoire.

About three hundred popular stories are still performed as classic *rakugo*, and many new stories have been created by living *rakugo* artists. Even these new stories conform to *rakugo* structure, so the essence of the art form has remained intact. Each story opens with a section called the *makura* (まくら pillow, in the sense of padding), which leads the audience into the *hanashi* (はなし story). The *makura* is the preparatory stage for entering into the moral or lesson of the *rakugo* story. The lines called *kusuguri* (くすぐり)—which literally means "tickle" but can be translated as "jab of laughter"—occur throughout the story, and at the end of the story comes the "punch line" (オチ *ochi*, which means both "to drop" and "to let down").

One might well ask why an audience would laugh at the punch line of a familiar *rakugo* story that people have heard many times before—especially in the case of a classic story. Partly it is because of the *kusuguri*. Each performer introduces original touches in performance, and especially in the successive "jabs of laughter." These may have to do with wordplay, the setting of the story, the exaggeration of performance, or characters' styles of conversation. After three hundred years, people still find amusement in the traditional stories, just as contemporary western audiences still enjoy classic operas, the plays of Shakespeare, or classic comedy routines.

The *kusuguri* occur throughout the performance—during both the *makura* and the following *hanashi*—in order to gauge and maintain the audience's interest. The *hanashi* is usually a humorous event or outcome designed to make the punch line more potent. It may be serious or sad, but it can still have humorous "jabs." Using technique and/or artistic skill, the *rakugo* performer must engage the audience in the imaginary story during the *hanashi* so as to ensure that audience members are taken by surprise when they encounter the punch line at the end of the story.

Rakugo is a unique form of storytelling that includes comic acting and mimicry as well as the art of narration. Japanese audiences appreciate the continuity of the style, structure, and rich tradition of *rakugo* as it has been passed on to succeeding generations; at the same time, they want to see social and cultural changes reflected in *rakugo*. Newer stories do reflect modern Japanese society and are as much appreciated as classic stories. Today's events will be history tomorrow, so reflections of today's society are blended into *rakugo* tradition.

In *rakugo* the performer must be able to play the role of each distinct character using only the conversations between them, without action. There are always several characters in a *rakugo* story, and each is played only by changing voice, facial expression, mannerisms, style of speech, and so on. In most cases the characters have strong, stereotypical personalities and characteristics so that the audience readily detects the change as the performer switches from one character to another. Some of the popular character stereotypes are: (1) stupid, hasty, rash, forgetful, clumsy; (2) smart, reliable, short-tempered; (3) pretentious, vain; (4) cunning, tricky, quick-witted; (5) authority figure, man in power; (6) canny, stingy, mean; (7) sexy; (8) liar, braggart, untruthful; and (9) nonhuman characters.[3] Each of these characters represents qualities found within all of us, or parts of the whole human personality, and each tends to emphasize just one simplified aspect of human nature. Since these exaggerated characters are performed without costume or disguise, *rakugo* is in a way the art of imagination: the audience is free to imagine the features of the characters and the background settings.

Conversational comedy is important to traditional *rakugo* in two ways, both of which mirror conventions of communication in Japanese. First, *rakugo* reproduces the Japanese "indirect" conversation style. It is the nature of Japanese language to employ idioms and euphemistic expressions to avoid direct conflict, argument, or the making of concrete decisions. This is why the stereotypical view has evolved that the Japanese do not make clear statements of "yes" or "no." However, in *rakugo* stories this indirectness is used to render the conversation, or sometimes the whole story, humorous. Many *kusuguri* depend on misunderstandings, on misleading deceptions between characters in the story, and on the exaggeration of such conversations. One typical example is a scene from the story *Sagitori* (鷺とり *Catching Herons*) in which an authority figure (AF) and a stupid man (SM) are having a conversation:

AF: Hey, seems like you are hanging out and not working recently. How do you feed yourself?

SM: Ah, I hold the rice bowl in my left hand and chopsticks in my right and, and . . .

AF: No, no. That's not what I mean. . . . Ah, how do you get that rice?

SM: Oh, I scoop some from the steamer.

AF: Right. Where does the rice in your steamer come from?

SM: My storage.

AF: What about the rice in your storage?

SM: The rice shop delivers it.

AF: That's the point! How do you make your payments to the rice shop?

SM: I don't![4]

In this example, asking a direct question such as "How do you earn money?" would be considered rude; therefore the first character asks an indirect question, "How do you feed yourself?" In normal communication, it is obvious to everyone that the question is intended to ask about work or a job. In the *rakugo* structure, however, the stupidity or literal-mindedness of the second character allows him to reply with answers that are factual but which avoid answering the question. While this style of humorous conversation takes place not only in *rakugo* but also in Japanese daily communication, in *rakugo* such a misleading conversation will be exaggerated and prolonged so that it goes on for quite a long time. It could also take a turn in an equally wrong different direction and continue in that way.

The other reason that conversation is such an important element in *rakugo* humor is that the purpose of joking together is for people to share a common understanding and to relate to each other to gain solidarity. Humor is not often completed by one person, but involves several people taking part by bouncing words back and forth. Therefore, jokes and humor do not usually function as "ice breakers" at people's first meeting in Japanese communication. Those present must be confident of sharing something in common to enjoy communicative humor.

Often, Japanese people are highly aware of the roles they are playing in humorous communication. Usually one among a group of people will undertake the role of the *boke* (ボケ the fool), and another will play the *tsukkomi* (つっこみ the "sharp man").[5] The *boke*'s role is to make stupid or out-of-context statements and to engage in cognitive misunderstandings (*boke* means "vague," "confused," "addled," or "fuddled"). By contrast, *tsukkomi* means "to thrust," "to poke," or "to be sharp or aggressive," so that role involves making statements to correct or to put down the *boke*. In conversation the *boke* is always followed by the *tsukkomi*, without whose responses the humorous conversation set cannot be completed in Japanese communication.

105

Although the roles of *boke* and *tsukkomi* are the ones most commonly adopted in humorous conversational exchanges, there are others that individuals and their conversational group may be aware of. These are special character roles in which one might be canny, another stingy or mean, and so on. People will deliberately establish and exaggerate their own chosen characters in order to make the conversation funny. Such categories of roles or characters match the popular stereotypical characters found in *rakugo*. Japan's long history of isolation (until roughly 1867) and its accompanying self-image of the Japanese as a homogeneous society did not encourage a rich development of ethnic or cultural stereotypes.[6] Therefore, Japanese humor in general has tended to favor stereotypes based on this type of exaggerated character with different personality traits.

Because of the use of conversation and character roles, it is quite difficult to employ the Japanese sense of humor in simple statements. The stereotypical belief that the Japanese lack a sense of humor does not necessarily come from such an actual deficit but rather from the way humor is expressed in Japanese communication. Nevertheless, the question still stands: Do the Japanese tell jokes? The answer is yes. However, they are not told in the way that western jokes are told—a short third-person narrative and a punch line. Only one type of joke can be told in the western style in Japanese: jokes depending on wordplay. Usually, Japanese jokes are told in story form, recounting a personal experience, preferably one that can be exaggerated. The story certainly does not have to true, or actually based on one's own experience, but it is considered much more humorous if it did indeed happen to the person telling it.

It is important to recall that the purpose of humor and of telling jokes among the Japanese is to share a common experience and a sense of relating to each other. Telling of personal experiences is an effective way of sharing something about oneself; for example, a person might say: "My grandpa is eighty-five years old and he loves candies. So I gave him a box of chocolates for Valentine's Day. And he ate them all in one day. I was about to tell him, 'Grandpa, if you eat so much chocolate at once, you will get toothache.' But I didn't, because he suddenly took all his teeth out of his mouth!"[7]

This story may well have been exaggerated from the real experience. Grandpa may not have actually taken his teeth out, or maybe the storyteller simply remembered that he does not have *many* teeth left, not that they are all gone. In fact, this story may not originally have been about the speaker's grandfather at all; it could have been about his neighbor's grandfather. But if this story was told as a story merely about some old man, it would be neither funny nor satisfactory for the purposes of humor. People present would not understand why the speaker was telling a story about somebody he doesn't know, since jokes are required to be something that the people present can relate to. Most commonly, people will tell funny personal experience stories as representing the experience of a friend; for example, in a conversation I recorded, one member of a group recounted the following story, to which everyone nodded agreement, acknowledging the punch line embedded in it: "A friend of mine has three sons. One day, she showed them a picture of herself in her high school days. The youngest son said, 'Mom, you haven't changed at all.' The middle one said, 'Does that mean she looks young now?' The oldest one said, 'No, it means she looked old when she was in high school.'"[8]

Jokes taking the shape of impersonal, fictional stories—for example, those that begin "A man said . . ." or "There were three men . . ." or "Have you heard the one about . . . ?"—are hardly ever heard in Japanese communication. This western style of joke would be understood but would not inspire much laugher. For Japanese communication, such ready-made jokes are inappropriate because they bear no relationship to the speaker or to anyone around the table or in the group and thus do not help to build closer relationships.

Another style of Japanese humor, however, is to tell *neta* (ネタ) jokes. *Rakugo* performers often use *neta* jokes in their *makura* before they start the actual *rakugo* story. *Neta* jokes are ready-made, popular jokes that are repeated many times, but they generally still take the story style rather than the condensed western joke form of a short narration and a punch line, as the following example shows: "Recent new technology has developed machines that talk. There is a set of scales at the gym that tells you your weight when you stand on it. When someone stands on the measure, it says, 'Pi pi pi . . . , You are . . . sixty-five kilograms.' Once when a middle-aged woman stood on the scales, it said, 'Pi pi pi . . . , Please, one person at a time.'"[9]

This joke turns on the stereotype of the Japanese middle-aged woman, who is considered heavy, talkative, loud, and meddlesome, but motherly. *Neta* jokes are usually told in public speeches or by comedians. Importantly, when a person is going to tell a *neta* joke to a group of people, the speaker begins by stating that he or she is going to tell a *neta* joke, thus ensuring that the audience is prepared to appreciate the story properly.

In a way, *rakugo* stories are a type of extended *neta* joke because the same popular stories are told many times in the same style by several different comedians. However, true *neta* jokes are frequently and easily made use of both by *rakugo* performers and by *manzai* stand-up comedians,[10] and this style of personal experience story has been popular with contemporary audiences as a device to connect the joke-teller and the audience.

In effect, *rakugo* embraces the full range of Japanese humor: it includes character stereotypes, humorous conversational devices, and the personal storytelling style. It is excellent material for an introduction not only to Japanese humor but also to Japanese culture and society, since the traditions and also recent developments in Japanese culture and society can be viewed through *rakugo*. Every year, new *rakugo* stories about contemporary Japanese culture and society are created by young, talented *rakugo* performers, thereby keeping the form current and lively.

NOTES

1. An earlier version of this chapter was published as "Rakugo: Sit-Down Comedy," *Humor and Health Journal* 8, no. 3 (1998): 9–12.
2. Aiba Akio, *Rakugo Nyūmon* (Tokyo: Kōbun Shuppan, 1991), 17–18.
3. Ōshima, "Rakugo: Sit-Down Comedy."
4. Katsura Shijaku, *Rakugo de Shijaku* (Tokyo: Chikuma Shobō, 1993), 14–15; my translation.
5. See also the discussion of these two roles in chapters 2 and 4.
6. Terry Morrison, *Kiss, Bow, or Shake Hands* (Tokyo: Macmillan Language House, 1999), 232–40.

7. This example is drawn from personal communications with family and friends.
8. I recorded this exchange during spontaneous conversation with family and friends.
9. I recorded this *neta* joke from the *rakugo* performance of Katsura Kaishi (during the *makura*) in Osaka on May 13, 2000.
10. For a more detailed discussion of *manzai*, see chapter 4.

8 Forgotten Women: Two *Kyōka* Poets of the Temmei Era

Rokuo Tanaka

Kyōka

The comic poetic genre of *kyōka* (狂歌) flourished in the Edo period (1600–1868) and reached its peak in the Temmei era (1781–89), when two women poets, Fushimatsu no Kaka and Chie no Naishi, were prominent. *Kyōka* uses allusion and poetic devices to create an exquisite subterfuge. This chapter examines how that deployment of deception is transformed into comic verse, and how the mixing of high and low language expresses freedom and radically redefines the traditional *waka* (和歌) form of thirty-one-syllable poems.[1]

Humor in Ancient Poetry

The Day of the Ox, July 30, is a special day in Japan. It is the traditional day for eating eel, and Japanese people consume tons of this delicacy on this day. Grilled eel is believed to bring vitality and to help fight the hot summer. Eel has been enjoyed in Japan since ancient days, as is evidenced from the first extant Japanese anthology, the *Man'yōshū* (万葉集), compiled in the eighth century. It records two *waka* poems by Ōtomo no Yakamochi (大伴家持) (ca. 718–85), one of the compilers of the *Man'yōshū* that employ incongruously pompous language to ridicule a courtier, Ishimaro, who was very lean. The poems are well worth quoting in full.[2] They are accompanied by a note explaining that Yoshida no Muraji Oyu, commonly known as Ishimaro, was extremely lean; although he ate and drank a great deal, he always looked famished.[3] They are introduced by the title "Two Poems Ridiculing a Lean Man."

111

Two Poems Ridiculing a Lean Man

石麻呂に	Ishimaro ni	To Ishimaro
我物申す	Ware mono mōsu	I say to you
夏痩に	Natsu yase ni	To prevent summer weight loss
良しといふものそ	Yoshi to iu mono zo	It's said you should eat eels
鰻捕りめせ	Munagi tori mese	Go and catch some!
痩す痩すも	Yasu yasu mo	No matter how lean you are
生けらばあらむを	Ikeraba aramu o	It is better to be alive
はたやはた	Hataya hata	But when you attempt
鰻を捕ると	Munagi o toru to	To catch an eel
川に流るな	Kawa ni nagaru na	Don't let the river wash you away!

Yakamochi composed these provocative poems to ridicule Ishimaro. They seem to anticipate a counteroffensive from Ishimaro, but there is no record of one. This suggests that Yakamochi and Ishimaro may have been at a banquet where guests took turns as targets of insults, being "roasted" in the contemporary American sense of being teased publicly.[4] These two poems are commonly categorized as *gishōka* (戯笑歌 playful and mocking verse). I have hypothesized that the spirit of *gishōka* lies at the foundation of humor in Japanese literature, and especially at the root of *kyōka*, the thirty-one-syllable comic verse form that developed from early comic *waka* such as these.[5]

Humor in the Edo Period

Various forms of popular literature developed during the Edo period (1600–1868), and they all attracted samurai (mostly of the lower ranks), merchants, and commoners as well as scholars of the Japanese and Chinese classics. The forms included *jōruri* (浄瑠璃 puppet theater); *kabuki* plays; *gesaku* (戯作 light literature), which includes a range from *manga*-esque *kibyōshi* (黄表紙) to *ninjōbon* (人情本 "cartoon" pictures depicting the Floating World of the geisha quarters); *senryū* (川柳 seventeen-syllable comic *haiku*);[6] *kyōshi* (狂詞 comic poems in Chinese); and *kyōka* (the thirty-one-syllable comic *waka*). *Kyōka* in particular was nurtured and reached its peak in the Temmei era (1781–1789). People enthusiastically engaged in *kyōka* composition as a pastime, and their works are included in the many *kyōka* collections extant today.

112

The basic technique of *kyōka* composition is the skillful use of literary allusion to create an exquisite subterfuge and also the use of poetical devices such as *kakekotoba* (掛詞 pivot words), *engo* (縁語 intertextually associated words), and *mitate* (見立 figurative language). *Kyōka* does not employ the traditional fixed epithets and decorative modifiers (枕詞 *makura kotoba*, or pillow words) that were so often integral elements of traditional *waka*.

Defining *Kyōka*

In his *History of Japanese Literature* (1899) William G. Aston, who pioneered the translation of Japanese literature into English, defines *kyōka* by comparison with *tanka*: "Kiōka (literally 'mad poetry') is a comic and vulgar variety of *tanka*. There is an absolute freedom both in respect of language and choice of subject. The *kiōka* must be funny, that is all."[7] In *Oriental Humor* (1959), R. H. Blyth offers more detail: "*Kyōka*, mad (light) *waka*, which had their flourishing time at the end of the eighteenth century, are usually a kind of parody, but not so much making a fool of the original writer as in European verse; rather 'lightening' it, in the sense of omitting all the seriousness that so easily falls into sentimentality."[8]

Blyth illustrates his point by presenting a parody of the following *waka* poem by the priest Saigyō (西行) (1118–90), which is included in the 1205 anthology known as the *Shin Kokin Wakashū* (新古今和歌集):

吉野山	*Yoshinoyama*	Mount Yoshino:
去年の枝折の	*Kozo no shiori no*	I will change my path
道かへて	*Michi kaete*	From last year's broken twig
まだ見ぬ方の	*Mada minu kata no*	And view cherry blossoms
花をたづねん	*Hana o tazunen*	I have not yet seen[9]

The author, Saigyō, had broken off a twig when visiting the previous year in order to show the way to the best spot for viewing the cherry blossoms, but this year he would purposely avoid the old path and explore a part of Mount Yoshino he had never been to before. The poem captures to perfection the delicate spirit of familiarity and change.

A *kyōka* poet of the eighteenth and nineteenth century,

Ki no Sadamaru (紀定丸) (1760–1841) parodied Saigyō's elegant *waka* poem as follows:

吉野山	Yoshinoyama	Mount Yoshino:
去年の枝折を	Kozo no shiori o	The flowers are in full bloom
見ちがえて	Mi chigaete	I wander around
うろつくほどの	Urotsuku hodo no	Having mistaken the twig
花盛りかな	Hanazakari kana	I broke last year[10]

Sadamaru skillfully crafted his *kyōka* so that the title and first two lines sound almost identical to Saigyō's (only two syllables in Sadamaru's version have been changed, as shown below in bold in the relevant lines), but as a result they give a totally different meaning:

Saigyō: *Yoshinoyama kozo no shiori **no** michi **ka**ete* (changing paths)
Sadamaru: *Yoshinoyama kozo no shiori **o** mi chi**ga**ete* (making a mistake)

The first three lines of the *kyōka* thus make one long and very elegant pun on an original poem familiar to the audience of the time.

The *kyōka* scholar Hamada Giichirō defines *kyōka* as traditional *waka* in a thirty-one-syllable verse form that expresses nontraditional, incongruous content and which eschews elegant diction and sophisticated prosody designed to move heaven and earth. In other words, he says, a satirically humorous perspective is invoked by, as it were, the heart of a poet who wears a "robe made of silk brocade" but who ties it with a "sash made of straw."[11] In my view this captures the genre exactly. Topics and vocabulary for *kyōka* are not as restricted as they are in traditional *waka*. Thus *kyōka* extracts wit and humor from materials found in ordinary daily life, invariably transforming elegance into plebeianism and seriousness into mockery by its improvisations.

Four Kyōka Poets of the Temmei Era

Among the well-known *kyōka* poets of the Temmei era, two of the greatest were women. One was Yamazaki Matsu (山崎まつ) (1745–1810), whose pen name was Fushimatsu no Kaka (節松嫁嫁). She was the spouse of Akera Kankō (朱楽管江) (1740–1800). The other was Kaneko Michi (金子通) (1745–1807), whose pen name was Chie no Naishi (智恵内子). She was the wife of a commoner, Watanabe Kisaburō (渡辺喜三郎) (1724–1811), owner of a public bathhouse in Edo, who himself excelled in *kyōka* compositions under the pen name Moto no Mokuami (元木網).[12] Both couples were partnerships of gifted *kyōka* poets whose works deserve individual discussion.

AKERA KANKŌ

Yamazaki Gōnosuke (山崎郷助) (1740–1800), also known as Akera Kankō, the husband of Fushimatsu no Kaka, was a retainer of the Edo Shogunate, and therefore a samurai, but one of low rank. Kankō and his wife, Fushimatsu no Kaka, led his group of *kyōka* enthusiasts, the Akera-ren (朱楽連), which was named for him and which comprised shogunal retainers who, like himself, were also samurai. Kankō was well versed in Japanese and Chinese classical poetry and prose. He became known as one of the three greatest *kyōka* poets, along with Karagoromo Kisshū (唐衣橘洲) (1743–1802) and Yomo no Akara (四方赤良) (1749–1823). Kankō excelled in writing *share-bon* (洒落本 "clever," "smart," or "stylish" books)[13] and *senryū*. He compiled the *kyōka* collection entitled the *Kyōgen Ōashū* (狂言鶯蛙集) in 1785 and also published two *share-bon*, the *Baika Shin'eki* (売花新駅), in 1776 and the *Taitei Goran* (大抵御覧) in 1779. Typical of his style is the following *kyōka*:

山かけに	Yamakake ni	Light snow in the spring
つもる豆腐の	Tsumoru tōfu no	On the shadow of mountains
淡雪も	Awayuki mo	Soon melts away
春のものとて	Haru no mono tote	As *tōfu* with grated yam
腹にたまらず	Hara ni tamarazu	Does not stick to the ribs[14]

Light snow that had rested on the shadowy side of the mountains seems to be almost gone as spring arrives. In a similar fashion, the poet reminds us, bean curd (*tōfu*) dressed with grated yam does not stick to the ribs but seems to melt away. Kankō employed *mitate* (figurative words) for *yamakake tōfu* (*tōfu* with grated yam on the top) and *awayuki* (light snow). This combination creates a novel and amusing synesthesia whereby the reader "feels" as well as sees the melting of the snow. Little is known about the life of Kankō, but his literary works in the genres of *kyōka*, *gesaku*, and *senryū* have been extensively recorded.

FUSHIMATSU NO KAKA

Fushimatsu no Kaka, the wife of Akera Kankō, was said to have started composing *kyōka* around the third year of Temmei (1783). She was expert in traditional *waka* and had a profound knowledge of the Japanese as well as the Chinese classics. In fact, she assisted her husband in instructing his disciples in *kyōka* composition. Her mastery of the form is demonstrated by examples of her *kyōka* such as the following:

FORGETTING TO RETURN HOME UNDER THE CHERRY BLOSSOMS

よしや又	*Yoshiya mata*	"After us the deluge!"
うちは野となれ	*Uchi wa no to nare*	You don't care for my house
山桜	*Yamazakura*	Unless the cherry blossoms fall
ちらずは根にも	*Chirazuba ne nimo*	Even to sleep
かへらざらなん	*Kaerazaranan*	You will not return home[15]

Fushimatsu no Kaka presumably composed this *kyōka* when her young husband left home to wander around enjoying the moon and the flowers. She cleverly crafted the poem to describe her husband's state of mind: "It doesn't matter to you whether the house reverts to a field or a mountain wilderness!" She uses a pivot word, the homophone "*ne*" to mean both "root" and "sleep," so that the poem means that her husband will not return home, even to sleep, until the beautiful cherry blossoms fall and return to their roots. She also used a cliché—"After us the deluge!"—as a pivot word with its alternate meaning of *yamazakura* (mountain cherry blossoms).

To fully appreciate this poem, one must understand the allusion to a phrase taken from a poem in the *Wakan Rōeishū* (和漢朗詠集 *Japanese and Chinese Poems to Sing*, ca. 1012), compiled by the late-Heian poet and critic Fujiwara no Kintō (藤原公任) (966–1041). The relevant poem is the following by the Chinese poet Po Chü-i:

SPRING INSPIRATION

花の下を	*Hana no moto o*	Beneath the flowers
変えらむことを	*Kaeramu koto o*	Forgetting
わするるは	*Wasururu wa*	To return home
美景に因てなり	*Bikei ni yotte nari*	Because of the lovely scene

116

樽の前に	Son no mae ni	Facing my wine cup
酔を勧むるは	Ei o susumuru wa	Urging me to drink
これ春の風	Kore haru no kaze	None other than spring wind![16]

The key phrases are "Beneath the flowers / Forgetting / To return home." Fushimatsu no Kaka's lines "Unless the cherry blossoms fall / You will not return home" echo Po Chü-i's without exactly duplicating them.

These references prompt the reader to reflect that an alternate meaning of the poem is that it was composed when Akera forgot to return home from the pleasure quarters of the Yoshiwara. The word "flower" also applied to a beautiful woman, a professional entertainer of the Yoshiwara. In either interpretation, this poem was about her husband's infatuation with some "scenic beauty," whether human or natural, and in it she uttered not a word of resentment or jealousy. This proves that she was a woman of the world, a woman of *sui* (粋) or *iki* (粋), which means she had a thorough acquaintance with human feelings and particularly a natural ability to recognize her own and to portray them in artistic form, as well as to hold her own in an artistic setting. A key Edo term, *tsū* (通 connoisseurship), would better fit her, and she was indeed a connoisseur of *waka* and *kyōka*—of their special vocabulary, their attention to detail, and their innate taste.

In another of her *kyōka,* she is bantering with a flirting man:

うかうかと	Ukauka to	Absentmindedly
ながき夜すがら	Nagaki yo sugara	All through the night
憧れて	Akugarate	Admiring
月に鼻毛の	Tsuki ni hanage no	The harvest moon
数やよまれん	Kazu ya yomaren	Can count your nostril hairs![17]

Men may spend the whole night gazing absently at the full moon. This looks as though the moon is teasing them, just as women tease them. "To count nostril hairs" is a phrase that means that a woman can easily make a fool of a man when she is familiar with his weak points, that is, when the man is infatuated with the woman. This interpretation leads the reader to an understanding of Fushimatsu no Kaka's poignant criticism (written

117

from the point of view of a woman who is not free to leave the house at night) of men drifting in the Floating World of pleasure and indulgence all night long.

The reference point for this *kyōka* is the following *haiku* by the famous poet Matsuo Bashō (松尾芭蕉) (1644–94):

明月や	*Meigetsu ya*	The harvest moon:
池をめぐりて	*Ike o megurite*	I stroll round the pond
夜もすがら	*Yo mo sugara*	Till the night is through[18]

A man spending a long night without sleep under the August moon is certainly captivated by the bright moonlight. Since Bashō, the master poet, invoked the harvest moon, it must necessarily be enjoyed all through the night by any man of taste. A man of dubious taste, however, wandering round absentmindedly viewing the moon, is thus playfully made sport of by the moon itself. Accordingly, Fushimatsu no Kaka's *kyōka* ridicules the man who merely goes through the aesthetic motions, aping the true artistic sensitivity of the ideal set by Bashō.

Here is another *kyōka* on the topic of a *sake* wine party on a spring night:

買はばやな	*Kawabayana*	The moon is clouded over
月はおぼろに	*Tsuki wa oboro ni*	At night in the misty spring
春の夜の	*Haru no yo no*	Cherry flowers are in full bloom
花も酒屋の	*Hana mo sakaya no*	I wish I could buy
かよい尋ねて	*Kayoi tazunete*	A bottle of *sake* on credit[19]

The time is the season for viewing cherry blossoms; the night is warm under the misty moon in spring. Under the fragrant cherry blossoms, the author would like to drink with her beloved. Alas, there is no money to buy a bottle of *sake*. She searches hurriedly for her credit book in the drawer. On such a night, instead of being full of poetic sensibility, perhaps even of romantic sentiment, she is prosaically looking for the credit book she will need to take with her to the store, thinking about money. Fushimatsu no Kaka blends the classical phrase *Kawabayana* ("I wish I could buy") with the realistic *kayoi* ("credit book"). This mixture of high and low language invites the reader to laugh. Here she also uses pivot words with two meanings: *sakaya* for "wine shop" and "in full bloom," and *kayoi* for "fragrance of cherry flowers" and "credit book." The purpose of the pivots is to collapse two sentences into one by exploiting the fact that they have dual meanings.

Here is another example of her work, entitled "Chrysanthemum in *Sake* Wine":

ひたすらに	Hitasura ni	With all my heart
薬と菊の	Kusuri to kiku no	I gaze at the shadows of
かげ見えて	Kage miete	Medicine and chrysanthemum
下戸も千歳や	Geko mo chitose ya	A non-drinker's wish for longevity
ふらすこの酒	Furasuko no sake	Reflects on the *sake* in a flask[20]

This *kyōka* evokes the seasonal image of the observation of *chōyō*, or the double *yang*, falling on the ninth day of the ninth month, when people customarily drank wine in which chrysanthemums were soaked, in token of their hope for longevity. The poet uses a homophonic pivot word, *kage*, to mean both "shadow" and "blessing," and she manifests her colorful sense of imagery by describing an up-to-date glass bottle, a "flask" (probably imported from abroad), and by combining it with such traditional *waka* rhetoric as references to chrysanthemum wine. This use of the foreign word "flask" (*furasuko*) marks an innovation in *kyōka* that was to help to shape future poetics.

After the death of her husband in 1800, Fushimatsu no Kaka went on alone to lead Akera Kankō's group of *kyōka* enthusiasts, the Akera-ren. Her works were included in two volumes of the *Toku Wakago Manzaishū* (徳和歌後萬載集) (1785), a collection of some eight hundred poems by about two hundred *kyōka* poets. Instead of holding the customary memorial service one year after her husband's death, Fushimatsu no Kaka built an obelisk commemorating *kyōka* poetry in Mukōjima in Edo. At the same time she published a *kyōka* collection entitled *Kozue no Yuki* (*Snow on the Treetops*). In her later years she lost her eyesight and became a nun, taking the name Kogetsu-ni (孤月尼).

Moto no Mokuami

Watanabe Kisaburō (渡辺喜三郎) (1724–1811), whose pen name was Moto no Mokuami (元木網), was the husband of Chie no Naishi and, as mentioned earlier, owned and operated a public

bathhouse in Kyōbashi in the heart of Edo. In 1781, having retired from his business, he and his wife formed a group of *kyōka*
poets called the Ochiguri-ren (落栗連) in Shiba (now in inner
Tokyo) and began teaching *kyōka* techniques to their disciples,
who were merchants and commoners. Mokuami was one of the
earliest leaders of the *kyōka* camp. Because he was a commoner
himself, his influence over these *kyōka* enthusiasts was strong,
and he was further empowered by his wife, whose assistance
was of no small value. Rumor had it that half of the *kyōka* disciples in Edo belonged to the Ochiguri-ren under the guidance of
Moto no Mokuami and Chie no Naishi. Mokuami compiled the
kyōka collection entitled *Shin Kokin Kyōkashū* (新古今狂歌集)
and other *gesaku* work.[21] He was well grounded in Japanese and
Chinese literature, and his style in *kyōka* was very precise, with
the source of the allusions easily identifiable in each case. The
result frequently approaches the western concept of parody, because of the exactitude of the mockery.

One example of his *kyōka*, on the inspiring topic of lice,
alludes to a poem by Ariwara no Narihira (在原業平), a handsome Heian court poet, one of whose poems appears in chapter
23 of the classical work *The Tales of Ise* (伊勢物語). The original
poem captures a charming domestic setting for a child's growth
over the period of the poet's absence:

筒井つの	*Tsutsuitsu no*	By the bamboo fence
井筒にかけし	*Izutsu ni kakeshi*	Around the well
まろがたけ	*Maro ga take*	Once I measured my height
過ぎにけらしな	*Sugi ni kerashina*	Time has passed
妹見ざる間に	*Imo mizaru ma ni*	Since I last saw her[22]

The parody by Mokuami, on the other hand, reads:

筒井づつ	*Tsutsuizutsu*	Bamboo fence:
いつもしらみは	*Itsumo shirami wa*	Always full of lice
あり原や	*Arihara ya*	Poor Ariwara
はいにけらしな	*Hai ni kerashina*	Be on guard
ちと見ざる間に	*Chito mizaru ma ni*	Don't let them crawl![23]

Here the handsome playboy Ariwara no Narihira is imagined as
infested with lice. Accordingly, a momentary lapse of attention

to his long and otherwise elegant hair (as when he is climbing through a bamboo fence on his way to a nightly assignation) will disturb the lice by brushing them off against the poles, encouraging them to crawl away. Those obnoxious parasites appear frequently in premodern humorous texts, and it is a striking idea to connect them with the handsomest of court poets. By parodying the language of the original poem so exactly (compare the detail of lines 1, 4, and 5), Mokuami brought a courtly love story down to the lowest, most incongruous level. This is a good example of the juxtaposition in *kyōka* of high and low language, which in this case is reinforced by especially careful linguistic parallels in the opening and closing lines.

Moto no Mokuami in his old age became a monk, yet he continued to guide the members of his Ochiguri-ren, teaching them principles of true *kyōka* composition.

CHIE NO NAISHI

Mokuami's spouse, Chie no Naishi, began to compose *kyōka* around 1769 when her husband joined a *kyōka* group in the early stages of the genre's development in the Edo period. Her rival, Fushimatsu no Kaka, also had her followers, but Chie no Naishi was undoubtedly the representative female poet of the Edo *kyōka* world. Many of her works were included in the *Kyōka Wakabashū* (狂歌若葉集) (1783), the *Manzai Kyōkashū* (万載狂歌集) (1783), and other collections. Her style was characteristically soft, delicate, and feminine.

Both Chie no Naishi and her daughter were *kyōka* poets and therefore adopted pen names with typically ironic meanings. "Chie no Naishi" means "Ignorant Girl," and her daughter's pen name, "Ikuji no Naishi," means "Spineless Girl." In 1794 both mother and daughter were recognized by having a number of their works published in the *Shin Kokin Kyōkashū* mentioned above.[24] Chie no Naishi later became a nun and composed a very subdued poem about that serious point of transition in her life:

今日よりは	*Kyō yori wa*	As of this day
つげの小櫛も	*Tsuge no ogushi mo*	Throwing away a small hair comb
うちすてて	*Uchisutete*	Made from a *tsuge* tree
木の端なりと	*Ki no hashi nari to*	I would rather people called me
人にいわれん	*Hito ni iwaren*	A piece of wood[25]

Hair combs made of *tsuge* (boxwood) were expensive and had long been favored by Japanese women. This poem describes the poet's state of mind as she abandons the material interests of the real world and enters the tranquillity of the Buddhist life.

The true *kyōka* of Chie no Naishi, however, also evidence her profound knowledge of the Japanese classics. Typical is the following, which depends upon classical allusions for its comic effects:

ON A RAINY NIGHT OF THE FULL MOON

明月の	*Meigetsu no*	The full moon does not shine
雲間にひかる	*Kumoma ni hikaru*	Even through clouds in the sky
君まさで	*Kimi masade*	Without the Shining Prince
さえぬ雨夜の	*Saenu amayo no*	How dull is storytelling
物がたりかな	*Monogatari kana*	On a rainy night![26]

Tonight is the night of the full moon; but it is raining so the full moon does not shine through the clouds. Since the Shining Prince (a personification of the moon) will not come, a gathering with dear friends for storytelling will not be very exciting. This is the argument of the poem. Chie no Naishi displays her special skill here in her use of *engo* (intertextually associated words that are rich in classical allusion). *Hikaru kimi* refers not only to the moon but also to the fictional Shining Prince, Hikaru Genji, hero of the classic *Tale of Genji*; and *saenu* is intertextually related both to "not shining" and to "an unexciting calculation done with an abacus." Because over time the word *kimi*, meaning "Lord," came to be used euphemistically or familiarly for "you" (as addressed to a boy or a younger male), a second meaning is embraced in which the poet conveys warm and homely feelings between herself and an unnamed companion. Although the theme is not particularly momentous or innovative, the wordplay with which Chie no Naishi constructed this poem justifies her reputation as one of the most talented *kyōka* poets of the time.

Conclusion

The basic technique of *kyōka* composition is the skillful use of allusion, which is really part of an exquisite subterfuge. The elements of humor, satirical comment, and parody in *kyōka* derive from altering in an incongruous way a part of the foundational material located in *waka, monogatari* (物語 tales), *nikki* (日記 diaries), and essays. The end result is not a crude reduction of the original with outright ridicule but rather a gentle mocking acknowledgment of the human realities beneath the elegant poetic ideal.

The Edo period saw the full flowering of *kyōka* verse as an accepted form of poetic composition. In a period of Neo-Confucian dominance, it is remarkable that two of the prime exemplars of *kyōka* verse were women, and commoners at that. Their compositions not only evidence a refined poetical taste and skillful use of the techniques of composition but also demonstrate complete familiarity with the Japanese and Chinese classics. Furthermore, their fame is not just retrospective, surfacing through modern scholarship: they were well known and well appreciated in their own milieu and time. Their reputations were independent of their husbands' despite the fact that both couples worked in partnership. Their achievements demonstrate that poetry could then, as it can now, empower a woman, allowing her to engage in discourse that is otherwise reserved for men. A woman can express her strength, pleasure, or anger through poetic allusion. Thus poetry emancipates and allows women an original voice. In the case of Chie no Naishi and Fushimatsu no Kaka, that voice is delightfully humorous.

NOTES

1. For a more detailed discussion of *waka* and its related poetic form *tanka*, see chapters 10 and 2, respectively.
2. In the poems quoted in this chapter, the romanization of the Japanese version follows the Hiragana readings in modern pronunciation (unless otherwise stated). The lines of English translation do not necessarily correspond exactly in word order or sequence with the lines of Japanese text. Unless otherwise stated, the English translations are my own. Further details are given in the Editor's Note at the beginning of this volume.
3. The poems and note are found in the fourth volume of the collection *Man'yōshū* and are published in a modern edition in *Nihon Koten Bungaku Zenshū*, ed. Kojima Noriyuki et al., vol. 5 (Tokyo: Shōgakkan, 1992), 140. The Japanese in which these beautiful and

ancient poems are written is naturally somewhat archaic in expression, but, following the conventions adopted for the rest of this chapter, archaisms have been modernized in the romanized version, except for *munagi*, which corresponds to the modern *unagi*, or eel.

4. George A. Test, *Satire: Spirit and Art* (Tampa: University of South Florida Press, 1991), 89–90.
5. Tanaka Rokuo, "Ishikawa Masamochi and the *Shokunin-zukushi Kyōka Awase*" (unpublished master's thesis, University of Hawaii, August 1977), 9.
6. For a more detailed discussion of *senryū* and *haiku*, see chapters 2 and 10.
7. William G. Aston, *A History of Japanese Literature* (1899; Tokyo: Tuttle, 1972), 297–98.
8. R. H. Blyth, *Oriental Humor* (Tokyo: Hokuseidō Press, 1959), 245–46.
9. Minemura Fumito, ed., *Shin Kokin Wakashū*, Book 1 (Spring: 1, Poem 86), in *Nihon Koten Bungaku Zenshū*, vol. 26 (Tokyo: Shōgakkan, 1992), 61. Alternate English translations of this and the following poem can be found in Blyth, *Oriental Humor*, 245–46.
10. Blyth, *Oriental Humor*, 246.
11. Yoshida Seiichi and Hamada Giichirō, eds., *Senryūshū Kyōkashū*, in *Nihon Koten Bungaku Zenshū*, vol. 33 (Tokyo: Chikuma Shobō, 1961), 345.
12. Pen names are traditionally comical in and of themselves, either orthographically, phonologically, or both. Thus "Moto no Mokuami" is actually a cliché meaning "to return home as wise as one set out": applied to a person, it might be rendered as "The Man of Much Ado about Nothing." "Akera Kankō" bears a close resemblance phonetically to the adverb *akkerakan* and thus gives a meaning of "Lord Blank Looks" or "Lord Vacant Stare." "Fushimatsu no Kaka" could be translated as "The Prodigal's Wife." For discussion of the pen names of Chie no Naishi and her daughter, see below.
13. *Sha-re* means "wordplay" as well as "elegance or style." For more on the technique of *sha-re* see chapter 5.
14. From the *Manzai Kyōkashū* (1783), in Kokumin Bunko Kankōkai, eds., *Kyōka Kyōgen* (Tokyo: Kokumin Bunko Kankōkai, 1913), 14.
15. From the *Toku Wakago Manzaishū* (1785), in Sugimoto Nagashige and Hamada Giichirō, eds., *Senryū Kyōshi*, in *Koten Nihon Bungaku Taikei*, vol. 57 (Tokyo: Iwanami Shoten, 1958), 319.

16. Quoted from Kawaguchi Hisao, ed., *Wakan Rōeishū Ryōjin Hishō*, in *Nihon Koten Bungaku Taikei*, vol. 73 (Tokyo: Iwanami Shoten, 1965), 51.

17. From the *Kyōgen Ōashū* (1785), in Kokumin Bunko Kankōkai, *Kyōka Kyōgen*, 205.

18. Ueda Makoto, *Bashō and His Interpreters: Selected Hokku with Commentary* (Stanford, Calif.: Stanford University Press, 1991), 143.

19. From the *Kyōgen Ōashū* (1785), in Kokumin Bunko Kankōkai, *Kyōka Kyōgen*, 413.

20. Ibid., 210.

21. The title of the *Shin Kokin Kyōkashū* parodies that of the *Shin Kokin Wakashū*, the classic anthology of *waka* referred to earlier.

22. Horiuchi Hideaki and Akiyama Ken, *Taketori Monogatari Ise Monogatari*, in *Shin Nihon Koten Bungaku Taikei*, vol. 17 (Tokyo: Iwanami Shoten, 1997), 104.

23. From the *Manzai Kyōkashū* (1783), in Kokumin Bunko Kankōkai, *Kyōka Kyōgen*, 110.

24. See note 21 above.

25. Nihon Koten Bungaku Daijiten Henshū I'inkai, eds., *Nihon Koten Bungaku Daijiten*, vol. 4 (Tokyo: Iwanami Shoten, 1984), 217.

26. From the *Manzai Kyōkashū* (1783), in Kokumin Bunko Kankōkai, *Kyōka Kyōgen*, 37.

Farce and Satire in *Kyōgen*

Marguerite A. Wells
and Jessica Milner Davis

Comic Terminology

In discussing the universality of certain forms of comedy found in the theater both east and west, it may be helpful to start by defining some terms, both in English and Japanese. *Comedy* (コメディー) applies specifically to performances (usually on a stage) intended to make an audience laugh. In Japanese, *kigeki* (喜劇)[1] refers both to comedy in general and to a specific genre of comedy on the Japanese stage. Within the English term *comedy*, English usage recognizes a range of styles and forms, from farce (ファース *faasu* or 笑劇 *shōgeki*) to satire (諷刺 *fūshi*), from romantic comedy to absurdism, and so on. A good illustration of absurdism is the work of the Japanese playwright Abe Kōbō (for example, *The Man Who Turned into a Stick*)[2] or the mid-twentieth-century plays of Eugène Ionesco and Samuel Beckett.

All genres of comedy deal with conflict—verbal abuse, battles of wit, quarrels, plots, deceits and trickery, even real fights—the results of which are not intended to be taken too seriously, and after which harmony is generally restored. The conflicts may be between equals; between authority figures and the rebels or those who would aspire to power; between colleagues, neighbors, friends, or sworn enemies; or between family members. The conflicts may be over totally trivial matters or over serious issues, such as love or infidelity, honesty or corruption; they may take the shape of words, deeds, or both. But whatever their form, in any comedy, the audience's sympathy will tend to lie with the side that stands for fun and festivity, not with that representing sour repression. And the outcome of any comedy is more likely to be a feast, a cheerful reconciliation, or a triumphant celebration of wit than a moralizing speech about the seriousness of life.

Different styles of comedy, however, approach their material in different ways, and they certainly generate different responses from the audience. Romantic comedy is very gentle, even tearful, in its laughter (hence the French term *comédie larmoyante*). Satire and absurdist comedy are more bitter, often with strongly marked messages or with moral comment intended for the viewers. Farce is cheerfully disgraceful, allowing its jokers to lark about with little intention of reform but ensuring that conventional authority is restored at the end of the period of indulgence and festivity.

Characteristics of Farce

Of all these comic forms, the lowest or simplest is farce. Because of its reliance upon physical slapstick, its "stock," or simplified, cartoon-like characters, and its lack of heightened, witty dialogue, farce has often been seen as the original comic form, the one upon which all others are based. In fact, "pure" farce is quite rare, and, far from being simple, is complex in its careful balance and patterning of both character and action. Farce is notoriously difficult to act and to produce onstage. In some ways its challenge to established authority and propriety makes it the most extreme of all comic forms, but in other ways it is the most conservative.

As Davis's study of farce has demonstrated,[3] this paradox is achieved by detailed attention to structure and balance and by careful justification for whatever mayhem is permitted. Both jokers and their targets are carefully chosen, the former to engage the audience's allegiance for their tricks and indulgence, the latter to justify with their ineptitude, weaknesses, and faults the aggressions and humiliations they will suffer. Both are usually lacking in self-awareness and in the ability to reflect on their plight, and they are more given to gesticulation than to instrumental action. Typically, farce plots conform to one of four patterns.[4] Each pattern is adapted to emphasize the limited nature of the aggression and usually ensures that the conventions under challenge in the comic conflict are safely restored by the play's end.

Following Davis's typology, the patterns are as follows:

1. *Humiliation or deception farces.* Here an unpleasant victim is exposed to his or her fate without opportunity for retaliation. These farces are unidirectional in their joking and require special justification for the pleasure taken in the sufferings of others.

2. *Reversal farces.* In this case the tables are turned on the original rebel or joker, allowing the victim retaliation in return. Often further reversals are permitted in order to prolong the mirth and ensure the "proper," conventional outcome.

3. *Equilibrium or quarrel farces.* Here the plot focuses upon a narrow, perpetual-motion kind of movement in which opposing forces wrestle each other—literally or metaphorically—in a tug-of-war without resolution, remaining in permanent balance.

4. *Snowball farces.* In this case all the characters are equally caught up as victims in a whirlwind of escalating sound and fury. Often these plots are driven by an elaborate series of misunderstandings and errors, giving rise to many "crossed lines" between the different parties. The source of the joke is frequently the power of nature, inanimate objects, tools, or machines to dominate mere humans.

These patterns are represented graphically in figure 9.1.

In various ways, all these patterns ensure that only a controlled and limited license to challenge conventional authority is given to the jokers, who are intent on getting their own way, indulging themselves, or revenging themselves on their betters. In addition, the style of acting in farce makes it obvious that no one is really getting hurt. In the case of humiliation farces, the sour representatives of authority and control frequently invite their own punishment, and their fate is unlikely to stir any protest from an audience out to enjoy itself at the theater. In reversal farces the final twist will bring about a return to proper social order, and for equilibrium farces the audience responds with little sympathy for either of the equally matched sides. Snowball farces sweep their audience along with fast-paced action, allow-

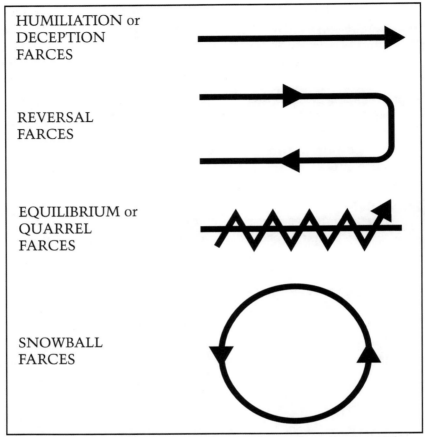

HUMILIATION or
DECEPTION
FARCES

REVERSAL
FARCES

EQUILIBRIUM or
QUARREL
FARCES

SNOWBALL
FARCES

Fig. 9.1 Schemata of basic farce plots (Redrawn from Jessica Milner Davis, *Farce*, rev. ed. [New Brunswick, N.J.: Transaction, 2003], 7)

ing no time for reflection or the development of empathy, and all characters alike are exposed to the cosmic joke—which extends to embrace the audience as well—that as members of the human race we are not in control of our own destiny.

When a person of empathy, moral comment, or aesthetic wit enters into the domain of farce, then the comic style will falter, transmuting to another form. If it is extended verbal wit, then we tend to label the style as high comedy or comedy of manners, what Osada Chūichi in 1894 called *jōryū no komedii* (上流のコメディー).[5] If empathy takes hold, then sentimental or romantic comedy is quickly at hand. But if there is reflective moral comment or criticism, then the style becomes satiric. This transition may be driven by the self-awareness of the characters, by the threat of serious consequences to the fooling on-stage, or by the intervention of an external character who points to the social evils of the characters and their joking. The result in any of these cases is that unease creeps into the audience's laughter as attention is diverted from "just having fun" toward the need for reform and change, whether in society or in human nature itself.

In examining the highlights of *kyōgen* (狂言), the comic genre native to Japan and its classical theater, it is instructive to ask if these western typologies of comic style and structure apply. Although the parent form with which *kyōgen* is associated, *nō* drama (能),[6] is famous around the world, its accompanying comic playlets, known as *kyōgen*, are less well known and rarely performed outside Japan.

Brief Description and History of *Kyōgen*

Kyōgen is the comic relief on the *nō* stage: *nō* is drama, whereas *kyōgen* is comedy. The two genres are performed by different actors but on the same stage and in the one program. Like *nō*, *kyōgen* took its present form in the Muromachi period of Japanese history, from the fourteenth to the sixteenth centuries.[7] Handed down in an oral tradition within schools that developed to train actors, the *kyōgen* texts were first committed to writing in the early Edo period. They are now preserved and interpreted by several schools, of which two still continue the unbroken tradition, the Ōkura and the Izumi.[8] The great actor and *nō* master Zeami (1363–1443), who started writing around the year 1400, provided the classic texts on the philosophy and interpretation of *nō*, and he also commented on the origins and acting of *kyōgen*, as a matter incidental to the *nō*. Scripts, characters, costume, settings, and acting style have been handed down from this period. Figures 9.2 and 9.3 give an idea of the traditional setting for a *nō* production (common to both genres). The first is a photograph of an outdoor *nō* stage at the Yasaka Shrine in the center of Kyoto,[9] and the second shows a floor plan of the stage itself.

Fig. 9.2 *Nō* stage at the Yasaka Shrine, Kyoto (photo by Marguerite Wells, 1989)

A full program today would be three *nō* plays interspersed with two *kyōgen* plays, although programs used to be longer. *Nō* has musical accompaniment, whereas *kyōgen* usually does not, although rejoicing, in the form of song and dance, often appears in *kyōgen*, as might be expected in any comedy. *Nō* is masked drama, but most *kyōgen* characters do not wear masks. The exceptions are demons, women, and characters in auspicious plays that approach the solemnity of *nō*. These pieces, like the auspicious *manzai* referred to in chapter 4, serve as quite serious ritual invocations of good fortune rather than as comic relief. In pace, costuming, and concept of character, we might typify *nō* as slow-paced, elevated, formal, and brocaded, whereas *kyōgen* is for the most part simplified, down-to-earth, and homespun, so that, although deliberate and highly polished, the actions of the actors are not quite as stylized as they are in *nō*.

Kyōgen as Farce

What kind of comedy is the comic relief of *kyōgen*? The repertoire is small, comprising no more than about 250 pieces.[10] Applying Davis's typology of farce in an analysis of the texts reveals

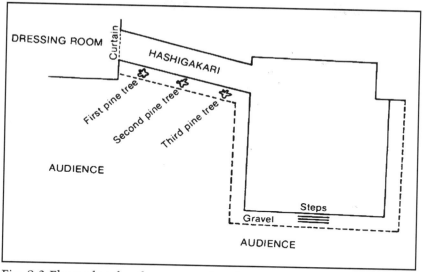

Fig. 9.3 Floor plan for the conventional *nō* stage (redrawn from P. G. O'Neill, *A Guide to Nō* [Kyoto: Hinoki Shoten, 1954], 6, 8ff.)

that all of the *kyōgen* plots fall into one or another of the four farce categories, except for a few that clearly are not comedy at all. These exceptions are the auspicious plays referred to above, which are not in the slightest bit funny but rather have religious or auspicious themes and serve an entirely different theatrical and social purpose from any form of comedy. They chiefly consist of songs and dances that are performed to bring down the blessings of the gods on the place and/or people. These are a distinct and atypical subset of *kyōgen*, but they are, however, a very small minority. For the majority of the texts, a single example of a typical farce plot in each category serves to illustrates how neatly the typology fits the main body of traditional *kyōgen*.

HUMILIATION OR DECEPTION FARCE

Hisshiki Muko (引敷婿 *The Covered-up Bridegroom*)[11] provides an excellent example of a straightforward plot in this category. A young man who is just married goes on a formal visit to his father-in-law's house. He does not have the dress trousers (袴 *hakama*) required for the occasion, so a friend ties a draped top on his front to look like trousers and lends him a leather loincloth for the back. His problem is to face toward everybody during the whole visit, but his father-in-law asks him to perform a dance for him. Even so, he manages fairly well to dance always facing the front until his father-in-law joins in the dance, views the rear, and the fraud is discovered. The young man runs off, humiliated.

A more complex case is *Asahina* (朝比奈) ("Asahina" is the name of a famous warrior). This is one of a number of plays in which the King of Hell, Emma, has to go out into the highways and byways to catch human souls because so many new religions are successful in getting sinners into heaven and the king is losing out on hell's regular share. Here, after much grumbling at the competitive pressures he is subjected to, Emma meets up with an unknown but doughty opponent—Asahina, of course. Asahina and the King of Hell do battle, and the king is beaten soundly. When Emma asks the secret of his strength, Asahina explains who he is and tells the story of one of his famous battles. He then obliges the King of Hell to carry his weapons for him and to act as guide to show him the way to heaven.

Although this is also undoubtedly a humiliation farce in that the King of Hell is cast as the victim throughout, and the play's purpose is to ridicule and humiliate him, it is significant that it borrows both the form and structure of many *nō* plays, without intending parody. In other words, it has beneath its fun a serious purpose. This lends the farce a reflective air, particularly in the recitation of the famous battle story. One of the great unresolved issues of Japanese society and art, and of *nō* in particular, was the moral status of the warrior. Japan in general—and the warriors in particular—adopted Buddhism. When the warriors took control of Japanese politics away from the aristocrats, the result was a society that honored the warrior but in which the prevailing Buddhist beliefs forbade killing. How were warriors to achieve salvation? Whereas *nō* plays agonized over the problem, this farce puts forward a simple and happy solution: overpower and humiliate the King of Hell, whose task it is to punish violent killers! The solution appears in many other *kyōgen*, turning the king into a stock comic character, always good for a laugh. Here, therefore, is a case of a farce approaching the borderline of this kind of farce.

REVERSAL FARCE

A classic and well-known *kyōgen* is *Busu* (附子 or ぶす).[12] Here the plot turns on the fact that a master goes off and leaves his two wily servants in charge of a terrible poison that he calls "Busu." They are terrified, but after a while they realize that it is actually sugar, which was a rare and precious substance in those days, when the only sweetener was honey. They eat the lot. Terrified at what they have done, they try to work out how to escape their master's wrath. Then one of them starts tearing the master's paintings and smashing the valuable pottery. When the master comes home he finds them sitting and crying. Their calculated story is that they were having a *sumō* wrestling match and accidentally smashed the valuable pottery and tore the priceless scroll, after which they tried to commit suicide by eating the poison—which of course did not work. They have hilariously turned the tables on the master.

EQUILIBRIUM OR QUARREL FARCE

In performance, *Yobigoe*, or *Yobikoe* (呼声 *Calling Voices*), is one of the funniest extant *kyōgen*. A servant who has not been turning up for work lately pretends not to be at home when his master and his overseer come to find him. Knowing that he cannot resist a rhythm, they stand outside his house and start chanting everything in time to a beat. He is caught up in the rhythm and emerges, dancing, but he still refuses to work. The result is a total standoff, with each side held in balance against the other. They all dance around the stage, talking to each other in chant, while those in the audience fall about in their seats, laughing at the antics. Equilibrium farces are often the most uproarious in their comedy and laughter, precisely because (as here) the audience's sympathy for one side is counterpoised by the other. The situation creates a kind of "perpetual motion" machine with it rapidly becoming evident that neither side will ever decisively prevail.

SNOWBALL FARCE

The play known as either *Fukurō Yamabushi* (ふくろう山伏 *The Owl and the Mountain Priest*) or simply *Fukurō* (ふくろう

The Owl)[13] takes the structure of a snowball farce. Here a younger brother becomes possessed by the spirit of an owl and behaves accordingly. When his older brother calls in the priest to exorcize the spirit, the two of them in turn become "infected" and, instead of the young man being cured, matters go from bad to worse. Eventually they all hop off, cheerfully hooting.

Complex *Kyōgen* Plots

A careful study of the *kyōgen* repertoire reveals that most plots fall neatly into one or other of the four farce types. Figure 9.4 presents classifications for some of the major plays found today in the repertoire of the Izumi and Ōkura schools. Identifying the principal structure is a relatively straightforward matter, but the plot frequently combines one overarching pattern with a number of twists and turns.

Because *kyōgen* are short plays (from twenty to forty-five minutes long), there is usually not sufficient time to develop elaborate snowball plots such as the classic five-act pieces of the nineteenth-century European stage. Despite this, it should not be supposed that all *kyōgen* are simplistic in their construction: complexity is still achieved within the strict time limitation. Quite sophisticated pieces result from the combination of various types of humiliation, reversal, and equilibrium plots to form elaborate farcical deceptions, revenge plots, and punishments. Some examples will serve to demonstrate the delightful farcical structures that can result from these kinds of combinations.

Bō Shibari (棒縛 *Tied to a Staff*) is a highly complex farce plot with a double humiliation, two reversals, and a final humiliation of two carefully selected victims.[14] It has the same fundamental plot as *Busu*, but here the master tricks his servants physically as well as verbally to prevent them from drinking his *sake* while he is out. The play makes good use of the traditional *kyōgen* pair of trickster servants, similar to the Graeco-Roman comedy tradition of the wily servant and the stupid servant that is familiar to theatergoers in the West. In *kyōgen* these two are stock characters, usually named Tarō Kaja and Jirō Kaja, and the audience knows to expect all kinds of mischievous complications and surprises when they appear.

This *kyōgen* starts with the master, anxious about trusting his servants not to misbehave while he is out, calling the two of

Humiliation or Deception Farces

Asahina	Awataguchi	Bakuchi Jūō
Bonsan	Chidori	Dobu Kachiri
Dongongusa	Gan Daimyō	Hagi Daimyō
Hanatorizumō	Hara Tatezu	Hige Yagura
Hikkukuri	Hisshiki Muko	Imajimmei

Reversal Farces

Akubō	Akutarō	Akutagawa
Awasegaki	Bakurō	Bō Shibari
Buaku	Busu	Busshi
Chigo Yabusame	Dontarō	Futari Daimyō
Hakuyō	Hoshi ga Haha	

Equilibrium or Quarrel Farces

Akagari	Bishamon Renga	Chasanbai
Chatsubo	Daihannya	Dochi Hagure
Domori	Ebisu Daikoku	Fuji Matsu
Fukitori	Fumi Ninsai	Fumi Yamadachi
Funa Watashi Muko	Fune Funa	Fuse Nai Kyō
Gan Karigane	Gan Tsubute	
Gyūba	Hachiku Renga	Iruma
Hana Arasoi	Hana Ori	Hana Nusubito
Haridako	Hi no Sake	Hito o Uma
Hōjō no Tane	Ima Mairi	Iroha

Snowball Farces

Imonji	Fukuro Yamabushi	Futaribakama
Hanago	Hikuzu	Hōchō Muko
Igui		

Non-farce Plots: Auspicious Plots

Bikusada	Daikoku Renga	Ebisu Bishamon
Echigo Muko	Fukube no Shin	Hachi Tataki
Iori no Ume		

Fig. 9.4 Classifications of *kyōgen* plots

them and asking Tarō Kaja (who loves to show off) to give a demonstration of fighting with the staff. In the process, the master, helped by the loyal but uncomprehending Jirō Kaja, thrusts the staff through the sleeves of Tarō Kaja's *kimono*, and he is tied up and rendered helpless. Figure 9.5, taken from a *kabuki* version of the *kyōgen* play, shows how the master then ties up Jirō Kaja in the same way and leaves, secure in the belief that they will not be able to drink his *sake* while he is gone. Thus far the play is a double humiliation farce, with a reversal against the foolish Jirō Kaja, who sided with his master.

Left to themselves, Tarō Kaja and Jirō Kaja figure out that if one of them holds a large *sake* cup, the other can pour the *sake* into it and then drink from the cup that the other is holding. By the time the master comes home they are very happily drunk, singing and dancing in ensemble, still attached to their staves. The tables are well and truly turned on their master in a complete reversal of trickery. So drunk that they do not even hear their master approach, they see his angry face only when it has come close enough to be reflected in the *sake* cup on which they are fixated. By this time, the two are so far gone that they sing a rude song about him: here they overreach themselves, provoking in turn their own second humiliation and punishment as their master chases them off, swearing vengeance.

Hōchō Muko (包丁婿 *The Bridegroom and the Carving Knife*)[15] is another play with a complex plot. (It is a significant, if minor, matter to note that although this is a very funny play, its traditional title has nothing to do with the actual content, demonstrating that some texts of *kyōgen* are corrupt.) In this play as it is performed today, a nervous and gullible bridegroom who is going to pay his first visit to his father-in-law is given a set of instructions on etiquette by a friend. But the friend determines to play a trick on him and gives him instead written instructions to follow, which the audience discovers are those for fighting a *sumō* match, not for paying a courtesy visit.

As the young man cannot read, his not-too-bright bride reads the instructions to him, and they follow them step by step. Realizing that the young man has been tricked, and not wishing to expose him to ridicule, the father-in-law kindly plays along. The wife is not sure whom to help, but she finally takes her husband's part: the sequence progresses to where the youngsters

Fig. 9.5 The comic servants Tarō Kaja and Jirō Kaja are outwitted by their master in a *kabuki* version of the *kyōgen* play *Bō Shibari*. (From *Shin'engei*, July 1918, n.p.)

together manage to throw the old man in a sort of *sumō* hold. Well satisfied with themselves, they exit, leaving the old man calling a mixture of complaints and threats after them.

This complex plot combines elements of a humiliation farce (the young man being victimized and making a fool of himself) with those of a snowball farce (a mistake draws all the characters into confusion), and it ends with a more challenging and humiliating reversal to conventional authority, whereby the fearsome formality of a visit to a revered in-law turns into a triumphant assertion of youth and vitality. The final status of the authority figure is full of ridicule, and a delightful touch is the ambiguity of the seeming naïveté of the bride.

Conditions Justifying Comic Punishments

While in snowball farces all the parties are exposed in turn—and consequently give as good as they get—and in equilibrium farces the parties are fairly equally matched, humiliation farces and reversal farces specialize in the focused victimization of one or more characters. When, as in *Hōchō Muko*, the victims might seem to be undeserving of their fate (after all, the father-in-law, however bearlike and frightening, was willing to play along with his foolish son-in-law, which might be supposed to merit some consideration), the audience needs special reasons to feel that those singled out for humiliation deserve their fate. In order to allow the audience to laugh freely at the chosen victims, *kyōgen* plots must and do pay careful attention to these aspects of motivation and characterization.

What, then, are the qualities that justify an audience in laughing at a victim in *kyōgen*, and do these tend to reinforce the carefree spirit of farce or the critical spirit of satire in their effects? In farce, typically, the failings of its comic victims are superficial and commonplace and their sufferings not so harsh as to provoke any implicit criticism of the society that allows such characters to flourish. In satire, on the other hand, the victims' failings are more serious and flawed and will typically result in enough suffering and bitter comment by them and/or others to encourage the audience in seriously criticizing the society that produces them.

Going through the *kyōgen* plays one by one, it is possible to produce a list of failings that Japanese audiences of the last six hundred years or so must have found psychologically convincing in liberating laughter. Figure 9.6 lists some of the major failings. There is no question that some operate as well in the twenty-first century as they would have at any time in the history of *kyōgen*; others, however, such as the matter of physical handicap, have acquired a more sympathetic appeal now than was traditional. In fact, a whole cycle of "blind man" *kyōgen* is rarely played these days, since contemporary mores do not hold that blindness justifies victimization. It should be noted, however, that in the annals of European farce this condition was also a traditional justification for mocking a comic victim.[16] As for the "physical failing" identified as "being Chinese," racial stereotyping also is not uncommon in joking and farcical comedy around the world. One need only reflect on the (long-lived) popularity of the famous Gilbert and Sullivan comic opera *The*

```
Moral Failings
trickery          malice          cowardice       trouble-making
dishonesty        gullibility     stupidity       bullying
cruelty           ineptitude      greed           boasting
theft             pretension      jealousy        shrewishness
infidelity        ignorance       nagging         drunkenness

Physical Failings
blindness                  ugliness (in women)
physical deformity         being Chinese

Religious Failings
ritual defilement          being the King of Hell
```

Fig. 9.6 Conditions justifying comic punishment in *kyōgen*

Mikado to see how things Japanese immediately qualified for comic ridicule in upper-class London in the late Victorian era.

Stylization in Acting, Costume, and Movement

Of course, all these failings of character, role, or body are highlighted by the style of acting employed by *kyōgen* actors, which exaggerates the characters onstage and makes them seem larger than life. Because of this distancing from reality, the audience is less seriously concerned for the characters' sufferings as "normal" people; it is invited to regard them as suitable victims for cheerful comedy in which people "don't really get hurt." In the context of its carefully balanced plots and unself-aware characters, *kyōgen* does not dwell upon its characters' failings or present those as serious subjects for reform. Indeed, the plots depend upon the fact that the stock characters will appear again and again as they return to their old tricks, having learned nothing from the last time round.

A vivid illustration of the exaggerated but homely acting style adopted for *kyōgen* is provided by an example from Mibu *kyōgen*, a subset of the genre, which is a form of masked dumb show played at the Mibu Temple in Kyoto twice a year. In the Mibu *kyōgen* play *Gakizumō* (餓鬼相撲 *The Hungry Ghosts'*

Fig. 9.7 The Mibu *kyōgen* play *Gakizumō* (*The Hungry Ghosts'*
Wrestling Match), performed at the Mibu Temple, Kyoto, April
1988. Here, the Hungry Ghosts cringe in a corner while Saint Jizō
agrees to wrestle with the King of Hell (photo by Marguerite Wells,
1988)

Wrestling Match),[17] the King of Hell and his team of Demons
challenge Saint Jizō and his team of Hungry Ghosts (human
souls in hell) to a prolonged and well-balanced wrestling match.
Of course, the team led by Saint Jizō ultimately wins, strength-
ened by the spiritual might of their captain, so this is a combination of a quarrel farce with a final reversal, in which the King of
Hell and the Demons are punished for being themselves—ma-
levolent braggarts.

The King of Hell and the Demons engage in plenty of blus-
ter. For their part, the Hungry Ghosts (illustrated in figure 9.7)
spend a great deal of the play cringing and shaking visibly with
terror, retreating to the *hashigakari* (walkway to the stage) in
order to get as far away from the Demons as they can. Both blus-
ter and cringing are of course visual signals of the cowardice
that justifies victimization in farce, but the events presented
here cannot be regarded as making a serious proposal that either
Hungry Ghosts or Demons reform their ways!

Indeed, as previously noted, the comic victims are *expected*
to maintain their traditional ways, with the King of Hell a popu-

Fig. 9.8 Emma, the King of Hell, before his defeat in the Mibu *kyōgen* play *Gaki-zumō* (*The Hungry Ghosts' Wrestling Match*), at the Mibu Temple, Kyoto, April 1988 (photo by Marguerite Wells, 1988)

lar villain who appears in several *kyōgen* plays. As noted in the discussion of *Asahina*, his role is usually to lament the declining number of sinners available for hell. He is a downcast figure, forced to go into the highways and byways to catch sinners and push them into hell. Here as elsewhere he fails, to the audience's great satisfaction: sinners mostly get away with indulgence in *kyōgen*. He is, however, an eye-catching killjoy, as is shown in figure 9.8.

The Borders of Farce

When a farce plot has strong elements of sentiment, morality, or empathy, it moves over the borderline of farce and verges on becoming another kind of comedy. In *kyōgen* this is rare, but there are a few examples. *Asahina* has been noted already as

Fig. 9.9 The *kyōgen* play *Utsubozaru* (*A Monkey for a Quiver*), showing the monkey (played by a child) performing (reproduced from a postcard, probably Taishō era, 1912–26).

introducing some elements of more serious reflection on moral issues. Other plays, such as *Utsubozaru* (靭猿 *A Monkey for a Quiver*),[18] sound a sentimental note. This piece could well be classified as farce-becoming-*comédie larmoyante*, as an examination of its plot demonstrates.

A landowner who is out hunting meets a monkey trainer with his monkey. The landowner decides that he will shoot the monkey and use its skin to make a quiver for his arrows. The monkey trainer is devastated and asks to be allowed to say goodbye to his friend. He also says that he will kill it himself, but the monkey, thinking the trainer is gesturing to it to perform, begins its act. The monkey trainer cries, the landowner relents, and all ends on a festive note with dancing, singing, gifts, and general rejoicing. This is a nice farcical reversal, but the balance of the dramatic action takes place on the borderline between farce and *comédie larmoyante*. As figure 9.9 reveals, the audience's empathy is engaged by the device of having a child actor play the monkey's part.

At the other end of the spectrum of comic style, there are a few examples of farce-becoming-satire. *Dochi Hagure* (東西はぐれ *Between East and West*)[19] is an unusual *kyōgen* for a number of reasons. A priest has received invitations to preach at two places. At one he will be given money, at the other a good meal. He argues with himself for so long about where to go that it becomes too late to go to either! The play concludes with his exit, as he moralizes to the audience quite openly about greed and indecision.

Despite the fact that this *kyōgen* is a rare one-hander, to be played solo, its structure is essentially that of a quarrel farce in which the struggle (or *débat*, as the technique is termed in comparable French medieval farce)[20] takes place between the two parts of the priest himself, each pulling him in a different direction. His two loves are so well balanced that he is unable to satisfy either one. However, the character's self-awareness during his debate shifts the comic tone away from the indulgence of farce toward a focus upon the relative seriousness of his failings. Given that he is a priest, his gluttony and cupidity take on a deeper significance, which is underlined by his own ability to draw the moral from his stupidity. At the close of the play, the comic tone shifts decisively toward satire, with a strongly critical message for the audience. In the *kyōgen* repertoire, this is rare.

The Concept of *Gekokujō*

The fact that both farce and satire specialize in comic rebellion and the shock of taboo violations of one kind or another is a confusing matter for commentators. In an article entitled "A Keepsake from the Tail-Wagging-the-Dog Society: Kyōgen,"[21] Sugiura Mimpei discusses the idea of "the tail wagging the dog," or *gekokujō* (下克上). This is a reference to any era when society is topsy-turvy, when the common people are rebelling and lording it over those above them in the social hierarchy. According to Sugiura: "In the laughter of the middle ages . . . the medieval peasants and townspeople . . . having seen the framework of order and class broken down by internal strife, were just beginning to know their own power."[22] Thus "the humour of *kyōgen* is nothing other than the humour of *gekokujō*,"[23] that is, the rebellious mockery of the upper classes by the lower. Sugiura acknowledges that *kyōgen* is not satire,[24] but the topsy-turvy, dog-eat-dog nature of the *gekokujō* world encourages some to argue that it really does stand for rebellion against the established social system. If *kyōgen* does not wield the critical knife of satire, it at least wields the bludgeon of *gekokujō*.

Of course, neither its representation as the theater of the bludgeon nor the term "farce" is a compliment to one of Japan's exquisite traditional arts where the finest performers are designated living national treasures.[25] Thus, despite some academic references like Sugiura's,[26] farce is not the usual way *kyōgen* is described by those with a proprietary interest in it, and the identification of *kyōgen* as satire remains current and widespread.[27]

It is true that the taboos which *kyōgen* choose to violate are largely not those of adult propriety but rather those of hierarchy. Ōkura Toraaki, the author of the great treatise on *kyōgen* completed in 1651, *Warambegusa (Jottings for the Children)*, complained that the *kyōgen* of his day was vulgar (いやしい *iyashii*) and that clowning and indecent things (道化 *dōke*; 尾龍なること *birō naru koto*) were the disease of *kyōgen*.[28] However, as Iizawa Tadasu points out (with apparent regret) in his 1972 essay "Vulgar *Kyōgen*," if that was so then, it is not now.[29] The vulgarity in the presently preserved texts and performances extends at most to devices such as that of an acolyte who comes upon a temple maid bending over a well (there is an additional joke here in that all the female roles are played by men) and seizes the opportunity to pinch her bottom.[30]

The emphasis on hierarchical "cheekiness" increases the temptation for Japanese writers to identify *kyōgen* as satire, because indeed the typical *kyōgen* plot is *not* about dirty jokes but about a master (often referred to as the *daimyō*) being tricked by his wily servants. *Daimyō* (大名) came to mean a feudal baron, so it is easy to conclude that *kyōgen* is a satire on feudal barons, just the sort of person who would have been its audience. But a different meaning is indicated by many facts, not the least of which is that two of the traditional divisions of *kyōgen* are called *daimyō kyōgen* (大名狂言) and *shōmyō kyōgen* (小名狂言), that is to say, "great-name *kyōgen*" and "little-name *kyōgen*." At the end of the Heian period and in the Kamakura period, as the *Kōjien* dictionary tells us, *daimyō* meant not a baron but a village landowner.[31] These terms therefore mean "plays about big landowners" and "plays about small landholders." Thus the plays are in fact about rustics—the sort of person whom the citified, aristocratic audience of the day might well have regarded with some contempt as country bumpkins, suited to being fooled by their own servants. The fooling, however, could by no stretch of the imagination be construed as any threat to themselves, requiring serious reform.

Thus *kyōgen* gave its aristocratic audience the emotional release of being allowed to look down on and laugh at country bumpkins, and to its commoner audience it gave the pleasure of seeing country masters being fooled by people of their own subservient station, so that they themselves were afforded the luxury of looking down upon and laughing at the people whom they served. In its original social setting, *kyōgen* was a comic release for the aggressions toward others of *both* those at the top *and* those at the bottom of the social hierarchy. The aggression was of course safely contained, never being directed at targets higher than the lower middle of the social structure, and, most importantly, being controlled (as we have seen) by the careful balances of the typical *kyōgen* farce plot.

As the plot classifications have demonstrated, the usual conclusion is that the master who has been tricked by his wily servant or servants ends up chasing him or them off, shouting threats of retribution. This is not satire's critique of corrupt social authorities; rather, it signals the end of farce's classic, festival-day release from the rules, showing that the laughter can conclude safely with a reassertion of normal, conventional social hierarchy.

Of course, there are some anomalies to this restoration of normal authority. First, as noted above, throughout the *kyōgen* repertoire there is the convention that human beings beat demons and even gods. A second major anomaly is that when husbands and wives fight, the woman wins. Although this is not the stereotype of Japanese society that is current either in Japan or elsewhere, it is a rueful and deeply comic acknowledgment of reality. No matter what the supposed social power of the man, either at the time of the composition of these plays or even now, his wife still had then—and has today—the power to make his life miserable. *Kyōgen* simply acknowledges this as fact, and as cause for laughter.

147

Expurgation and Containment

In her book *Japanese Humour,* Wells has argued, as have many other scholars, that humor has its negative aspects. It can be used in ridicule, blasphemy, and obscenity; it can bring down governments and destroy reputations. Therefore every civilized society faces, explicitly or implicitly, the need to control those types of humor that have the potential to cause conflict. The main means of control of negative types of humor are fundamentally ethical rules that Wells labels *expurgation* and *containment.*

In the culture that accompanies the English language, there is social permission for humor at almost any time, provided it is expurgated. That is, although it is possible, indeed encouraged, to provoke laughter on almost any occasion, there are complex rules surrounding it—for example, that dirty jokes must not be made in mixed company and that it is rude to use satire or sarcasm against someone who is present. English speakers are also taught from childhood not to laugh at people who should be pitied; not to make "toilet jokes" (which are fit only for children of a certain age); and not to take pleasure in humiliating others or offending others' religion. Thus English speakers expurgate or censor their humor. However, such expurgation is not the only means of controlling the negative aspects of humor.

Another major means of control is containment, and it is this means that has been preferred in the Japanese tradition. Here, social permission for humor is given principally in particular situations or "containers," such as in performances, or in the presence of alcohol. The result (for those societies where humor is chiefly contained) is that there will be only very mild humor found or offered in ordinary social situations, while the humor found in the "containers" may very well be broad and crude. This is true for Japan.

As a means of control, containment aligns much better with farce than with satire. The aggression inherent in farce is highly contained in a fantasy release, normally with a reassertion of the social structure and the social rules at the end. At the end of the festival, we all go back to our daily drudgery feeling more cheerful—but reality has not changed. The aggression of satire, on the other hand, is intended to change reality and consequently threatens to escape from any container. This may be one reason for the extreme caution with which Japanese humorous style approaches the practice, as opposed to the notion, of satire.[32]

It should therefore be no surprise that *kyōgen*, as the age-old, popular, light relief for the *nō* drama, avoids the dangerous ground of satire in favor of the tried-and-true safety of farce. It did well to avoid the dangers inherent in satire and to exploit the structural advantages of the contained rebellion of farce. As a final touchstone for the classification of *kyōgen*'s comic style as farce, Davis's summary analysis of the kind of joking and rebellion that characterizes farce can be read as an accurate description of this hugely funny genre:

Firstly, [farce] invites laughter by the violation of social taboos, whether those of adult propriety, or those of hierarchy. It nevertheless avoids giving offence (which would diminish the laughter), usually by adhering to a balanced structure in which the characters and values under attack are ultimately restored to their conventional positions. Structural stylization and mechanical patterning also help to distinguish the festive licence under which these attacks are carried out. The aggression is both sufficiently precise to be psychologically valid and sufficiently delimited to qualify as play.

Secondly, these jokes are not designed primarily as dramatic vehicles for satirical comment upon the way of the world. Their spirit tends rather to an indulgent, perhaps an ironic acceptance of the human condition.

Thirdly, the participants in the joking are not usually self-aware characters who reflect upon their mischief and its consequences. They are type-characters whose automatism is obvious and whose playful plight demands little sympathy, whether they are the first or last victim of the round.

Essentially, the comic spirit of farce is one which delights in taboo-violation, but which avoids implied moral comment or social criticism, and which tends to debar empathy for its victims.[33]

This aptly summarizes the kinds of comic plots, characters, acting style, and humorous concerns found in the vast majority of *kyōgen* plays. The use of stock characters and larger-than-life stylized acting is marked, as we have seen, and such characters are rarely reflective or particularly sympathetic.[34] The plots conform to the typical European farce plot structures, emphasizing the balance and circularity of the trickery with a careful restoration of authority at the end. Except in its avoidance of vulgarity, *kyōgen* conforms in every way to this analysis of the characteristics of European farce. *Kyōgen* is unequivocally farce, and *gekokujō* can be properly seen as a characteristic of farce during its limited period of indulgence rather than as a symptom of the state of Japanese society at any particular period.

After all, *kyōgen* has long functioned as comic relief for the seriousness and high drama of the *nō* theater. If the briefly licensed topsy-turvydom of *kyōgen* were as serious in its own way as *nō*, and if the plays intentionally used *gekokujō* to take the knife to social evils among the ruling class, by definition *kyōgen* could not function well as comic relief. We may safely conclude that the *gekokujō* of *kyōgen* is just a game, contained in a brief and comic flourish on the stage, as farce is all over the world.

NOTES

An earlier version of this chapter was presented at the twelfth Conference of the International Society for Humor Studies at Kansai University, Osaka, July 2000.

1. The term *kigeki* is usually found with a qualifier such as *shin* ("new"), as is discussed in chapter 2. Further discussion about the terminology of humor and laughter in Japan can be found in the introduction and in chapter 12.
2. Abe Kōbō, *Bō ni Natta Otoko: The Man Who Turned into a Stick; Three Related Plays*, trans. Donald Keene (Tokyo: University of Tokyo Press, 1975).
3. Jessica Milner Davis, *Farce* (London: Methuen, 1978).
4. Ibid., 25–84. See also the introduction to Jessica Milner Davis, *Farce*, rev. ed. (New Brunswick, N.J.: Transaction, 2003), 6–7.
5. Osada Chūichi [Osada Shūtō], "Futsukoku Engeki Genjō," *Waseda Bungaku*, March 1894, 26–44, and "Futsukoku Kigeki," *Waseda Bungaku*, May 1894, 53–70.
6. *Nō* is frequently transliterated *Noh*. Using the Hepburn system of romanization (which is easiest for English speakers to read) the correct transliteration is *nō*, the accent being a macron, representing a long vowel (see the Editor's Note).
7. Different histories give different dates for the periods or eras of Jap-

anese history. Some of the dates given for the Muromachi period are 1392–1568 (Sansom); 1336–1568 (Reischauer); 1473–1568 (Art Dealers' Association); 1392–1573 (Nelson); 1333–1573 (Suwa); and 1333–1568 (*Encyclopaedia of Japan*). As quoted in Andrew N. Nelson, *Japanese-English Character Dictionary* (Tokyo: Tuttle, 1978), 1016–17.

8. The Sagi school is presently undergoing a revival.

9. Plays can be staged both indoors and outdoors.

10. Synopses of the plots of virtually the whole *kyōgen* repertoire can be found in Don Kenny, *A Guide to Kyōgen* (Kyoto: Hinoki Shoten, 1968).

11. The script of this play is found in Sasano Ken, ed., *Ōkura Toraaki, Nō-kyōgen*, 3 vols. (Tokyo: Iwanami Bunko, 1942, 1943, 1945), 2:203–11.

12. The script of this play is found in Koyama Hiroshi, ed., "Nihon Koten Bungaku Taikei," in *Kyōgenshū*, 2 vols. (Tokyo: Iwanami Shoten, 1960, 1961), 1:315–23. For an English translation see Sakanishi Shio, *Japanese Folk-Plays: The Ink-Smeared Lady and Other Kyōgen* (Tokyo: Tuttle, 1960), 84–89.

13. The script of this play is found in Sasano, *Nō-kyōgen*, 1:483–86.

14. For the script of this play see ibid., 1:306–14. For an English translation see Izumi Motohide, ed., *Kyōgen: Traditional and Shakespearean of Izumi School* [sic] (Japan: Izumi Souke [sic], 1993), 30–53.

15. The script of this play is found in Sasano, *Nō-kyōgen*, 2:203–11.

16. An equivalent collection of medieval farce texts exists from sources in Europe, especially the Tournai region of France; see Davis, *Farce* (1978), 11–12, and *Farce* (2003), 77.

17. Because Mibu *kyōgen* is a dumb show there are no scripts, but a synopsis is found in the program for the performance at the Mibu Temple, Kyoto, Mibu Kyōgen Dainembutsukō, eds., *Mibu Kyōgen Kaisetsu* (Kyoto: Ishihara Ōbundō, 1999), 8–9.

18. The script of this play is found in Koyama, *Kyōgenshū*, 1:170–80.

19. An alternative reading is *Tochi Hagure*.

20. For further discussion on this technique, see Barbara Bowen, *Les Caractéristiques Essentielles de la Farce Française et leur Survivance dans les Années 1550–1620* (Urbana: University of Illinois Press, 1964), 37–38.

21. Sugiura Mimpei, "Gekokujōteki Shakai no Katami: Kyōgen," *Bungaku* 32 (1964): 640–51.

22. Ibid., 649–50.

23. Ibid., 650.

24. Ibid., 649.

25. The lowly status of both the term and the genre in its European aspects is discussed in Davis, *Farce* (1978), 1–24, and in its Japanese aspects in Marguerite Wells, *Japanese Humour* (Basingstoke: Macmillan, 1997).
26. For example, Andō Eriko, "Kyōgen, Shōgeki to Shite no Shiten Yori," *Engekigaku*, March 1977, 91–97; Oda Shōkichi, *Nihon no Yōmoa: Koten Setsuwahen*, 2nd ed. (Tokyo: Chikuma Shobō, 1987), 148–50; Sugiura, "Gekokujōteki Shakai no Katami: Kyōgen," 649; Kurahashi Ken, *Engeki Eiga Buyō Terebi Opera Hyakka* (Tokyo: Heibonsha, 1983), 384.
27. For example, see references by Izumi Motohide (*Kyōgen*, 8) to a "shrewdly satiric thrust"; see also Dan Furst, "*Omoshiroi Mono ja:* Kyōgen as Universal Comedy," *Kyōto Journal*, Winter 1987, 27–35.
28. *Ōkura Toraaki: Warambegusa*, ed. Sasano Ken (Tokyo: Iwanami Bunko, 1962), 345.
29. Iizawa Tadasu, "Gehin na Kyōgen," in *Shibai: Miru Tsukuru* (Tokyo: Heibonsha, 1972), 27–33.
30. This play is *Mizu Kumi* (*Drawing Water*) or *Ocha no Mizu* (*Water for Tea*). The script of this play is found in Koyama, *Kyōgenshū*, 2:290–95.
31. Shinmura Izuru, ed., *Kōjien*, 2nd ed. (Tokyo: Iwanami Shoten, 1955), 1349.
32. For a more extended discussion of this and related points, see chapter 12.
33. Davis, *Farce* (1978), 86–87, and *Farce* (2003), 141.
34. For a rare exception, as has been noted, see the discussion above of the priest in *Dochi Hagure*.

Senryū: Japan's Short Comic Poetry

Masashi Kobayashi

Senryū and *Haiku*

Haiku (俳句), short Japanese poems of seventeen syllables that capture a moment in time, are well known outside Japan. However, Japan's short comic poetic genre *senryū* (川柳) is not so well known. *Senryū* verses have the same seventeen-syllable form as *haiku*, and both poems derive from the same origin. Since ancient times, the combination of lines of five and seven syllables has been the most natural syllabic pattern for Japanese poetry. The ancient poems *waka* (和歌 Japanese songs) or *tanka* (短歌 short songs) restrict themselves to thirty-one syllables, patterned in three lines of 5.7.5 (totaling seventeen syllables) plus two more lines of 7.7 (for a total of 17 + 14 = 31). *Haiku* and *senryū*, both of which developed from *waka*, retain the verse form of seventeen syllables arranged in the 5.7.5 pattern, following this ancient syllabic structure, but drop the last couplet.[1]

During the Nara (710–94) and Heian periods (794–1185), verse-capping, or composing linked verses, was a popular game among aristocrats. Someone would make up a short verse, and someone else had to finish it. This was called *renga* (連歌 linked verses). The first part of the verse, known as the *hokku*, was a triplet with three lines in the 5.7.5 syllable pattern. *Hokku* triplets later came to stand alone as poems in their own right, and the genre *haikai*, the ancestor of later *haiku*, is said to have originated in 1499 when *Chikuba Kyōginshū*, the first anthology of *haikai*, was published.[2]

There was another form of the game of linking verses, a reversed form, in which the first player composed two lines of seven syllables each (the *last* couplet of a poem) and the second player had to compose the *first* triplet. This was called *maeku-zuke* (前句づけ), or "adding the second verse," a practice I shall discuss later.[3] *Senryū* developed from these three-line verse

153

combinations. It is said to have started in 1757 when a broad-sheet was printed giving the winning poems from a *maeku-zuke* competition; thus *senryū* made its appearance 258 years later than *haikai*.[4] *Haikai* was renamed *haiku* in the Meiji era (1868–1912) by Masaoka Shiki (1867–1902), a great poet who made innovations and named the resulting poetic form *haiku*. For simplicity's sake, in this discussion we will not distinguish historically among *haikai*, *hokku*, and *haiku* but will call them all by the modern name *haiku*.

    Senryū was hugely popular, especially among the common people in the city of Edo, now Tokyo. Although the warrior class comprised about 60 percent of the population of Edo, most of the verses were composed by the common people, who sometimes even used *senryū* to caricature the warriors. Around 200,000 of the *senryū* poems composed during the Edo era survive today. The poems of this era are now called Edo *senryū, senryūten*, or *kosenryū* (old *senryū*) and are considered the classics of the genre, to the extent that even now they may be quoted in the daily conversation of older people. A number survive in the *rakugo* story-telling genre, which is discussed elsewhere in this volume.[5]

    Senryū remain popular throughout contemporary Japan. Poems contributed by readers are published in many daily newspapers and magazines, so for a long time *senryū* has been the poetry of the common people of Japan.[6] It is certainly more down-to-earth than the classical, formal style of *haiku*. To illustrate some of its comic possibilities, it is helpful to contrast some matched examples of the two forms. In his recent study *Haiku to Senryū (Haiku and Senryū)*, Fukumoto Ichirō[7] makes an extensive comparison, showing the intertextual relationship between *haiku* and *senryū*. There is room here for only a small sample of his enlightening examples.

    The first *haiku* he selects is an extremely famous one by Matsuo Bashō, composed in 1686 in a mostly serious vein:

古池や	*Furuike ya*	An old pond
蛙飛び込む	*Kawazu tobikomu*	A frog jumps in
水の音	*Mizu no oto*	The sound of water[8]

Fukumoto compares it with the following, more relaxed poem:

芭蕉翁	*Bashō-ō*	At the splash
ぽちゃんというと	*Pochan to iu to*	Old Bashō
立ち止まり	*Tachidomari*	Stands still[9]

This poem is an archetypal *senryū* in both spirit and structure. It builds upon the poem by Bashō, capturing the moment in time before he composed the *haiku* that was his masterpiece. Master Bashō, out for a walk and hearing the splash (*pochan*, a delightfully onomatopoeic word), suddenly stops still, expecting an excellent new poem to flash into his mind just as his famous *haiku* had done. The effect of the *senryū* is not so much to evoke awe at the master's genius but rather affection for the memory of the "Old Man," bringing the reader closer to the man himself.

The next *haiku* is also by Bashō. This time it is he himself who is in a humorous mood:

いざさらば	*Iza saraba*	Now I'll go
雪見にころぶ	*Yuki-mi ni korobu*	Snow viewing
ところまで	*Tokoro made*	Till I fall over[10]

Bashō composed this *senryū*-like *haiku* in 1687, the year after he composed the "frog jumps in" poem. It couples the sublime rapture of aesthetic experience with the all-too-real dangers of coming to grief in the snow. This image forms the basis for the next poem, by the *senryū* poet Chikushi, who visualizes Bashō on his snow-viewing excursion to great comic effect:

ひざや手を	*Hiza ya te o*	The Old Man, patting
はたいて翁	*Hataite Okina*	Knees and hands
一句読み	*Ikku yomi*	Composes a verse[11]

(*Okina* is a respectful name for an old man and refers to Bashō, the Grand Old Man of *haiku* poetry.) This is a typical *senryū* in that it is more openly comic than the original *haiku* above. Clearly the *senryū* depends for its full effect upon knowledge, not just of who the "Grand Old Man" was, but of the specific snow-viewing *haiku*. This linking is why *senryū* are sometimes said to be parodic of their *haiku* originals, but the actual relationship is a great deal more delicate than can be conveyed by the western term *parody*.

Origins of *Senryū*
and the Birth of the *Haifū Yanagidaru*

The originator of *senryū* poetry was Karai Senryū (1718–90), who became the first of a line of persons bearing that name as a title or office. Senryū was one of his pen names, his real name being Karai Hachiemon. He was born in the city of Edo and began as a *haiku* poet. In 1757 he became a selector of *maekuzuke*. He does not seem to have composed many poems himself, but as a literary critic he conducted competitions for *maekuzuke* poetry and enjoyed great popularity in his role as adjudicator and editor of anthologies comprising poems submitted for the competitions. The poems he selected for his anthologies came to be called *senryūten* (or *senryūden*) after him, and in the Meiji era the whole genre came to be called *senryū*. His great enthusiasm for *senryū* and his excellent judgment led *senryū* in the right direction just when the genre was blooming in the city of Edo, with the result that many excellent poems were composed by the ordinary people.

The verse-capping game called *maekuzuke* ("adding to the front verse") was very popular in Kamigata (the Kyoto-Osaka area) and had spread to the city of Edo by the late 1680s. A measure of its popularity is that competitors had to pay an entry fee of twelve *mon* per verse (this was one and a half times the price of adult entry to a bathhouse at that time). At the close of the Meiwa period (1764–72) the fee was increased to sixteen *mon* per verse.[12] The winners' poems were printed and distributed in broadsheet form, and prizes were awarded. In the earlier, aristocratic game of *renga*, a poet would compose the first triplet (of seventeen syllables in a pattern of 5.7.5) on the spot and then pass the poem to the second player, who would compose the last couplet, totaling fourteen syllables (7.7). The complete poem was thus in the form of a *tanka* or *waka* (a structure of 5.7.5.7.7). Participants would then go on to compose 5.7.5 and 7.7 verses alternately, producing a series of connected poems. This is why *renga* are called linked verses. In the later form of the game, *maekuzuke*, the linking order is reversed: the game starts with the couplet of the poem (7.7), and the player provides the triplet

(5.7.5). Thus in *maekuzuke* no long chains are produced, only a single link in which the first two lines are given out in advance by the organizer of the competition.

For example, the organizer might give a couplet (usually the same line repeated) consisting of two lines of seven syllables each:

| ずるいことかな | *Zurui koto ka na* | How cunning! |
| ずるいことかな | *Zurui koto ka na* | How cunning![13] |

This is the subject for the competition. It is called the *maeku* (前句 front verse). Then the competitors demonstrate their skill and wit by adding three lines of 5.7.5 after the *maeku*; for example:

朝寝する	*Asane suru*	To wake someone	5
人を起こすは	*Hito o okosu wa*	Sleeping in	7
昼と言い	*Hiru to ii*	Say it's noon	5

The seventeen-syllable triplet was called the *tsukeku* (付け句 added verse). Putting the two together, the poem now reads:

ずるいことかな	*Zurui koto ka na*	How cunning!
ずるいことかな	*Zurui koto ka na*	How cunning!
朝寝する	*Asane suru*	To wake someone
人を起こすは	*Hito o okosu wa*	Sleeping in
昼と言い	*Hiru to ii*	Say it's noon

In final published format the order of the *tsukeku* and *maeku* would be reversed, which had the effect of highlighting the new and original poetic composition. This practice was well received by the audience.

Maekuzuke was not just a literary amusement; it also served as practice for poets who wanted to study and improve their technique for composing linked verses, or *renga*. In *renga* both parts of the verse were equally important, each being composed on the spot by an accomplished poet. In *maekuzuke*, however, the couplet given by the promoter of the competition was common to perhaps thousands of verses, so it was naturally the *tsukeku* triplet that was of most interest. The popularity of putting the *maeku* after the *tsukeku* effectively created a brand-new poetic form, and over time the couplet disappeared, leaving only the triplet (5.7.5). In this way the form of *senryū* was established.

During the Hōreki period (1751–64), with interest gradually shifting to the *tsukeku* triplet, demand grew for a poem that could be appreciated fully without the *maeku* couplet. Goryōken Arubeshi, a friend of Karai Senryū, sensed this and, since Karai's anthologies of winning material had become so voluminous, together with a publisher named Hanaya Kyūjirō, urged Senryū to publish a new anthology of shortened poems. In 1765, Goryōken and Hanaya finally brought out the first edition.[14] It comprised 756 poems that could be understood on their own without their *maeku* couplet and which were still interesting and amusing as independent poems. The poems in the new anthology were all excellent, although it is said that the selectors sometimes edited the poems they published in order to improve the quality. Later, the *maeku* couplet was dropped altogether.

The First Karai Senryū died in 1790, one year before the publication of the twenty-fourth edition of the *Haifū Yanagidaru*. Following his death, his name and the headship of his "school" of *senryū* were passed down from generation to generation of his chief disciples. They continued publication of the anthology under the title of *Yanagidaru* until 1838, when it had reached its 146th edition.[15] It seems that publication ceased in either 1839 or 1840 with the 167th edition (authorities vary on this detail), but from 1841 onward volumes of the *Shinpen Yanagidaru* (*Newly Edited Yanigidaru Collection*) appeared (it is difficult to ascertain the full publishing history of this period).

The History of the *Maekuzuke* Competition

In the first competition, held in 1757, only 13 of the 207 poems submitted were selected. These were published in the first anthology, which was then entitled *Mankuawase* (or *Yorozukuawase*). In 1762, five years later, there were three competitions, and more than 10,000 poems were entered in each. On September 25, 1767, the number of entries reached an amazing 23,348 (the total number of poems entered for *maekuzuke* competitions in that year was about 140,000). In 1779, the year the fourteenth anthology (by now entitled *Haifū Yanagidaru*) was published, the number of poems entered in the October 25 competition alone was 25,024.[16]

One of the reasons for the enormous popularity of the *maekuzuke* competitions among ordinary people was that the subjects (the couplets given in advance) were mostly very simple and often given in repeated form. This simplicity seems to have given poets great freedom in both content and expression. There was no need to be a specialist to compose *senryū*. In addition, in the first twenty-five anthologies, poems were published anonymously, which further encouraged ordinary people to take part in the competitions. If you were poking fun at someone or some social institution, you might like to win a prize, but perhaps you would have preferred not to sign your poem.

Of course, the First Karai's enthusiasm, talent for selecting winning poems, and personal popularity greatly contributed to the phenomenal success of the competitions during his lifetime. However, by the Temmei era (1781–89), standards were declining somewhat and, according to one authority,[17] the simplicity of the subject matter resulted in increasingly mediocre, stereotyped verses. From the twenty-sixth anthology on, poems were signed by the poets, and the fact that the author now had to bear the responsibility for the poem and its comic criticisms meant that there was a reduction in freedom of expression, so the original spirit and vitality of the anonymous poems were lost. It is also said that only the first twenty-four *Yanagidaru* anthologies, selected by Karai Senryū himself, were of true literary value.[18]

Examples of Classical *Senryū* Poems

One well-known *senryū* from the *Yanagidaru* anthologies makes fun of officials who take bribes:

役人の子は	*Yakunin no ko wa*	The civil servant's baby
にぎにぎを	*Niginigi o*	Is very good at learning
よく覚え	*Yoku oboe*	How to grasp[19]

One of the things babies learn early is to close their fists and to grip things, which suggests the idea of grasping at bribes. Given that the *maeku* to which this triplet was linked was "Un no yoi koto / Un no yoi koto" ("How lucky! / How lucky!"), this *senryū* can be read as implying harsh criticism of public officials who customarily took bribes. And since those officials would have held samurai rank, it is also an example of the common people using *senryū* as a humorous critique of the warrior class. However, one modern commentator has seen it as implying envy rather than satire.[20] Whatever the case, this poem was originally published anonymously, and later it was struck out of the *Haifū Yanagidaru*.[21] Japan had a very efficient censorship bureaucracy, and *senryū* poetry, like other forms of literature, was closely watched by the establishment, especially during the Kansei Reforms (1787–93) that were implemented by the statesman Matsudaira Sadanobu (1758–1829). Therefore publishers of *senryū* anthologies revised or struck out poems that might be censored or which might render their publications liable to confiscation by the authorities. These reforms undoubtedly contributed to the *senryū* losing some of its original vitality. Both in anthologies appearing during the reforms and even in 1800, after the reforms were completed, administrators struck out or revised some of the poems, as, for example, in the twenty-ninth edition of the *Haifū Yanagidaru* (1800).[22]

In technical terms, one of the chief challenges of a successful *senryū* is to exploit the limitations of the form. Like the *haiku* poet, the *senryū* writer must pack large amounts of information into seventeen syllables. Abbreviation and compaction are common techniques, as the following example shows:

国の母	*Kuni no haha*	Mother in the country
生まれた文を	*Umareta fumi o*	Walks cuddling
抱き歩き	*Dakiaruki*	The newborn letter[23]

This touching poem captures the moment in time when a woman in the country receives the long-looked-for letter telling of the birth of her grandchild. Lost in her joy and unaware of what she is doing, she walks home cuddling the letter as though it were the newborn baby.

Other *senryū* use the same technique of compaction, collapsing into one portmanteau expression two contrasting images or thoughts, as in the following example:

| 祭りから戻ると
連れた子を
配り | *Matsuri kara modoru to*
Tsureta ko o
Kubari | Back from the festival
Distributing the children
We took with us[24] |

The children who have been taken to the festival are being handed out like playing cards or presents to the parents who have stayed at home, reversing the process of gathering them up to take them to the festival in the first place.

Another such example introduces a note of realism and ironic comment to a romantic, "postcard" image:

| うちわ売り
少しあおいで
出して見せ | *Uchiwa-uri*
Sukoshi aoide
Dashite mise | The fan seller
Fanning himself a little
Shows off his wares[25] |

The fan seller is a nostalgic image from Old Japan, and the round fan (*uchiwa*) is still used in the humid Japanese summer. This *senryū* blends two purposes or motives for the fan seller, who uses his fans both to cool himself and to promote his sales.

Another poem about *uchiwa*:

| 寝ていても
うちわの動く
親ごころ | *Nete ite mo*
Uchiwa no ugoku
Oyagokoro | Though she's asleep
The fan keeps moving:
Motherly love[26] |

This poem deftly conjures up the family scene of the children, sprawled under the mosquito net, their skin glistening with perspiration on a hot and humid summer night, with the fan moving languidly as the mother sits, propped up on her arm but nonetheless asleep herself. Even as she sleeps, she is tending to her children's welfare. As the poem says, this is the heart of a mother.

In effect, these *senryū* are vivid and comical snapshots of ordinary life. In the next example it is important to remember that the Japanese summer is so terribly humid that children always want to run around naked. Japanese mothers would often chase after their children, shouting, "If you're naked, the thunder god will take your navel away!" Accordingly, a familiar image presents itself in the following charming poem:

かみなりを	Kaminari o	Imitating the thunder
まねて腹がけ	Manete haragake	At last managing
やっとさせ	Yatto sase	To get his bib-waistcoat on[27]

The bib-waistcoat was worn to prevent the child from getting cold while asleep, and fastening it requires quite a lot of cooperation from a struggling toddler.

When a summer shower did come on, people in the street without umbrellas would rush to shelter under the eaves of nearby shops or the main gate of a Buddhist temple. The following poem uses that image to offer an excellent illustration of the extremes to which the technique of compaction can go:

雨やどり	Amayadori	Sheltering from the rain
頭の上へ	Atama no ue e	Above [my] head
餌を運び	E o hakobi	Carrying food [to the nest][28]

The expression is so condensed here that there is no actual mention of either birds or nest in the original poem. The word *"e"* in *"E o hakobi"* means "fodder." It is used only to refer to food for animals, never for humans. And what could be carrying fodder "above my head" but a bird, most probably a sparrow? Awareness of the fact that grammatical subjects are not usually needed in Japanese is a great help in condensing the poem into a few words that carry a lot of meaning. In English it is necessary to put some of the subjects in, as, for example, the line "Above [my] head." It might be above *his* head, *her* head, *its* head, *your* head and so on, depending on the context provided by the other lines of the poem.

The experience of sheltering from a sudden downpour is the subject for several other well-known *senryū* poems:

雨やどり	Amayadori	Sheltering from the rain
きせるを出して	Kiseru o dashite	Taking out [his] pipe
叱られる	Shikarareru	[He] was scolded[29]

Japanese houses were made of wood and paper, and many of them were thatched. In the cities they were very close together and fire was a major hazard, so that at the time smoking under the eaves was prohibited. The *kiseru* was a long pipe, made for shredded tobacco and quite liable to drop sparks.

However, there might also be a more playful reason for leaving the shelter:

雨やどり	Amayadori	Sheltering from the rain
ちょちょっと出ては	Chochotto dete wa	Stepping out a moment
濡れてみる	Nurete miru	To see how wet he gets[30]

Meanwhile, the boredom of waiting continues; but in the temple grounds themselves, certain distractions can be found, as the next two poems record:

雨やどり	Amayadori	Sheltering from the rain
ごおんとついて	Go-on to tsuite	Striking the gong
叱られる	Shikarareru	He was scolded

雨やどり	Amayadori	Sheltering from the rain
額の文字を	Gaku no monji o	Memorizing
よく覚え	Yoku oboe	The letters on the tablet[31]

The gong is temptingly at hand, although to strike it will draw attention to the misdemeanor. Or else there is a big tablet, perhaps with a Buddhist motto or poem, framed and hung on the gate of the temple. When there is nothing else to do, people who can read will peruse the same tablet over and over again until it is stuck in their memory forever.

A housewife, sheltering under the eaves of a shop, also finds it impossible to do nothing and stay silent; here is her picture:

要りもせぬ	Iri mo senu	She asks the price of things
物の値を聞く	Mono no ne o kiku	She doesn't want
雨やどり	Amayadori	Sheltering from the rain[32]

The shopkeeper, for his part, cannot refuse to answer, so our mind's eye shows him reluctantly replying.

Finally, here is a *senryū* that reflects on the irony of nature's little ways:

本降りに	*Honburi ni*	Going out just as
なって出て行く	*Natte dete yuku*	It comes down in earnest
雨やどり	*Amayadori*	Sheltering from the rain[33]

"Oh no," we cry. "I should have left earlier!" These are fine sketches of human behavior, with comic (if rueful) comment on the universal human condition.

Differences between *Haiku* and *Senryū*

Although it is not easy to draw a clear and definite line between *haiku* and *senryū*, it is axiomatic that *haiku* primarily deals with nature, frequently with the beauties of nature represented by the term *ka-chō-fū-getsu* (花鳥風月), which literally means "flowers, birds, wind, and moon." *Senryū*, on the other hand, primarily deals with human beings—their nature, character, and life—as we have seen. It humanizes other creatures and even nature itself. *Senryū* deals with people in casual, everyday situations, and it usually handles subjects comically or with mild satirical observation.

Further, in *senryū* there is certainly much more freedom in choice of subject and means of expression. In composing *haiku*, poets are supposed to use, somewhere in the poem, a word or short phrase called a *kigo* (季語), that is, one which indicates a season or seasonal event; but there is no such rule in *senryū*. Even when a *kigo* occurs in a *senryū*, it is often not there to indicate the season. Other forms of expression that are required in *haiku* but not in *senryū* include *kireji* (切字), that is, "cutting words" or "sentence final words" which are taken from the literary Japanese language and thus indicate an elevated tone.[34] The casual nature of *senryū* poetry is reflected in its use of the language of the common people, which can sink even into coarseness, while *haiku* poets must use more tasteful, refined, literary language. Thus, while *senryū* verse is sometimes said to be less refined, it is by the same token more humorous, more cynical, and more satirical.

Although not all *senryū* are comic, even the more remote and classical *senryū* convey an immediate sense of humanity to their readers. For example, the striking visual imagery of the following sketch of country life speaks clearly to today's reader:

道問えば	Michi toeba	I ask the way:
一度にうごく	Ichido ni ugoku	The rice planters' bamboo hats
田植え笠	Tauegasa	Move all at once[35]

Also from the countryside comes this image:

ひんぬいた大根で	Hinnuita daiko de	With the radish
道を	Michi o	He had pulled he pointed
教えられ	Oshierare	The way[36]

The radish referred to is a Japanese radish, or *daikon* (also read *daiko*),[37] which looks like a very large white carrot. It can be twenty inches or so in length.

Interestingly enough, a similar vivid effect arising from the same subject is achieved by the famous *haiku* poet Kobayashi Issa (1763–1827), who is well known for his introduction of humor. In the following *haiku* he uses the more formal structure with all its proper rules of prosody, including the requirement to incorporate an element of personal emotion. The emotion is often evoked, as here, by the use of a *kireji*, such as the verbal suffix *-keri*.

大根引き	Daikohiki	The radish puller
大根で道を	Daiko de michi o	Using the radish
教えけり	Oshiekeri	Told me the way[38]

Comparing these two poems, Fukumoto Ichirō comments[39] that Issa was so moved by the scene of the farmers pulling up the radishes that he composed a poem illustrating the affinity between the farmer and his crop. It is the suffix *-keri* in the last line which shows that the poet was aesthetically moved by the scene. Thus this *haiku* is mostly serious, whereas the preceding *senryū* is humorous, with the radish there playing a major part in evoking laughter at the visual incongruity of the farmer's gesture.

A similar immediacy of viewpoint is achieved in the following two comical poems about animals:

にわとりの	Niwatori no	The way a rooster walks
なにか言いたい	Nani ka iitai	As if it were going
足づかい	Ashizukai	To say something[40]

A rooster puts its head on one side as it steps forward. Its movements are humorous and even look somewhat philosophical. Kanda considers this one of the best of the *Yanagidaru* poems.[41] A similar visual quality is created in the second example:

つき当たり	Tsukiatari	Bumping into each other
なにかささやき	Nani ka sasayaki	And whispering something
蟻わかれ	Ari wakare	The ants part

Personification is one of the characteristics of *senryū*, and the way this poem and the one about the rooster use it to capture a visual image of the animals' motion illustrates its power. Many such *senryū* can be successfully illustrated because of the strength and delicacy of the visual humor.[42]

The following is a rather more serious *senryū*, invoking a deathbed scene with strong visual and emotional effects:

遺言の	Yuigon no	The last words
次第次第に	Shidai shidai ni	Gradually sinking
低くなり	Hikuku nari	Lower and lower[43]

Praising the extreme concision and subtlety of emotions captured here, R. H. Blyth says, "This verse is the Zen of *Senryū*."[44]

Exactly the same technique, however, can embrace ironic and detached comment on an emotional scene, as in the following poem:

泣き泣きも	Nakinaki mo	Crying and crying
よい方をとる	Yoi hō o toru	While taking the best ones:
形見分け	Katami-wake	Sharing the keepsakes[45]

Although the loved one has only just died, the relatives are dividing up the spoils, taking care to keep the best possessions for themselves, even while weeping for their lost family member. This is human nature with all its selfish contradictions.

A similar derogative alliance of ideas can be used to critique, gently and ironically, other common human behaviors, as in the following examples:

孝行の	*Kōkō no*	Just when you want to show
したい時分に	*Shitai jibun ni*	Filial piety
親はなし	*Oya wa nashi*	You have no parents

抱いた子に	*Daita ko ni*	Getting the baby
たたかせてみる	*Tatakasete miru*	She is holding
惚れた人	*Horeta hito*	To pat her sweetheart[46]

It can also be used to create a short visual image that sums up the complex emotional interplay which has preceded the scene, as in the following example:

よっぽどのりんき	*Yoppodo no rinki*	Extreme jealousy:
亭主が	*Teishu ga*	The husband
飯を炊き	*Meshi o taki*	Cooking the rice[47]

In the Edo era, Japanese husbands certainly did not do the cooking. On this occasion, however, the wife has become so jealous that she was probably not even talking to him and has refused to cook, thus obliging the husband to cook for himself.

On a similar theme, the following *senryū* shows that the form can be quite philosophical and abstract:

女房のやくほど	*Nyōbō no yaku hodo*	Husbands are not
亭主	*Teishu*	As popular with women
もてもせず	*Mote mo sezu*	As their wives are jealous[48]

The wife's jealousy is totally out of proportion to the degree to which the husband is attractive to women. The origin of this famous *senryū* is unknown, but its fame apparently spread in Japan, since it often appears in *rakugo* (comic storytelling) when episodes about jealous wives are being narrated. There are many *senryū* like this that exist as folklore and are retold both by professional entertainers and by older people. Some may have been composed by *rakugo* narrators themselves.[49]

Human behavior supplies many *senryū* with their subjects, mostly sympathetic accounts of our fallible condition. This example strikes a timeless note:

飲まぬやつ	*Nomanu yatsu*	The bloke not drinking
時々笑う	*Tokidoki warau*	Laughs now and then.
ばかりなり	*Bakari nari*	That's all.[50]

Although drinking in Japan, as in other cultures, releases easy laughter, a significant proportion of Japanese people lack the gene that produces the enzymes allowing digestion of alcohol. Although drinking is culturally expected of Japanese men, if one says "I can't drink," people *will* understand that you will have violent digestive problems if you do. Nevertheless, you are required to join in by laughing occasionally, even though you are not drunk: hence the image of somewhat modified hilarity from the odd man out. On the other hand, if you do drink, the following *senryū* neatly captures the effects:

二日酔い	*Futsukayoi*	Hangover:
飲んだところを	*Nonda tokoro o*	Trying to think
考える	*Kangaeru*	Where I drank[51]

And for the truth on gambling and the family man, this example sums up the situation:

勝った日は	*Katta hi wa*	Days when I win
意見言わぬが	*Iken iwanu ga*	She doesn't tell me off:
女なり	*Onna nari*	That's women for you![52]

How a lucky win changes the mood at home! The poem invites us to reflect on both domestic scenes at once, good and bad, with a wry smile about human nature.

But if the wife is having an affair, the poor husband is likely to be a victim in more than one way, as the following example makes clear:

店中で	*Tanajū de*	All over the shop the only
知らぬは亭主	*Shiranu wa teishu*	One who doesn't know
一人なり	*Hitori nari*	Is the husband[53]

Senryū sometimes takes up subjects from history, and usually it treats its subjects irreverently in order to emphasize their humanity. The following example is about the most famous author of the Heian era, the Lady Murasaki, author of *The Tale of Genji*.[54] She was staying at the Ishiyama Buddhist temple, where the monks, of course, were celibate. The poem captures a situation in which the acolytes, despite their vows, were allured by the presence of a beautiful lady writing love stories and used any excuse to talk to her:

石山の所家衆	*Ishiyama no shokeshū*	The acolytes
短冊など	*Tanzaku nado*	Of Ishiyama ask
ねだり	*Nedari*	For autographs[55]

A *tanzaku* is a long, narrow piece of decorative card used for writing poems, so the poem evokes an image of the acolytes lining up like adolescents to ask the Lady Murasaki for her autograph, thus giving themselves an excuse to talk to a beautiful woman famous both for her love affairs and for her writing.

Eventually, the Oshō himself (the senior Buddhist, or what would be called in the West the abbot) becomes restless. Deciding to visit the room the Lady Murasaki is staying in, he produces a more intellectual excuse for the rendezvous (from one bibliophile to another):

何冊ものに	*Nansatsumono ni*	How many volumes
なりますと	*Narimasu to*	Will it be?
和尚きき	*Oshō kiki*	The Oshō asks

The ancient lay *The Tale of the Heike*[56] recounts many battle exploits of heroes, among them Musashibō Benkei (d. 1189), who was a mighty warrior in the days of the Japanese civil wars. He was a loyal retainer of the famous Yoshitsune of the Minamoto clan (1159–89). Benkei is said to have borne seven kinds of arms on the battlefield, bristling with them so that the weapons on his back looked like a windmill. It could be said, commenting via the form of a comical *senryū*, that

武蔵坊	*Musashibō*	Musashibō was apt
とかく支度に	*Tokaku shitaku ni*	To take time
手間がとれ	*Tema ga tore*	Getting ready[57]

This *senryū* humanizes Benkei the revered leader by adopting the viewpoint of his soldiers, all ready for the fight. They must have been irritated by how long it took for their leader to array himself in his battle dress and strap on all his weapons. Here is a quiet joke made at the expense of a legendary hero.

Ugachi in Senryū

Critics commonly recognize three elements to senryū: okashimi (おかしみ humor), karumi (軽身 lightness), and ugachi (penetration or insight). Ugachi, from the verb ugatsu (穿つ), means to dig,[58] and it captures the gentle mocking tendency so well exhibited in the examples above. One haiku poet, Hino Sōjō, who advocated composing even haiku without kigo (seasonal words), observed in 1952 that senryū essentially is the literature that makes readers "nod in agreement."[59] This suggests that the essence of senryū is ugachi,[60] whereas haiku makes readers "feel" when they read the poem.

Other writers agree that senryū is characterized by this element of witty critique or observation. Tanabe Seiko, a popular Japanese novelist and a devotee of senryū (she has written a number of specialized books on senryū poetry), has said that there are two kinds of senryū: one is what she calls ta-ha-ha-ha senryū, and the other is ūn senryū.[61] Ta-ha-ha-ha of course is a burst of laughter; ūn means "nodding in agreement," that is, being so deeply impressed and in such total sympathy with someone or something that one has to nod.[62] For Tanabe, ta-ha-ha-ha senryū relate more strongly to okashimi (laughing humor), whereas ūn senryū relate to ugachi (penetrating wit).

The following poem, which captures the pathetic bravado of the coward saving his skin, is a fine example of ugachi:

逃げしなに	Nigeshina ni	Before running away
覚えていろは	Oboete iro wa	"Remember that!"
負けたやつ	Maketa yatsu	Shouts the bloke who lost[63]

The Future of Senryū Poetry

After its period of glory in the Meiwa (1764–72) and An'ei (1772–81) eras, senryū poetry gradually declined. However, it was revived in the Meiji era principally through the efforts of two senryū poets, Sakai Kuraki (1869–1945) and Inoue Kenkabō (1870–1934), and the senryū of that time were called "new sen-

ryū." As a result, the poetic form has survived to the present day.

The differences between *haiku* and *senryū* remain somewhat unclear. There are not so many "laughing" or *ta-ha-ha-ha senryū* these days, and some *senryū* poets even seem to look down on humor and laughter from a literary point of view. *Senryū* poets always seem to be conscious of *haiku*, but *haiku* poets are almost indifferent to the world of *senryū* poetry. Therefore it is important for *haiku* and *senryū* poets to give careful thought to their identity as poets and to the differences between the two genres.

These days, however, there are many *senryū* enthusiasts and many magazines for them throughout Japan. The biggest (and oldest) is the monthly magazine *Bangasa*, established in 1913, whose title means "a coarse oiled-paper umbrella." In May 2001 a new monthly general *senryū* magazine also started.[64] In addition there are many books about and anthologies of *senryū*. An excellent and accessible selection from the *Haifū Yanagidaru* was published in Japan with English translations by Utsuo Kiyoaki in 1998.[65]

Although the poetic form of *haiku* and the name of its most famous poet, Matsuo Bashō, are well known outside Japan, the same is not true for *senryū*. The first International Haiku Symposium was held in Yamanashi Prefecture by the Nihon Dentō Haiku Kyōkai (The Association for Japanese Classical Haiku) in August 1989. They have been held regularly ever since. It is true, as Fukumoto Ichirō has pointed out,[66] that for international audiences some finer points that characterize *haiku* are neglected because they are too deeply dependent on the structure of the Japanese language to be successfully used in other languages. However, the essential nature of the form is still widely appreciated.

In fact, *senryū* requires neither *kigo* nor *kireji*. It is a casual form of poetry that deals with human beings—how they think, their traits, and their behavior. *Senryū* poets also take up current events with humor and depict those strange, inconsistent, but lovable creatures called human beings with sympathy, or sometimes with irony or criticism. *Senryū* is the art of people-watching with a combination of both warm and cool eyes. Its subject matter, style, and tone are epitomized in this final example:

171

人間万事	*Ningen banji*	Human beings do
さまざまの	*Samazama no*	Every single kind
馬鹿をする	*Baka o suru*	Of stupid thing[67]

Senryū undoubtedly has the potential for wide international appreciation.

NOTES

1. For further discussion of these structural developments, see chapter 1.
2. Fukumoto Ichirō, *Haiku to Senryū* (Tokyo: Kōdansha, 1999), 51.
3. For additional discussion of this practice, see chapter 1. Its purpose was to demonstrate one's wit by adding seventeen syllables to another person's *maeku* (couplet). It was effectively the ancestor of *senryū.*
4. Fukumoto, *Haiku to Senryū,* 108.
5. For more discussion of *rakugo,* see chapter 7.
6. The popularity of *senryū* is also discussed in chapters 1 and 11.
7. See note 2 above.
8. The poem is said to have been written by Bashō in 1686, when he was forty-three. It is here quoted from Fukumoto, *Haiku to Senryū,* 135, who asserts that more than a hundred English translations of this famous poem exist (136). All translations into English in this article are original, unless otherwise stated. However, in view of the shortness of the poetic form under discussion, close similarities to other copyright translations cannot always be avoided (see the Editor's Note) and in this particular case must certainly exist.
9. The original poem appeared in the 17th edition of the *Haifū Yanagidaru,* published in 1782; it is here quoted from Fukumoto, *Haiku to Senryū,* 136. Another translation is found in Utsuo Kiyoaki, *Edo Senryū: Haifū Yanagidaru* (Osaka: Yōbunkan Publishing, 1998), 242.
10. The original poem appeared in *Hanatsumi* (1690), a collection associated with Takarai Kikaku, a famous disciple of Bashō; it is here quoted from Fukumoto, *Haiku to Senryū,* 137; a translation by R. H. Blyth appears in his *Haiku,* 4 vols. (Tokyo: Hokuseidō Press, 1981), 4:1196.
11. The original poem appeared in the 74th edition of the *Haifū Yanagidaru* (1822); it is here quoted from Fukumoto, *Haiku to Senryū,* 137.
12. To provide some indication of the value of the *mon,* sixteen *mon*

purchased an ordinary dish of *kake soba* (buckwheat noodles in soup), according to Shimoyama Hiroshi, *Edo Ko-Senryū no Sekai* (Tokyo: Kōdansha, 1994), 72. The price of adult bathhouse entry was eight *mon*, with children admitted free, according to Suzuki Katsutada, *Senryū Zappai Edo Shomin no Sekai* (Tokyo: Miki Shobō, 1996), 41. By 1775, when the 10th edition of the *Haifū Yangidaru* was published, the *maekuzuke* entry fee had risen to sixteen *mon*, according to Okada Asatarō, *Kansei Kaikaku to Yanagidaru no Kaihan* (Tokyo: Isobe Kōyōdō, 1927), 155–56.

13. The original *tsukeku* poem appeared in the 7th edition of the *Haifū Yanagidaru* (1772); it is here quoted in a version with minor changes from Ōmi Sajin and Fujiwara Seiken, *Senryū Nyūmon* (Osaka: Hoikusha, 1977), 101–2, where the composition process is also discussed.

14. The anthology, titled *Haifū Yanagidaru*, was edited by Goryōken Arubeshi and published by Hanaya Kyūjirō. According to *Senryū Sōgō Jiten*, ed. Sanryū Bitō (Tokyo: Yūzankaku Publishing, 1984), s.v. "Ryūso," Goryōken edited this collection from the 1st edition in 1765 until the 22nd edition in 1788 (the year of his death). From 1765 to the 24th edition in 1791, the source of the poems was the *Senryūhyō Mankuawase*, which circulated between 1757 and 1789 (in 1790 the First Karai Senryū died and a change of administration ensued). A modern edition is Okada Hajime, ed., *Haifū Yanagidaru Zenshū*, 12 vols. and index (Tokyo: Sanseidō, 1976–78, 1984).

15. However, according to Donald Keene, *World within Walls: Japanese Literature of the Pre-modern Era, 1600–1867* (Tokyo: Tuttle, 1978), 531–32, the 167th edition appeared in 1838 under the Fifth Senryū. There are many different views on these points.

16. Kanda Bōjin, *Edo Senryū o Tanoshimu* (Tokyo: Asahi Shimbunsha, 1989), 319, 326; Fukumoto, *Haiku to Senryū*, 76.

17. Kanda, *Edo Senryū o Tanoshimu*, 319.

18. Ōmi and Fujiwara, *Senryū Nyūmon*, 105.

19. The original poem appeared in the 1st edition of the *Haifū Yanagidaru* (1765). It is here quoted from Keene, *World within Walls*, 530, where a different translation can be found.

20. Yamaji Kanko, *Kosenryū Meiku Sen* (Tokyo: Chikuma Shobō, 1968), 26–28.

21. Kanda, *Edo Senryū o Tanoshimu*, 327; the poem was struck out, and other *senryū* in the 23rd edition of 1789 were substituted. Such deletions from the original volume's contents continued between 1801 and 1803 according to Okada, *Kansei Kaikaku to Yanagidaru no Kaihan*, 192–93.

22. Kanda, *Edo Senryū o Tanoshimu*, 327. Keene also comments on the dispiriting effects of censorship (*World within Walls*, 531–32), citing Teruoka Yasutaka and Gunji Masakatsu, *Edo Shimin Bungaku no Kaika*, in the *Nihon no Bungaku* series (Tokyo: Shibundō, 1967), 275. Okada Asatarō (1868–1936) has made a full study of the process of publication of revised editions; see note 12 above.

23. The original poem appeared in the 1st edition of the *Haifū Yanagidaru* (1765); it is here quoted from Keene, *World within Walls*, 530, where a different translation can be found.

24. The original poem appeared in the 1st edition of the *Haifū Yanagidaru* (1765); it is here quoted from Ōmi and Fujiwara, *Senryū Nyūmon*, 110.

25. The original poem appeared in the 2nd edition of the *Haifū Yanagidaru* (ca. 1767); it is here quoted from Blyth, *Haiku*, 1:198, where a different translation can be found.

26. The original poem appeared in the 1st edition of the *Haifū Yanagidaru* (1765); it is here quoted from Kanda, *Edo Senryū o Tanoshimu*, 273. A different translation can be found in Utsuo, *Edo Senryū*, 82.

27. The original poem appeared in the 1st edition of the *Haifū Yanagidaru* (1765); it is here quoted from Blyth, *Haiku*, 1:198, where a different translation can be found.

28. The original poem appeared in the 1st edition of the *Kawazoi Yanagi* (1780); it is here quoted from Kanda, *Edo Senryū o Tanoshimu*, 184.

29. The original poem appeared in the 5th edition of the *Haifū Yanagidaru* (1770); it is here quoted from R. H. Blyth, *Edo Satirical Verse Anthologies* (Tokyo: Hokuseidō Press, 1961), 250, where a different translation can be found.

30. The original poem appeared in the 13th edition of the *Haifū Yanagidaru* (1778); it is here quoted from Okitsu Kaname, *Edo no Warai*, vol. 24 of *Shōnen Shōjo Koten Bungakukan* (Tokyo: Kōdansha, 1992), 242.

31. The originals of these poems appeared in the 12th and 1st editions, respectively, of the *Haifū Yanagidaru* (1777 and 1765). The first poem is here quoted from Kanda, *Edo Senryū o Tanoshimu*, 184, and the second from Utsuo, *Edo Senryū*, 53, where a different translation can be found.

32. The original poem appeared in a volume of the *Senryūhyō Mankuawase* and then in the 3rd edition of the *Haifū Yanagidaru* (1768); it is here quoted from Blyth, *Edo Satirical Verse*, 232, where a different translation can be found.

33. The original poem appeared in the 1st edition of the *Haifū Yanagi-*

daru (1765); it is here quoted from Utsuo, *Edo Senryū*, 85, where a different translation can be found.

34. For more discussion of these technical terms, see chapter 1. Keene, *World within Walls*, 527 ff., discusses the differences between the two forms and points out that the *kireji* serve in *haiku* to separate the essential two elements of the poem, whereas in *senryū*, being the simpler form with only one element, there is no such requirement for demarcation.

35. The original poem appeared in the 1st edition of the *Haifū Yanagidaru* (1765); it is here quoted from Blyth, *Haiku*, 1:198, where a different translation can be found.

36. The poem originally appeared in the circular of the winning poems selected by Karai Senryū from the competition (*Senryūhyō Mankuawase Kachikuzuri*) and then in the 1st edition of the *Haifū Yanagidaru* (1765). It is here quoted from Utsuo, *Edo Senryū*, 63.

37. *Daiko* is an alternative reading for the now universal *daikon*.

38. The original poem appeared in Issa's *Shichiban Nikki* (Diary) of 1814. It is here quoted from Fukumoto, *Haiku to Senryū*, 98. Since it was composed later than the *senryū* quoted above, this *haiku* can be presumed to take the former as a point of reference.

39. Fukumoto, *Haiku to Senryū*, 97–98.

40. The original poems are found in the 1st and 101st editions of the *Haifū Yanagidaru* (1765 and 1828, respectively). The first is here quoted from Blyth, *Edo Satirical Verse*, 6, where a different translation can be found, and the second from Kanda, *Edo Senryū o Tanoshimu*, 3.

41. Kanda, *Edo Senryū o Tanoshimu*, 81.

42. Examples are the delicate pen-and-ink sketches reproduced as figures 12.1–12.3. They capture exactly the visual essence of the *senryū* that they are intended to illustrate, which are discussed in chapter 12.

43. The original poem appeared in the *Senryūhyō Mankuawase* (1765); it is here quoted from Tōi Jun, *Edo Senryū no Jojō o Tanoshimu* (Osaka: Shinyokan Publishing, 2004), 45; a different translation may be found in Blyth, *Edo Satirical Verse*, 233.

44. Blyth, *Edo Satirical Verse*, 233.

45. The original poem appeared in the 17th edition of the *Haifū Yanagidaru* (1782); it is here quoted from Kanda, *Edo Senryū o Tanoshimu*, 266. A variant of this poem is in Blyth, *Edo Satirical Verse*, 253.

46. Utsuo, *Edo Senryū*, 261 and 87, respectively, reproduces these two poems, with different translations. They originally appeared in

the 22nd (1788) and the 1st (1765) editions of the *Haifū Yanagidaru.*

47. The original poem appeared in the 48th edition of the *Haifu Yanigidaru* (1809); it is here quoted from Okada, *Haifu Yanagidaru Zenshū,* 4:150.

48. Quoted from Kanda, *Edo Senryū o Tanoshimu,* 117–18.

49. Kanda, *Edo Senryū o Tanoshimu,* 117–22, discusses the use made by *rakugo* narrators of traditional *senryū* folklore. For more information on *rakugo,* see chapter 7.

50. The original poem appeared in the *Senryūhyō Mankuawase;* it is here quoted from Blyth, *Edo Satirical Verse,* 233, where a different translation can be found.

51. The original poem appeared in the 7th edition of the *Haifū Yanagidaru* (1772); it is here quoted from Kanda, *Edo Senryū o Tanoshimu,* 287.

52. The original poem appeared in the 7th edition of the *Haifū Yanagidaru* (1772); it is here quoted from Blyth, *Edo Satirical Verse,* 255, where a different translation can be found.

53. The original poem appeared in the 7th edition of the *Haifū Yanagidaru* (1772); it is here quoted from Utsuo, *Edo Senryū,* 176, where a different translation is found.

54. Murasaki Shikibu [the Lady Murasaki], *The Tale of Genji,* trans. Edward G. Seidensticker (Tokyo: Charles E. Tuttle & Co.), 1978.

55. This poem and the following are quoted from Okitsu, *Edo no Warai,* 279 and 280, respectively. The original of the first poem appeared in the 2nd edition of the *Yanaibako* (1784), and that of the second in the 44th edition of the *Haifū Yanagidaru* (1808).

56. A good modern edition is *The Tale of the Heike,* trans. Kitagawa Hiroshi and Bruce T. Tsuchida (Tokyo: University of Tokyo Press, 1975).

57. The original poem appeared in the 1st edition of the *Haifū Yanagidaru* (1765); it is here quoted from Utsuo, *Edo Senryū,* 21, where a different translation is found.

58. *Kōjien,* 5th ed. (Tokyo: Iwanami Shoten, 1998), s.v. "Ugatsu."

59. Hino Sōjō quoted in Fukumoto, *Haiku to Senryū,* 216–17, my translation.

60. Bitō, *Senryū Sōgō Jiten,* 137, refers to remarks by Ebara Taizo to the effect that all other specific characteristics of *senryū* are subordinate to *ugachi.* This certainly accords with the fact that the First Karai Senryū's criteria for the verse form laid down *ugachi* as essential, and that early *senryū* of this period (*kosenryū,* or old *senryū*) are sometimes called "the literature of *ugachi*" (Bitō,

Senryū Sōgō Jiten, s.v. "San Yōso"). Compare also the opinion of Fukumoto, *Haiku to Senryū*, 245, who sees the real appeal of *senryū* as lying in the attractions of *ugachi*.

61. Tanabe Seiko, *Senryū Dendendaiko* (Tokyo: Kōdansha, 1988), 20, 23–25.
62. *Kōjien*, s.v. "Ūn."
63. The original poem appeared in the 3rd edition of the *Haifū Yanagidaru* (1768); it is here quoted from Utsuo, *Edo Senryū*, 146, where a different translation is found.
64. *Bangasa* is published by Bangasa Senryū Honsha, Osaka; *Senryū* is published by Shinyōkan Publishing, Osaka.
65. Utsuo Kiyoaki's book (*Edo Senryū*) appeared in 1998 with excellent translations of *senryū* into English, a preface by Donald Keene, and editorial assistance by Alan Crocket. For the small but important role of *senryū* in contemporary daily newspapers, see chapter 11.
66. Fukumoto, *Haiku to Senryū*, 234–49, advocates enhancing the international appreciation of *haiku* by recognizing the concepts of the "base" (*shubu*) and the "leap section" (*hiyaku setsubu*), which are two separate structural elements of *haiku*.
67. The original poem appeared in the 117th edition of the *Haifū Yanagidaru* (1832); it is here quoted from Kanda, *Edo Senryū o Tanoshimu*, 271. Interestingly, this *senryū* has an atypical structure of 7.5.5, not 5.7.5.

11

Humor in Japanese Newspapers

Hiroshi Inoue

An Uneasy Match?

Important news breathes life into newspapers. Headlines on the "extra" edition reach heights of excitement, such as "Heavens!" or "Don't you recognize this?" Their outcry is designed to capture our hearts and our attention. Newspapers have two important functions: coverage and comment. They cover changes in society in the form of news, and at the same time they offer comments, including interpretation of or opinions on the news. Although the most important aspect of coverage is to present the facts with utmost accuracy, there are of course a variety of ways to cover the news, including coverage from an objective point of view (for example, investigative reports), comment made in headlines, comment sought in discussions and interviews.

Yet another way is to cover the news with laughter and with humor, but it seems newspapers are not interested in undertaking this. Newspapers are by and large trapped in the idea that they should be serious and tense and that laughter is taboo. The size of any correction article that is deemed necessary shows their uneasiness about disappointing readers by making mistakes. They cling to the belief that seriousness brings trust. This is particularly true in Japan.

However, although (in comparison with western media) Japanese newspapers may not devote much space to humorous comment, they are not completely occupied with serious articles. Some efforts to provide a balance between seriousness and humor can be observed. Japanese newspapers do introduce such things as political caricatures in articles on politics, comic strips, and also *senryū* (川柳 a seventeen-syllable poem that is often mildly satirical about contemporary times and issues).[1] Each newspaper has a regular short column permitting a touch of humor, such as "Funsuitō" (ふんすい塔 "Fountain"),[2] "Ka-

179

taekubo" (かたえくぼ "Dimple"),[3] and "USO Hōsō" (USO 放送 "Pseudo-Broadcasting").[4] I confess I am a fan of these columns, which in most cases are written by individual readers and not by regular news writers. They are allowed to satirize the news with jokes and to make humorous comments. The columns are certainly entertaining, but they are not given very much weight in the newspaper, either in column-inches (see the examples in figures 11.1, 11.2, and 11.3) or in being featured as important items. Since they are not particularly encouraged and their writers are not professional, they tend to stick to an established form, which rather restricts their development. Nevertheless, even their limited success shows that although it is not easy to impress readers by coverage imbued with laughter and humor, if it *can* be done, newspapers can certainly become more attractive to the reader.

Figure 11.1 shows the "Funsuitō" column from the *Mainichi Shimbun* of February 23, 2001, with romanized Japanese text and English translation beneath. The writer has chosen to pick up on then-current news about a high official from the Japanese Ministry of Foreign Affairs who had been arrested for improper spending of ministry funds. Although this criminal behavior had been detected, the recipients of the payments could not be detailed, because the money was drawn from an officially classified "secret fund," and therefore what it had been spent on could not be disclosed. The Tax Office acknowledged itself puzzled by the problem. The column wonders, in the shape of a quotation attributed to the Tax Office, what the ramifications of such a situation might be.

Another wry comment is delivered by the column in figure 11.2, taken from "Kataekubo" in the *Asahi Shimbun* of January 25, 2001. News stories had been appearing about large hospitals making medical errors (a situation common to all nations) and how this was causing increasing alarm among the ranks of Japan's elderly people. Hospital attendance was falling. Since the elderly enjoy cheap medical insurance in Japan, they normally visit hospitals very frequently, almost regarding their trips as an opportunity to meet others in the same situation. Now they are becoming isolated, preferring to stay at home to avoid exposure to medical risk—unless things get desperate. Hospitals had

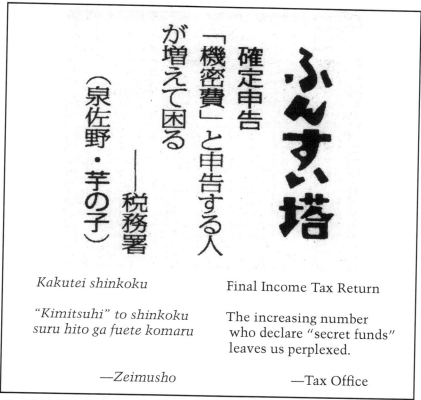

Kakutei shinkoku

"Kimitsuhi" to shinkoku
suru hito ga fuete komaru

—Zeimusho

Final Income Tax Return

The increasing number
who declare "secret funds"
leaves us perplexed.

—Tax Office

Fig. 11.1 "Funsuitō" column by "Sweet Potato Child of Izumi
Sano" (from *Mainichi Shimbun*, February 23, 2001; reprinted with
permission)

remarked on the depressing difference in the kind of patients
they were seeing. The irony of the situation encourages one to
say, "But of course! Should it ever have been otherwise?" But
the implications for the future are alarming, and there is a grim
undercurrent to this joking.

In March 2001, when television footage of the Japanese
Diet in session showed members slumbering in their seats, the
column in figure 11.3 from the *Yomiuri Shimbun* (March 18,
2001) commented acidly on such indulgence, which is usually
available to hardworking Japanese people only on their holidays
(in the spring blossom-viewing break, for example). The serious-

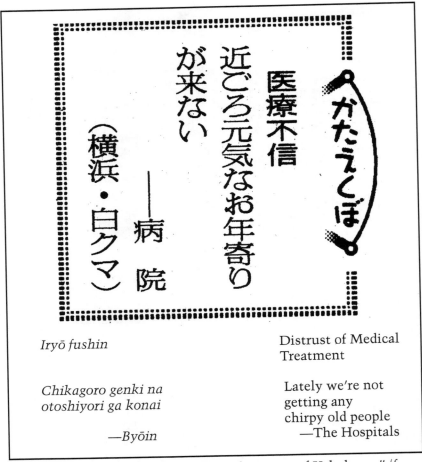

Iryō fushin	Distrust of Medical Treatment
Chikagoro genki na otoshiyori ga konai	Lately we're not getting any chirpy old people
—Byōin	—The Hospitals

Fig. 11.2 "Kataekubo" column by "White Bear of Yokohama" (from *Asahi Shimbun*, January 25, 2001; reprinted with permission)

ness of the nation's political and economic situation was then (and remains years later) common knowledge, and it is not difficult to read into this sarcastic little remark some deeply felt resentment of politicians living in their dream world of privilege with little concern for the lot of ordinary people.

There are several interesting structural features about these columns. First is the fact that the writers use pen names in order to remain anonymous. This is an age-old Japanese tradition for

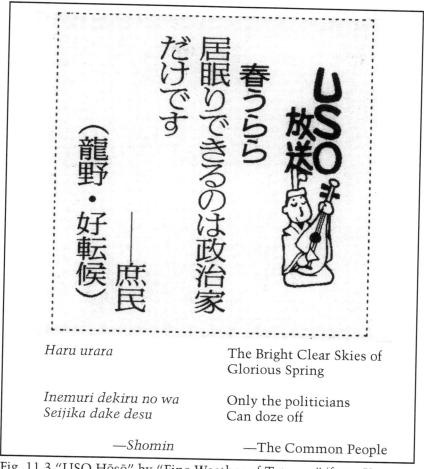

Haru urara	The Bright Clear Skies of Glorious Spring
Inemuri dekiru no wa Seijika dake desu	Only the politicians Can doze off
—Shomin	—The Common People

Fig. 11.3 "USO Hōsō" by "Fine Weather of Tatsuno" (from *Yomiuri Shimbun*, March 18, 2001; reprinted with permission)

writers, and such names frequently encapsulate a jest or a wry twist.[5] The device is a way of disguising the fact that a critical or reforming comment is being made.[6] Second, the chosen format for these "critical jests" should be noted. In each case they take either a genuine "quotable quote" from previous news items or something that could plausibly be such a quote; and, in a form familiar to the west from student reviews and parodies of newspapers, the quote is reflected upon by using a combination of an invented title or heading and an attributed source. In some cases the source may actually be provided by the real news item (such as the "hospital" quote); in others (such as the reflection upon politicians) it is what everyone is thinking and/or saying in private. These are in effect cartoon captions without the accompanying cartoon, leaving readers to supply the appropriate illustration from their own imagination.

These tiny pieces of satirical remarks—not much larger than a postage stamp—are quite powerful in their commentary on contemporary problems and issues. In fact, they have an intensity of emotion out of all proportion to their size. In terms of visual presentation, they fall into a tradition of the printed page that was established by the technique of wood-block print, where a small, unrelated square block might be used to fill the last remaining unoccupied space on a page. Simple, compact, and independent in voice and tone, the resulting message draws the reader's attention with considerable force.

Laughing Away Stress

Conventional cartoons can also be very direct in their comment. An interesting comic strip named "Mr. Sarari" (サラリ君 "Mr. Salary")[7] appeared in the *Sankei Shimbun* on January 14, 2000, just after the holidays for the New Year (see figure 11.4). The artist of this cartoon is Nishimura Sō (西村宗). This episode shows the hardworking Mr. Sarari waking up at home early in the morning and getting dressed for work. The first frame shows him jolting awake in bed and saying to himself:

| ン!? | *N!! [sound]* | Oh!!!? |

In the second, as he chooses a suit, he asks himself:

初出勤は	*Hatsushukkin wa*	Now, when should I go
きょうだったかな	*kyō datta ka na*	back to work? Is it today
あしただったかな	*ashita datta ka na*	or tomorrow?

In the third, his wife appears at the bedroom door, saying:

| いずれにしても | *Izure ni shite mo* | Whichever it is, at least you |
| 出勤日があるのね！ | *shukkinbi ga aru no ne!* | still have an office to go to |

Fig. 11.4 Mr. Sarari is off to the office (from *Sankei Shimbun*, January 14, 2000; reprinted with permission)

He replies (looking annoyed and checking his pocket diary):

あたりまえだ	*Atarimae da*	Of course I do!

In the final frame, his wife speeds off delightedly to tell the rest of the waiting family (grandmother and two children):

ヨカッタ、ヨカッタ	*Yokatta, yokatta*	Goody! Goody!

The joke here depends upon the reader's having some knowledge of the poor economic situation in Japan, in which, both at the time of the cartoon's first appearance and still some years later, a great many people were fired (because of the recession) but often could not admit it to their families, so they dressed to go to work as usual each morning. The joke also turns upon the ambiguity of communication between husband and wife: does he really have a job and is just confused about the length of holidays, or is he only pretending? What is he checking in his diary—which office to pretend to go to? Or his actual business appointments? Or is he just absentminded? Was she right to be worried, or was she worrying unnecessarily? This joke hits very close to home: people who had been or who were worrying about being fired would find this cartoon directly addressing their dilemma. If they laughed at it, it might help a little to relieve their stress.

The topical *senryū* column in the *Yomiuri Shimbun* can be equally direct. It is a full column of five poems, but easy to read, presenting short poems or wordplays in the classic *senryū* model. The week before, the "Mr. Sarari" cartoon appeared in the *Sankei Shimbun*, the *Yomiuri Shimbun* published an interesting example of a humorous poetic comment on the sad state of economic affairs and the lack of political action:

超赤字	*Chōakaji*	Even I
予算案なら	*Yosan'an nara*	Can draw up
わたしでも	*Watashi demo*	This mega-deficit budget[8]

How succinctly it expresses the writer's feelings of "What's going on! What hugely notable expert does it take to draw up this appalling national budget!" The writer shares with the reader his dismay about the current economic situation, while allowing him- or herself to laugh it off.

News coverage should be unambiguous and easy to understand. Therefore its style must be simple to avoid misunderstandings, especially for coverage from an objective point of view. However, when it comes to the sports sections or the local news pages, a quick comparison of expression shows that more adjectives and adverbs are used and that illustrations or cartoons are introduced more frequently. Although these adaptations are clearly intended to try to appeal to readers, the results still lack a sense of laughter.

In fact, a stiff, formal style can never persuade people. When criticizing the authorities or the government, a solemn, monotonous tone does not attract our attention. Criticisms that make the public laugh—in other words, those with a touch of irony—will actually be more successful in convincing society to change its opinions. An old military story tells how, after the leader of the army formally announced his name to the enemy, he cracked jokes and roared with laughter.[9] He made fun of the enemy to his soldiers and tried to frighten the enemy's own leader with his bravado. In the old days, leaders needed not only skill with weapons but also the ability to abuse their enemies and to make them a laughingstock. Today, if criticism about politics were humorous enough to make people laugh, it would certainly attract more public attention, and the satisfaction of laughing at the criticism would purify our souls as well as persuade us more effectively.

Positive Laughter

Newspapers reflect the negative side of society more than the positive side because when something bad happens, newspapers must cover it as news; thus if the event has a negative aspect, it is automatically called "news." This kind of news, which we see every day (such as scandals in the political or business world, horrible cases of murder, and so forth), makes us depressed. We cannot blame the newspapers, because we know they are merely presenting the truth. However, is it really acceptable to make us feel gloomy just because they are covering the truth? We would really benefit if the newspapers could offer us something positive, such as humor and laughter, while at the same time conveying accurate details to us.

Nowadays we recognize newspapers as part of our daily life and thus as influencing our feelings on a regular basis. It is true that we can choose our news broadcast by selecting our preferred television channel, but since all television stations broadcast the news at a fixed time (for instance, at 6 P.M.), everyone has developed the habit of watching the news at the same hour. Thus when a big news event occurs, all the stations broadcast it again and again, with no effective choice between programs either in terms of time or subject. Our own expertise or level of interest is also irrelevant: we simply have to accept the given form, which unavoidably exercises its influence over us. What makes the negative impact worse is that a person who follows the news from both television and newspapers will notice repetition of the same information, which catches our sight without warning as we turn the printed page. Negative news of this type about vicious crimes and other events leaves us very depressed, and the strong visual appeal of television is highly influential in affecting our environment and our perception. Because society is flooded with a repetition of news about vicious crimes, some people become convinced that society is in fact full of crime.

Such effects are counterproductive in helping individuals and society at large face up to difficulties and deal with them energetically. That is why satire is badly needed as an integral part of contemporary newspapers. We need to laugh off the problems in front of us, and newspapers should play an important role in encouraging us to do so. What is needed is more valuing of the expression of humor, so that when this is successful in inviting the readers' laughter, newspapers can both express sharp criticism and at the same time purify the "poison" of the depressing matters weighing on our hearts.

Humorless Leaders?

It is often said that, compared to foreign politicians, Japanese politicians lack a sense of humor. It is true that the latter prefer not to express themselves elaborately. Since Japanese newspapers always try to detect and to criticize politicians' slips of the tongue, rather than making an effort to understand them sympathetically, politicians are afraid of making mistakes. They tend to express their ideas without any wit or humor. They should not be so timid: history teaches us that humor can be very helpful politically.

Former U.S. president George H. W. Bush visited Japan in 1992. When he suddenly fell ill at a dinner party in the Royal Palace, his wife, Barbara, impressed others present very favorably with her witty repartee. She responded with the joke, "I think I can blame Mr. Armacost [then U.S. ambassador to Japan]. Because at the tennis match today, my husband and the Ambassador were soundly defeated by the Emperor and the Crown Prince: the Bush family is not accustomed to being beaten at tennis!"[10] Even the Japanese media admired her sense of humor and her ability to defuse diplomatic and social tensions. A greater attention to humor in Japanese newspapers would help politicians learn to be more adventurous in this area and would provide a good balance for readers.

Laughter Models Can Work for Newspapers

In our daily conversations we often refer to subjects taken from the newspaper or television, because when the news makes an impact on us we want to share the feeling with people at the office or at home. Equally, every time we find an interesting comic strip or *senryū*, we want to share it with somebody. When that person also finds it interesting, the conversation grows lively. Surely this is the fundamental purpose of newspapers, offering not only information but also something special, including humor, to invite the reader's attention or laughter.

Of course, newspapers need to keep their distance and objectivity in order to observe, report, and comment on the news. Such a stance is not incompatible with humorous comment, as is illustrated by some popular contemporary comment columns. Each of these manages to show a light touch but also to maintain composure. These columns are "Tensei Jingo" (from the *Asahi Shimbun*),[11] "Yoroku" (*Mainichi Shimbun*),[12] "Henshū Techō" (*Yomiuri Shimbun*),[13] and "Sankeishō" (*Sankei Shimbun*).[14] These columns tend to deal critically with social and economic issues in the individual voice of the journalist, who is permitted some playful remarks by the newspaper publishing company. However, they do remain somewhat formal in their expression, which does not go very far in promoting laughter and humor.

189

Since the writers have been given the freedom to express their views in their columns, it would be good if they would go further to write the fully developed comic expressions and phrases that heal readers' feelings. After all, newspapers take up the issues of social confrontation, but if they developed comment with humor they would help ease the tensions thereby created.

It will not be easy to realize this aim. Laughter must first be regarded with respect as a valuable means of communication, and the newspapers must then present it to the readers as a new model of communication. The writer's own sense of humor will be a crucial ingredient. Part of the problem is that full-time newspaper writers are selected by entrance examinations that attach importance only to a serious attitude and never to a sense of humor. Those who pass the tests must be very prosaic. More value needs to be placed on the evaluation of a sense of humor. When it comes to humorous writing, newspapers currently depend on outside specialists, which separates laughter from the mainstream of the newspaper. Humor needs to be internalized both into the structure of the paper and also into the style of the permanent writers themselves, since if they lack an appreciation of humor they will be able neither to write columns with good wit nor to find something humorous in another's words. If Japanese newspapers can move in this direction, they will surely become more interesting and effective than ever. In the meantime, readers will continue to enjoy the small satisfactions offered by the cartoons, the *senryū*, and the restrained ironic comments that already exist.

NOTES

1. For more detail on *senryū* and its history, see chapters 1 and 10.
2. "Funsuitō" is typically 1½ column-inches (3.7 centimeters).
3. "Kataekubo" is typically 1⅙ column-inches (3.0 centimeters). The name derives from a proverb: "A samurai dimples one cheek once in three years"; that is, this small amount of unbending is permitted at times.
4. "USO Hōsō" is typically 1¼ column-inches (3.2 centimeters).
5. For discussion of the pen names of some of the most famous classical writers of comic poetry in the form of *kyōka*, see chapter 8.
6. See chapter 10 for more detailed discussion of the impact of censorship—for example, during the period of the Kansei Reforms

(1787–93).

7. Japanese office workers (stereotypically male) are called *sararii-man*. In addition, *sarari to* means "lightly," so the name is a pun: he is Mr. Golightly (*Sarari-kun*) the Salary-man (*Sararii-man*).

8. *Yomiuri Shimbun*, January 5, 2000.

9. Versions of this traditional tale are found in both Japanese and Chinese literature and history.

10. "Sankeishō," *Sankei Shimbun*, January 10, 1992.

11. "Tensei Jingo" (天声人語 "The voice of heaven is the voice of the people") is an extremely well-known column and is much used as reading material in most western university-level Japanese courses. Typically it is 11⅚ column-inches (30 centimeters).

12. "Yoroku" (余録 "Extra Jottings") is typically 11½ column-inches (29 centimeters).

13. "Henshū Techō" (編集手帳 "The Editor's Notebook") is typically 8⅔ column-inches (22 centimeters).

14. "Sankeishō" (産経抄 "The Sankei Selection") is typically 12⅔ column-inches (32 centimeters).

Satire and Constraint in Japanese Culture

Marguerite A. Wells

Humor goes by fashions. In European cultures, for example, we could trace the rise and fall of the pun or the flourishing and decline of satire. Certain types of humor develop or fail to flourish at certain times within a particular culture, and it is equally true that certain cultures seem to favor the development of one type of humor over another. Sometimes the reasons for this are clear. The Japanese and Korean writing systems, which are based on the Chinese, have been fantastically fertile fields for punning, to the extent that in Korean a written poem, read in Chinese, may be a staid and trite celebration of the beauty of the moon, but the same poem read in Korean may be filthy or scurrilous, or both.[1] It seems unlikely that punsters engage in feats of such virtuosity in other languages. But not all cultural preferences in humor are so easily explained. Japan has an immensely rich comic tradition, but one of the forms of humor least seen in modern Japan is satire. This chapter will put forward some cultural reasons for this relative lack of satire and for the mildness of the satire that is seen.

For well over a century, one of the main themes in Japanese scholarship has been the classification of Japanese phenomena in terms of categories inherited from Europe. Since the categories usually do not fit very well, this makes the game great academic fun: there is infinite scope for rethinking and reclassification. This game of classification and reclassification is perhaps particularly complex in studies of humor or humorous genres. In this respect, one of the most vexed of the humorous genres is that of *kyōgen* (狂言), the comic interludes that intersperse the *nō* (能) plays. A day spent at the *nō* theater takes you, literally and intentionally, from the sublime to the ridiculous and back again.

As discussed elsewhere in this volume, the classification of *kyōgen* is vexed precisely because it is funny.[2] I have been asked very politely by a distinguished Japanese theater scholar, "Excuse me, but is *kyōgen* really comedy?" A native speaker of English who has seen a good *kyōgen* play will not have the slightest doubt that this is comedy, but in Japanese there is doubt, and the reason is that the Japanese word for comedy, *kigeki* (喜劇), has come to be applied to a particular theatrical genre not at all like *kyōgen*.[3] Words have different semantic coverage in different languages, and the Japanese word for comedy is such a word. This applies to many of the Japanese words relating to humor, including the word "humor" itself, *yūmoa* (ユーモア).[4] This is particularly true of the Japanese concept of satire.

Satire, in its English meaning, is humor (including ridicule, irony, sarcasm, and so forth) directed at the faults, vices, or follies of individuals or institutions, always with the intention of exposing and correcting them. In his useful handbook on *Satire*, Arthur Pollard briefly surveys how *satire* has been historically defined in English by its great classical writers:

> Dr. Johnson in the Dictionary defined satire as "a poem in which wickedness or folly is censured." Dryden and Defoe went further than this, the one in claiming that "the true end of satire is the amendment of vices" (*Discourse Concerning Satire*), the other that "the end of Satyr is Reformation: and the Author, tho' he doubts the work of Conversion is at a general Stop, has put his Hand to the Plow" (*Preface* to *The True Born Englishman*).[5]

The latter remark acknowledges that the satirist suspects that he or she may not convert the audience but is going to try anyway. In the preface to his satire *The Battle of the Books* (1704), Jonathan Swift wrote wryly of the reasons for this: "Satire is a sort of glass, wherein beholders do generally discover everybody's face but their own, which is the chief reason for that kind of reception it meets in the world, and that so few are offended with it."[6]

Pollard explains that in 1728 Swift "saw satire as at best a kind of moral policeman restraining the righteous but helpless against the wicked, assisting 'to preserve well inclin'd men in the course of virtue but seldom or never reclaiming the vicious.'"[7] The eighteenth-century poet Alexander Pope also extolled satire in this regard:

> Oh! sacred Weapon! left for Truth's defence
> Sole Dread of Folly, Vice and Insolence![8]

Despite some lugubriousness among the satirists about their chances of effectively turning the depraved from wickedness to virtue, the satirist in the European tradition is nonetheless, as Pollard says, "the guardian of ideals."[9]

The Japanese word for satire is *fūshi* (諷刺). It is an old word that came into Japanese from Chinese, and the characters with which it is written mean (the first character) to hint, suggest, insinuate, satirize, or lampoon, and (the second character) to stab. While there may be rather a wide spread of meaning in the first character, the second is unambiguous: satire, in both Japanese and Chinese, involves using the knife. A recent Japanese-Japanese dictionary[10] defines *fūshi* as: "Criticism of the faults of society or persons, wrapped in humor. Formerly abundant in and an important expressive device in *rakushu, senryū, kyōka* etc. (落首 ； 川柳 ； 狂歌)."[11] The dictionary goes on to give the English gloss *Satire*. The Japanese encyclopedic dictionary *Basic Knowledge of Words Used in the Literary Arts* gives the glosses *Satire* (English), *Satire* (German), *Satire* (French), defining them as follows:

> A category of humor. Intellectual and hostile, it involves attack. It stands at the opposite pole from humor, with irony between them. That is to say, the element of attack is strong and in contradistinction to the altruism of humor. . . . The works it designates expose the faults and illogicalities of times and societies. It became a category of literature in Western Europe with Lucilius and Horace[12] and in more recent times, famous authors have included Heine, Voltaire, Swift and Shaw.[13]

From this it would seem that the Japanese and European definitions mean satire in the same sense. However, the older encyclopedic dictionary *Kōjien*, which was the standard for the twentieth century, gives the following, much broader definition:

1. To criticize the faults and evils of society or persons by "roundaboutation."
2. To disparage without seeming to do so. Innuendo.[14]

In 1909, Natsume Sōseki published an essay entitled "Bungaku Hyōron" ("Literary Criticism").[15] Sōseki was lecturer in English literature at Tokyo Imperial University and was later to become Japan's greatest novelist (certainly its most famous: two of his earliest works were the comic and mildly satirical novels *I Am a Cat* and *Botchan*).[16] Sōseki had studied English literature in England and specialized in that of the eighteenth century.[17] This period was the heyday of satire in English, and Sōseki naturally gave it some attention in his lectures. As part of an extended discussion of Jonathan Swift's satire, he wrote:

> To sum up my own view of it in a word, I think the most appropriate would be callous (*reikoku* 冷酷). I even feel I could rate it as "cold cynicism." Basically the subjects of satire can be variously distinguished as how we look at human life and how we view society, but if we try to analyze the motives of those who go in for satire we can make several interesting distinctions. The first is the satire of good will. The satire itself may be harsh, but it derives from the good intention of making the person who is the object of the satire desist from evil and change to good. Addison and Steele, particularly Steele, have this tendency.[18]
>
> The second is that of ill will, and it is simply a cynical means of hurting that person's feelings, of sticking out one's tongue at him behind his back. Addison tended to do this sometimes.
>
> The third is of neither good nor ill will. People go in for it simply because satire itself is amusing. In order to achieve that end, anything is permissible, and no questions asked. As a child rejoices in chasing a dog around, satire has no object apart from satire.[19]

Sōseki gave this description of satire in about 1905 to a class of Japan's future authors, scholars, and literary critics, all assembled in his lecture theater at Tokyo Imperial University; it is also the description he left to future generations in his published works. Strictly speaking, only Sōseki's first type of satire is truly satire by European definitions, because it is the only one of the three with the intention to correct. His second type corresponds more closely to the lampoon, or put-down, and his third to slapstick, or farce. Perhaps, however, the Japanese word *fūshi* had a wider meaning than *satire* has in English. No matter what the reason, Sōseki was enshrining a definition of satire so broad that it ensured that something quite substantial, somewhere in the Japanese humorous tradition, could be classed as satire.

It is not surprising that, as a result, later authors have struggled with the classification of various Japanese genres. In 1942, for example, Furukawa Hisashi recounted that he had been asked to write an article in the place of another academic who had fallen ill. The topic he was assigned was "The satire of *kyōgen*" (*kyōgen no fūshi*). He was glad to have the chance, but "from what I had seen and read to date, you just couldn't classify *kyōgen* as satire."[20] He asked the editor if he could change the title and was told that he could change it to "The comicality and satire of *kyōgen*." Since he knew what the editor's motivation was in insisting on the word *satire*, "I took it into my head to come at the argument from the angle of the Western European–type view that humor is valueless if it is not satire."[21]

This theoretical stance gave him some trouble. As Wells and Davis note in chapter 9, *kyōgen* certainly makes fun of groups of people—country gentlemen, wily servants, priests, doctors, and the blind, for instance—but the implication is not that any of these groups ought to reform their ways, only that sometimes they can be funny. If one thinks of the scene in the *kyōgen Calling Voices* (呼声)[22] where the country landowner and his overseer dance around the house of a lazy serf, trying to coax him to come out by capturing him in the beat of a song, one realizes that *kyōgen* typically does not wield the knife or seek to correct faults. Its intentions are not really satirical but rather farcical, making mischief without a serious challenge to authority.

In his article, Professor Furukawa applied Sōseki's wide definition of satire to *kyōgen* and argued: "Thus we see that the satire of *kyōgen* is born of a nonchalant attitude on the part of the (anonymous) author, as a result is somewhat lacking in realism, and it does not occupy an important place in *kyōgen*."[23] By definition, satire is never nonchalant; it is not done simply for the sake of amusement and it is not joyful. Rather, it is deadly serious, and, above all, it is utterly bound up with reality. If the "satire" of *kyōgen* proves somewhat lacking in realism, then it is not really satire. It must be concluded that the main extant Japanese genre that is generally classified as satire is not so at all.

The dictionary definition quoted above mentions the comic poetic genres *senryū* and *kyōka* as employing satire as an important expressive device.[24] Chapters 1 and 10 in this volume give some examples of the humor of *senryū*. Of these, one, the verse about the official's baby being good at grasping, is satire. A few others, such as that about the samurai out walking with his spear carrier and turning around to look, or the one about the bereaved family dividing up the keepsakes and grabbing the best, might perhaps be construed as satire, but really are rueful comment on humanity. Two books of *senryū* edited by R. H. Blyth provide some ready examples of the types of humor found in *senryū*, in addition to those already discussed elsewhere in this volume.[25] Blyth classifies his selection and their translations under headings intended to give some guidance to the reader about the styles or topics of humor in the original poems. Thus, for "Grim Humour" (what might in European terms be called "Gallows Humor") he gives as a good example the following:

すっぽりと	*Suppari to*	He is completely
なおりましたが	*Naorimashita ga*	Cured but
はながおち	*Hana ga ochi*	His nose has fallen off[26]

This is a wry joke about syphilis and is quite explicit about its unappealing subject.

For "Tragic Humour," Blyth provides this touching verse:

吉原へ	*Yoshiwara e*	Facing the Yoshiwara
むいて上野で	*Muite Ueno de*	At Ueno
くびをつり	*Kubi o tsuri*	He hanged himself[27]

The Yoshiwara was the brothel quarter of Edo where young men misspent their youths and their families' life savings. Again the humor combines romance with grim reality to produce an ironic comment on the follies of youth.

Blyth includes a category that he calls "Kindly Humour" and illustrates it with the following:

わがせこが	Waga seko ga	It is the evening
くべきよいなり	Kubeki yoi nari	When my dear one is to come
しちをおき	Shichi o oki	Having pawned something[28]

The speaker here may be a *geisha* whose lover must find the money to pay for the time he spends with her. The romantic sentiment involved serves perhaps to soften the low burlesque of the situation, which descends rapidly from the evocation of romantic twilight to the unpleasant reality of life, money. Once again, the poem is not very severe in its criticism of human folly. It is certainly less humorously critical than what Blyth terms the "Humour of Exposed Pretence," as in the following:

うぬぼれて	Unubore o	When he stops loving himself
やめればほかに	Yamereba hoka ni	There will be no one else
ほれてなし	Horete nashi	To love him[29]

This attacks a common form of vanity and anticipates its future reform, which is indeed the business of satire.

A satisfyingly comic and subtle picture is also achieved by an example of the "Humour of Indirectness," where much must be inferred from key words in the text:

しからずに	Shikarazu ni	Not scolding but
となりのよめを	Tonari no yome o	Instead praising
ほめておき	Homete oki	The bride next door[30]

This is a Japanese mother-in-law joke. Since mothers-in-law had the job of training young brides in the ways of the household and were notorious for taking advantage of their almost life-and-death power over their daughters-in-law, the poem is a comment on a subtle mother-in-law manipulating her newly acquired daughter-in-law.

In the category of what Blyth labels the "Humour of Stupidity," he includes what seems almost an existential joke, which is here translated into Australian terms (which may also serve to communicate its essential "earthiness" to American readers):

つるやつも	Tsuru yatsu mo	The blokes fishing and and the blokes
つるやつみる	Tsuru yatsu miru	Watching the blokes fishing
やつもやつ	Yatsu mo yatsu	Are all blokes[31]

These *senryū* are all funny (in Japanese), and all are clever, but how many of them are unambiguously satire? Which wield the knife or seek to correct? Most are actually rueful comments on the human condition rather than corrective attacks on personal or social faults. "When he stops loving with himself" is admittedly a mild satire on vanity. "The blokes fishing" is more the broadly wielded bludgeon than the surgical knife: it is certainly a put-down, but since it does not really seek to correct anything or anyone it is difficult to class as satire. Rather, it is a wry observation on the limited nature of human beings.

Further insight into the kind of humor embodied by *senryū* can be gained by studying the style of illustration typically used to accompany the poems. The results tend to confirm the diagnosis of "the wry ironic comment" rather than the "sharp satirical knife." The reproductions that accompany these poems (figures 12.1, 12.2, and 12.3) are cartoons from a collection entitled *The Hundred Faces of Society.*[32] The author/artist has taken *senryū* both old and new and illustrated them, turning the moment captured by the poem into a cartoon or picture. Significantly, the style tends toward gentle burlesque rather than caricature. Figure 12.1 shows an illustration accompanying a poem by one Santarō:

涼み台	Suzumidai	Garden seat
うしろでがまが	Ushiro de gama ga	Behind them a toad
きいて居る	Kiite oru	Is listening[33]

Both poem and illustration can be classified in form as burlesque in that they make little of the great.[34] But like most *senryū*, this one does not particularly criticize or seek to correct faults. It presents the viewpoint of the sympathetic and unaggressive observer rather than that of a savage critic.

Two examples from this illustrated collection qualify as satire in the sense that they carry a clear implication that "things ought to be otherwise." One (illustrated in figure 12.2) is an "old *senryū*" describing a couple who will argue about anything:

Fig. 12.1 The garden seat in the cool of the evening (pen-and-ink drawing taken from multi-image pages of the collection *Senryū Manga to Banzuke Iroiro: Shakai Hyakumensō* [Japan: Dai Nihon Yūbenkai Kōdansha, 1931], unpaginated)

Fig. 12.2 The garden seat and the stars (pen-and-ink drawing taken from multi-image pages of the collection *Senryū Manga to Banzuke Iroiro: Shakai Hyaku-mensō* [Japan: Dai Nihon Yūbenkai Kōdansha, 1931], unpaginated)

涼み台	Suzumidai	Garden seat
又はじまった	Mata hajimatta	They're at it again
星の論	Hoshi no ron	Arguing about the stars[35]

Another "old *senryū*" (illustrated in figure 12.3) concerns a mild case of female vanity:

男なら	Otoko nara	A man would
直ぐに汲もうに	Sugu ni kumō ni	Fill his water bottle
水かがみ	Mizu kagami	The water is her mirror[36]

Fig. 12.3 The hikers and the pool (pen-and-ink drawing taken from multi-image pages of the collection *Senryū Manga to Banzuke Iroiro: Shakai Hyakumensō* [Japan: Dai Nihon Yūbenkai Kōdansha, 1931], unpaginated)

202

Overall, however, rueful comment on the common human lot seems to be more typical of the traditional *senryū* than does satire. By way of proof from the exception, however, one example of political satire can be found in the following poem. This time it is a *kyōka* that circulates orally in today's Japan:

このよには	*Kono yo ni wa*	In this world
かほどうるさき	*Ka hodo urusaki*	There is nothing
ものはなし	*Mono wa nashi*	More irritating than a mosquito
ぶんぶと言て	*Bumbu to yūte*	It goes "bumbu"
よるもねむれず	*Yoru mo nemurezu*	So you can't sleep at night.[37]

This seems pretty innocuous, until you realize that *ka hodo* not only means "as a mosquito," but also "as this" and that the poem can therefore be read, using this sly pun, as follows:

In this world
There is nothing
More irritating than this:
Going "bumbu"
So you can't sleep at night.

This may still look innocuously unsatiric, and indeed the evident superficiality of the poem serves to indicate that there must be more than meets the eye. Is there, as it were, a "secret language" in operation here?

To decode the satire, one more piece of information is necessary, which is that for some centuries Japan, ruled by the warrior class, was at peace. During that time, the warriors gradually ceased to be fighting men and became administrators. One morning, therefore, they woke up as it were and found that they were no longer knights of old but had become pen- (or rather, brush-) pushers. If flagging egos were to be boosted, some rationalization of this descent from armor to the white collar was needed. One means of doing this was the invention of the famous slogan "The Literati and the Military," or "The Pen and the Sword." This gives an acronym of *bumbu* (文武).

Rereading the poem with this in mind, it becomes evident that not everybody was fully impressed by the political slogan:

In this world
There is nothing
More irritating than this:
People who buzz around saying *bumbu, bumbu*
So you can't sleep at night.

Here is real political satire indeed, but subtle and rare.

Undoubtedly, then, *senryū* and its sister genre *kyōka* can extend to satire in the true meaning of the word, but that comic style is distinguished by its rarity, and its pointedness is typically quite limited. This may be in part because of the shortness of the poetic form itself, in part because of the observational viewpoint adopted. Whatever the reasons, poetic humor is usually quite general, not the most biting, and the rare touches of satire make up only a very small part of the corpus. It is ironic that the few examples of satire that *do* exist crop up again and again in discussions and analyses as "representative" of their genres.[38]

From these examples, however, two conclusions are clear. First, satire in Japan, when it has existed, has been typically mild in comparison with what it *can* be when the knife is wielded with deadly corrective intent. And second, much of what has usually been identified in Japan as satire is not really satire at all by European standards. Given the wide definition proposed by Sōseki and laid down in the dictionary quoted above, this is perhaps not surprising.

Of course, there is no reason why Japan should have to have biting satire solely because Europe does. Indeed, we cannot and should not use European-derived standards to judge Japanese culture. At this point a comparison with Japan's next-door neighbor, Korea, may be enlightening.[39] Korea has a long tradition of scathing political and social satire, to the extent that in 1970 a writer on the history of Korean humor complained: "Even today, Korean playwrights are writing satires on society and politics instead of dealing with the humour found in healthy everyday life or that which bespeaks nature and intuition. Their work, for the most part, is aggressive satire."[40]

The bite of Korean satire is certainly not exaggerated. In 1987 a television series on the state-run Korea Broadcasting Service called *You're Right, Mr. Chairman* was enormously successful and popular. It depicted the relationship between a greedy, illiterate, and deeply insecure conglomerate president who had married into the company and the groveling board members who sought his favor. There was a move to take the program off the air, but this backfired: "Telephone calls from irate viewers persuaded the station to continue the series, but comedian Kim Hyong-gon, who created the series and takes the starring role, had grown impatient with television censorship. 'You can't say everything you have in mind on TV. There are too many restrictions. I was seeking ways to communicate directly with the audience,' Kim said."⁴¹

Pursuing this aim, he invested his life savings in a theater version and doubled his investment in the first four weeks alone, during which more than ten thousand people came to see the play, and to be pelted by the conglomerate president with apples "representing the 'apple bomb' tear-gas grenades South Korean police have used to disperse striking workers."⁴² With their first direct presidential election in sixteen years only two months away, the audience reacted readily to political jokes. Park describes how "in one exchange the Chairman orders more illegal campaign funds to the Opposition Party because he fears 'something unexpected might occur' and the Opposition could win."⁴³

By anyone's standards this is satire: it requires no redefinition of terms or watering down of definitions. The length of the Korean tradition is moreover attested to by a number of essays dealing with humor in Korean literature, as the following example shows:

The laughter provoked by the Enlightenment literature is a laughter, sarcastic by nature, thrown against the social reality of that time. Therefore, the objects of ridicule are mainly government officials and their followers, the aggressiveness of Japanese imperialist intervention and sometimes the bogus enlightenment itself, while those who deride or expose corruption are low-class people or even allegorised animal figures.⁴⁴

This example is sufficient to demonstrate the presence of the most biting satire in modern Korea. Yet it would be difficult to give a single Japanese example of such uncompromisingly

205

scathing satire, satire so clearly intended to address contentious, even dangerous, issues and to correct the faults of Japanese people, society, and institutions.[45] The satire that appears in the Japanese newspapers (discussed in chapter 11) is certainly satire, but it is mild by comparison, even though it has the protection of anonymity. Why might contemporary democratic Japan have only mild satire at the same time that neighboring Korea, under a repressive government, had the most biting of satire?

We could speculate about a number of reasons. The first reason, and the one typically given in Japan, is the argument from political oppression. As Wells and Davis discussed in chapter 9, Sugiura uses this argument to explain the absence of satire from *kyōgen:*

> When *kyōgen* was all the rage among the populace the sharp thorns of satire must often have appeared, and we cannot deny that the exposure of contemporary reality was one of the most important functions of *kyōgen,* even though it might not be such as to be called satire. This function was simply killed off by the link with *nō.* . . .
>
> However, in the Muromachi era [fourteenth to sixteenth centuries], when civil strife and insurrection made *gekokujō* the normal thing, toppling so many decrepit social relationships and ideas, loud laughter rather than satire was the weapon appropriate to the newly risen classes. Therefore it can be said that it was extremely natural that *kyōgen* developed and flourished as farce rather than as satire.
>
> Of course it is unthinkable that such dangerous humor passed the Tokugawa government's severe and rigorous thought censorship. Not to mention the fact that *kyōgen* was receiving patronage as the ceremonial of the Shogunate.[46]

Writing about satire in the early modern period in England, Conal Condren has shown that the argument from political oppression is fallacious as a general principle, or at least inadequate.[47] On closer inspection, this is as true in the case of Japan as in the case of Europe and European-derived cultures. Although an efficient censorship system operated in Japan at times, it was no more efficient or oppressive than the censorship system operating in England at a time when satire flourished.[48] As Condren points out, the case of Eastern Europe makes it clear that there are circumstances where oppression actually gives rise to humor rather than stifling it.[49] This is undoubtedly true of Asia as well. For example, the comments of the Korean writers Shin-yong Chun and Jae-son Lee, quoted above, specifically mention Japanese imperialism as stimulating Korean satire. Thus the existence of censorship does not explain the relative absence of satire and the almost total absence of biting satire from Japan's rich comic tradition.

A second possible reason for the paucity of satire is the fact that among the many types of humor, satire undoubtedly holds a special place. Research shows that it is an acquired taste with a problem of circularity affecting its appreciation. An audience needs to be familiar with the content or subject matter in order to interpret a comment as satire and not as serious comment or merely straightforward humor.[50] At the same time, the audience needs to know that something *is* satire in order to understand the comment that is being made.[51] Low dogmatism scores are associated with a positive ability to perceive the point of satire.[52] For these reasons, in experimental studies, even among those who know a piece is satire, only a small percentage of people interpret an intended satirical message accurately.[53]

Therefore, even in societies that have a rich satirical tradition, the production and appreciation of satire has tended to go by fashions. In eighteenth-century England, the reading public was accustomed to recognizing that a comment was satire and to interpreting it as such. Yet today, although there is satire to be found in our daily lives (the political cartoon featured in most newspapers, weekly current affairs commentary on television, animated cartoons, cult films, novels, and so on), it occupies only a small band of the spectrum of our everyday communication and entertainment. Its popularity is limited to its special followers. It seems that a society has to evolve the habit of "reading" satire without misunderstanding or taking offense, even when legal sanctions are not in question.

A third reason for the paucity and mildness of satire in Japanese humor may have to do with the way individuals or societies accommodate aggression. Some people do not like the attack that is essential to satire. After all, wielding the knife requires aggression. Yet as Yong Suk-kee points out, quoting the theater critic Eric Bentley, farce (which is certainly well represented in Japan)[54] is also a comic form that features aggression, and he goes so far as to say that "if farces are examined they will be found to contain little 'harmless' joking. . . . Without aggression, farce cannot function."[55] It is certainly true that among the funniest and most popular of Japanese *kyōgen* are the humiliation farces that depend upon aggressive punishment of their chosen victims.[56] If both satire and farce, as types of humor, depend on aggression, why should farce be favored in the Japanese cultural tradition and not satire?

Furukawa Hisashi said that "satire" was not really important in *kyōgen* because those plays were "somewhat lacking in realism." He points to an important characteristic of satire: that it is firmly based in reality, indeed in contemporary reality. It criticizes and seeks to correct the real faults of its (at that time) real world. On the other hand, because it is a risky business, and precisely in order to mute the impact of this aggression, satire often disguises itself by being set in a fantasy world. This is true, for example, of the English classical satires *Gulliver's Travels* and *Erewhon*.[57] A comparable Japanese example is Akutagawa Ryūnosuke's novel *Kappa*, a mild satire set in the world of the water sprites whose faults mimic those of the human world.[58] Another device for muting the aggression is extended metaphor. Thus Ibuse Masuji's short story "The Charcoal Bus," first published in 1952, may (according to its translator, Ivan Morris) be read as a political satire on Japan during the last years of the Pacific War,[59] but readers who do not know this will think it is simply a funny story about people on a rickety old bus who have to get out and push it. But wherever a work may be set, or however it may be disguised, if it does not in some sense present criticisms about the real world, then it is not true satire.[60]

Farce, on the other hand, provides a safely contained fantasy release for aggression. It is based in emotional indulgence, not in critical reflection on reality. By definition, as we have seen, satire is highly intellectual humor, while farce functions at the level of the emotions or instincts. In its original social setting, the *kyōgen* farce was an indulgence or a release for the aggression of those at both the top and the bottom of the social hierarchy. Its aggression is safely contained as a kind of fantasy release, because although superficially a farce plot appears to be set in the real world, this is a world in which to some extent the social rules are relaxed—temporarily. As the discussion by Wells and Davis has shown,[61] with very few exceptions, the usual social hierarchy reasserts itself at the end of each play.

A society that allows itself nothing more than such temporary "festival-day" release from the rules is by any measure a highly structured and controlled society. Farce, wherever it is found, serves as emotional release for highly controlled people, people in whom aggression is normally suppressed. In farce this aggression can be safely released against fantasy objects that are not so unrealistic as to lack psychological veracity but which do not connect with any serious message of needed reform. In satire, on the other hand, aggression is awakened and released against real objects that correspond to the contemporary reality surrounding the audience (or the original audience). The pen is wielded as a sword, with skill and intelligence, to criticize and to correct. Although farce ends with all as it was before the opening of the play, the end of satire is meant to bring about a permanent change in reality, or at least in the audience's perception of reality. Thus it is easier for many to feel comfortable with the fantasy release of aggression that is offered by farce rather than with the deliberate and real aggression of satire.

As I argued in *Japanese Humour*,[62] two of the main means of social control of negative types of humor are expurgation and containment. The former depends upon individuals regulating their personal use of humor across most (if not all) social settings, according to an internalized set of values, while the latter marks out particular locales, structures, and times as those in which humor can—largely unrestricted—be indulged. Japanese society displays a clear preference for the containment of humor and also a clear preference for farce and wry humor over satire. There would seem to be a logical connection between these two preferences.

Although the aggression inherent in farce is highly contained through various devices and structures (not least the fact that it is played onstage at specific times),[63] the nature and structure of available containers may not be adequate to contain the negative aspects of knife-wielding satire. Putting satire on the imaginary world of the stage or in the condensed and formal structure of a *senryū* poem will not prevent that satire from affecting, or at least from deliberately trying to affect, the real world. Although farce is, as it were, a little naughty, it is nonetheless always and only play. In the case of wry humor, ironic reflection on human folly leads only to a quiet chuckle and a shake of the head. But satire is deliberate rudeness, an overt challenge to social norms.

On the other hand, neither can expurgation operate to constrain the negative aspects of satire. Humor fully expurgated of all matter that may offend is no longer satire. Societies that have a preference for the control of humor by expurgation get around this problem of the deliberate discourtesy of satire by elevating the value and purposes of the genre, thus giving a dispensation for its aggression owing to its high moral purpose of reform and social change. While the writer or performer of farces cannot claim to be much more than an entertainer, the satirist is the guardian of ideals. Satire as a genre places society's overall good above any immediate need for constraint on antisocial behavior. We have a moral right to be rude and to enjoy the rudeness of satire if it is for a good cause.

However, guarding ideals requires that those ideals be clearly communicated, as Pollard points out:

> The best satire, that which is surest in tone, is that which is surest in its values. In our own literature, the age of Pope [eighteenth century] . . . provided the best satire . . . because . . . men felt sure of the standards to which they could refer. Indeed, much of the sorrow and the anger in Pope's last works derives from the feeling that those standards had collapsed:
>
> Truth, Worth, Wisdom daily they decry—
> Nothing is Sacred now but Villainy.[64]

A society that does not have fixed, stable values will not be any sort of hunting ground for the satirist. More importantly, to serve as benchmarks against which the satirist may measure the society and find it wanting, the values must indeed be ideals; like truth, worth, and wisdom, they must be above mere humankind. Thus an age or culture in which values are considered absolute and independent of human beings will be an age or culture in which satire can flourish, while an age of moral relativism, or one of swift social change and dislocation, or even one of multiculturalism, should be less conducive to satire.

The cultural tradition of Europe that has been inherited by speakers of English is one in which ideals like truth, worth, and wisdom, as well as concepts like villainy and evil, make some sort of sense. Although in our age of relativism they may be much muted, we have nevertheless millennia of tradition in which it has been assumed that there is something called "good" and something called "evil" and that these are to be ascertained by reference to something above the merely human. For most people, and for most of written history, this something has been interpreted as God, but even atheists or agnostics still believe in and strive for moral ideals. We are trained from childhood to internalize these standards, to measure and judge ourselves according to them. We have, in short, even if we consider ourselves relativists, inherited a tradition of moral absolutism, in which satire can find standards against which to measure us and find us wanting.

Not all cultures work this way. In some cultures, people are trained from childhood to measure themselves not against internalized standards but against externalized standards. They are trained to judge their own behavior according to the expectations of those around them, not according to absolutes that are above humankind. The arbiter in these cultures is not, to put the matter hyperbolically, the eyes of God; but rather the eyes of the Other. Anthropologists have a name for this dichotomy: cultures principally ruled by internalized standards are called "guilt cultures," and cultures principally ruled by externalized standards are called "shame cultures."

Of course, these are broad terms that must not be taken too literally. There is infinite variety among humankind, and any subculture—or any family or any individual—may operate on the one principle or the other or according to a combination of the two principles, with infinite gradations. It would be a strange member of a European or European-derived culture who did not know the feelings of both guilt and shame. Nonetheless, the distinction is useful; and most importantly, if the concepts of guilt and shame are applied to the prediction of behavior, by and large they work. Even though human beings are infinitely varied, and cultures are amalgamations of huge numbers of infinitely varied human beings, over a large population things tend to average out, and some societies show a definite preference for internalized standards and others for externalized standards. Japanese culture has traditionally shown a definite preference for externalized standards.

In addition, Japanese culture has undergone a number of major shifts in values and cultural dislocations in the last century, the most major having been the loss of national beliefs and standards in the face of defeat in the Pacific War. Many people who believed, the day before the surrender, that they knew what was right found suddenly, within a short time after the surrender, that right was now defined as wrong. This may seem hyperbolic, but it is not. Social change has been swift in Japan during the last 150 years, and mores have changed just as swiftly.

As early as 1898, Tsubouchi Shōyō, the literary critic whose book *The Essence of the Novel* inspired the development of Japan's modern literature, wrote that "in an era when ideals are not fixed, there can be no grand laughter; in an era of research there can be no grand laughter."[65] The fluidity of values that has accompanied Japan's last century and a half of change, on top of the cultural preference for externalized standards, has meant that the twentieth century has provided stony ground for Japanese satire. In fact, by the beginning of the twenty-first century, Japan's economy was in a state of recession and frank disarray that would have been unthinkable a decade before. The flourishing economy and the era of material plenty that grew out of the ashes of World War II had been, to many Japanese people, a source of pride. But by the beginning of the new century, and in retrospect, this can be seen to have been somewhat complacent.

For the most part, Japanese people had, in the second half of the twentieth century, been happy enough to leave politics to the politicians. With the support of an overwhelming percentage of the population, because they were presiding over an era of plenty, the politicians were accepted without question as doing a good job. As the economy declined, however, people became less and less patient with the increasingly transparent decadence that they came to perceive in Japanese political institutions, and also with the procession of prime ministers falling like skittles before substantiated accusations of corruption. In the course of this volume there have been a few hints that (particularly in the *senryū* tradition, and more particularly in humor in contemporary newspapers)[66] the complacency of previous decades has to some extent given way to cynicism. Whether the future will bring reform that will satisfy the Japanese people's aspirations for personal and social stability and prosperity remains to be seen. If it does not, the future may prove a richer field for Japanese satire.

Rather than providing a neat and predictive set of answers about humor in Japan and elsewhere, this chapter may have served to prompt a set of broader questions through which to reflect on the material discussed in this volume. What forces determine the kinds of humor that develop in certain cultures during certain periods? To what extent do the whims of chance (producing particularly gifted individuals at particular times), of individual choice, and of fashion dictate the development of particular humorous genres? What is the overarching role of social, cultural, linguistic, and historical forces? When we better understand these issues, we better understand ourselves, as well as our neighbors.

NOTES

1. See, for example, Richard Rutt, "Kim Sakkat, the Popular Humorist," in *Humour in Korean Literature,* ed. International Cultural Foundation (Seoul: International Cultural Foundation, 1982), 35–54.
2. See chapter 9, which identifies the comic style of *kyōgen* as predominantly that of farce.
3. That is, to the theatrical genre *shinkigeki.* For further mentions of this form of comedy, see chapters 2 and 4.
4. See also the discussion of comic terminology in the introduction.
5. Arthur Pollard, *Satire* (London: Methuen, 1970), 2. This concise analysis of the genre summarizes the conventional definitions of satire in English critical usage. Other relevant studies are Leonard Feinberg, *The Satirist* (Ames: Iowa State University Press, 1963); Gilbert Highet, *The Anatomy of Satire* (Princeton, N.J.: Princeton University Press, 1962); Matthew Hodgart, *Satire* (London: Weidenfeld and Nicolson, 1969); and Conal Condren, *Satire, Lies, and Politics: The Case of Dr. Arbuthnot* (Basingstoke: Macmillan, 1997).

6. Quoted in Pollard, *Satire*, 2. A "glass" is a mirror.

7. Ibid.

8. Alexander Pope (1688–1744). Quoted by Pollard, *Satire*, 2.

9. Ibid., 3.

10. Umesao Tadao, Kindaichi Haruhiko, et al., *Nihongo Daijiten* (Tokyo: Kōdansha, 1989). Unless otherwise noted, all translations are my own.

11. Of these three genres, *kyōka* and *senryū* are discussed more fully in chapters 8 and 10, respectively. I return below to discussion of the definition of satire and its application to these genres.

12. Gaius Lucilius, c. 180–c. 102 or 101 B.C.; Quintus Horatius Flaccus, 65–83 B.C., author of *The Satires*.

13. Kokubungaku Kaishaku to Kanshō, *Bungei Yōgo no Kiso Chishiki* (Tokyo: Tōbundō, 1983), 527.

14. Shinmura Izuru, ed., *Kōjien*, 2nd ed. (Tokyo: Iwanami Shoten, 1955), 1915; my translation.

15. Natsume Sōseki, "Bungaku Hyōron," in *Sōseki Zenshū*, vol. 10 (Tokyo: Iwanami Shoten, 1966), 19–455.

16. *I Am a Cat*, trans. Aiko Ito and Graeme Wilson (Tokyo: Tuttle, 1972); *Botchan*, trans. Sasaki Umeji (Tokyo: Tuttle, 1968).

17. A readable account of Sōseki's life and works is found in Donald Keene, *Dawn to the West* (New York: Henry Holt and Co., 1987), 305–54.

18. Richard Steele (1672–1729), poet, playwright, and editor of the early newspapers *The Tatler* and *The Spectator* and a number of other periodicals; Joseph Addison (1672–1719), contributor to *The Tatler* and *The Spectator*.

19. Sōseki, "Bungaku Hyōron," 306.

20. Furukawa Hisashi, "Kyōgen no Fūshi," in *Nōgaku Zensho*, ed. Nogami Toyoichirō (Tokyo: Tōkyō Sōgensha, 1980), 134. Reprinted in Furukawa Hisashi, *Kyōgen no Kenkyū* (Tokyo: Fukumura Shoten, 1948), 15–37.

21. Furukawa, "Kyōgen no Fūshi," 134. Whether this ever was a European view is a moot point. He was struggling with the problem of the value of humor, which is discussed at length in *Japanese Humour* (Basingstoke: Macmillan, 1997).

22. This *kyōgen* is discussed in detail in chapter 9.

23. Furukawa, "Kyōgen no Fūshi," 126.

24. For detailed discussion of the two forms, see chapters 1 and 10 on *senryū* and chapter 8 on *kyōka*.

25. R. H. Blyth, *Edo Satirical Verse Anthologies* (Tokyo: Hokuseido Press, 1961) and *Japanese Life and Character in Senryū* (Tokyo: Hokuseido Press, 1960). Translations in the following are my own.

26. Ibid., 31.
27. Ibid., 314.
28. Ibid., 320.
29. Ibid., 322.
30. Ibid., 323.
31. Ibid., 325.
32. *Senryū Manga to Banzuke Iroiro: Shakai Hyakumensō* (Tokyo: Dai Nihon Yūbenkai Kōdansha, 1931), unpaginated.
33. Ibid., 6.
34. See John D. Jump, *Burlesque* (London: Methuen, 1972).
35. *Senryū Manga to Banzuke Iroiro*, 2.
36. Ibid.
37. I record this poem as it was recited to me some years ago. For more detailed discussion of the form and for other examples of classical *kyōka*, see chapter 8.
38. The *senryū* about the official's baby, for example, is quoted by several commentators, including Donald Keene, *World within Walls: Japanese Literature of the Pre-modern Era, 1600–1867* (New York: Holt, Rinehart and Winston, 1976), 530.
39. I would like to thank Dr. Roger Goodman of St. Antony's College, Oxford, for drawing my attention to the following material.
40. Gun Sam-lee, *Humour in Drama*, in "Report on P.E.N. Congress in Seoul," ed. International Research Centre, *Korean Quarterly* 12, no. 3 (1970): 22–27.
41. Park C. K., "Biting Satire on Conglomerates a Hit," *Korea Herald*, November, 5, 1987, 10.
42. Ibid.
43. Ibid.
44. Chun Shin-yong, "Introduction," in International Cultural Foundation, *Humour in Korean Literature*, 11–12; see also Lee Jae-son, "Laughter in the Literature of the Enlightenment Period," ibid., 80.
45. Wartime propaganda produced truly biting satire, although the seriousness of the context leaves room to doubt how funny the audience may have found it. I am grateful to Ron Stewart of Nagoya University for providing the following information:

    The Ono Hideo collection of 600 wartime posters is available for viewing in digital form at the ISICS Library (Shakai Jōhō Kenkyūjo Library) at Tokyo University's Hongō campus. Part of the collection (but as yet no Japanese wartime posters) may be viewed on the website <http://www.lib.isics.u-tokyo.ac.jp/ono/wg-index-e.html>.

Many of the posters made in Japan and by local artists were for audiences in countries that Imperial Japan controlled. They covered topics from grim life under American or British imperial oppression to a glorious future within Japan's Greater Asia Co-prosperity Sphere.

Tokyo University's War and Media Research Group (Sensō to Media Kenkyūkai) is in the process of putting together a database of Japanese wartime propaganda materials from the Ono Collection, and it is hoped to make them available on the internet in about 2006 (contact: Professor Yoshimi Shun'ya, Institute of Socio-Information and Communication Studies, Information and Society Division, Tokyo University).

Other works dealing with Japanese propaganda include John Dower, *War without Mercy* (New York: Pantheon Books, 1986) and *Japan in War and Peace* (London: Fontana Press/Harper Collins, 1995); Shimizu Isao, *Taiheiyō Senki no Manga* (*Cartoons of the Pacific War Period*) (Tokyo: Bijutsu Dōjinsha, Tokyo, 1971); and Sakuramoto Tomio, *Sensō to Manga* (*War and Cartoons*) (Tokyo: Sōdosha, 2000).

46. Sugiura Mimpei, "Gekokujōteki Shakai no Katami: Kyōgen," in *Bungaku*, vol. 32 (Tokyo: Iwanami Shoten, 1964), 649–50.
47. Conal Condren, "Between Social Constraint and the Public Sphere: On Misreading Political Satire in Early-Modern England," *Contemporary Political Theory* 1, no. 1 (2002): 79–101.
48. Marguerite Wells, "The Decline of the Japanese Laugh" (unpublished paper given at the Nissan Institute of Japanese Studies, Oxford University, January 23, 1987).
49. The same point is made by George Mikes, *Humour in Memoriam* (London: Routledge and Kegan Paul, 1970), and many other writers.
50. Anthony J. Chapman and Hugh Foot, *Humour and Laughter: Theory, Research, and Applications* (London: Wiley, 1976), 297, commenting on Charles Gruner, "An Experimental Study of Satire as Persuasion," *Speech Monographs*, no. 32 (1965): 149–53.
51. Chapman and Foot, *Humour and Laughter*, 301.
52. Ibid., 298 and 306. See also E. Cooper and Marie Jahoda, "The Evasion of Propaganda: How Prejudiced People Respond to Anti-prejudice Propaganda," *Journal of Psychology*, no. 23 (1947): 15–25; C. R. Gruner, "Dogmatism and the Understanding/Appreciation of Satire" (unpublished paper presented at the Convention of the Speech Communication Association, Chicago, 1974); G. R. Miller and P. Bacon, "Open- and Closed-mindedness and Rec-

ognition of Visual Humour," *Journal of Communication*, no. 21 (1971): 150–59.

53. Chapman and Foot, *Humour and Laughter*, 297 and 301.
54. See both the introduction and chapter 9.
55. Yong Suk-kee, "Laughter in the Korean Traditional Drama," in International Cultural Foundation, *Humour in Korean Literature*, 92. The reference is to Eric Bentley, *The Life of the Drama* (London: Methuen, 1996), 240.
56. See, for example, the discussion of *Asahina* in chapter 9.
57. Jonathan Swift, *Gulliver's Travels* (1726), in which Gulliver visits the lands of Lilliput and Brobdignab, as well as the country of the Houyhnms, virtuous horses plagued by the Yahoos (who are brutish humans). Samuel Butler, *Erewhon* (1872); Erewhon ("Nowhere" badly spelled backwards) is a mythical land hidden behind the mountain ranges of the South Island of New Zealand, where Butler lived from 1859 to 1864.
58. Akutagawa Ryūnosuke, *Kappa*, trans. Geoffrey Bownas (Tokyo: Tuttle, 1971).
59. Ibuse Masuji, "The Charcoal Bus," in *Modern Japanese Stories*, trans. Ivan Morris (Tokyo: Tuttle, 1962), 211–22.
60. This characteristic is widely acknowledged by writers on satire; see, for example, Feinberg, *The Satirist*, 7; Highet, *Anatomy of Satire*, 324–25; and Hodgart, *Satire*, 11–13. Condren, in *Satire, Lies, and Politics*, 13–26, argues that his subject (Arbuthnot's short satirical pamphlet *The Art of Political Lying*, 1712) was an intentional and effective Tory political tract.
61. See chapter 9.
62. See also chapter 9 for more detailed discussion of these concepts.
63. See chapter 9 and Jessica Milner Davis, *Farce*, rev. ed. (New Brunswick, N.J.: Transaction, 2003).
64. Pollard, *Satire*, 3.
65. Tsubouchi Shōyō, "Ikanaru Hito ga Mottomo Yoku," *Waseda Bungaku*, January 3, 1898, 127. The "era of research" was the Meiji era (1868–1912), when Japan was intently studying industrialized societies and planning its own modernization.
66. See chapter 11.

CONTRIBUTORS

GOH ABE is Professor in the Department of Literature, Tokushima Bunri University in Kagawa, where he teaches in comparative cultures, intercultural communication, and media discourse. His research interests are in interethnic communication (both between and within nations), cultural anthropology (particularly in Micronesia), and ethnic humor and disaster jokes. He has researched topics as disparate as humor festivals in Japan and Nepal, "Kerryman" jokes in Ireland, and jokes told in Australian Aboriginal communities against white Australians. In 2000 he was co-chair of the Organizing Committee of the International Society of Humor Studies' twelfth Conference in Osaka. He is a member of the Editorial Board of *Humor: International Journal of Humor Research*.

HIROSHI INOUE is Professor Emeritus at Kansai University, Osaka. He taught in communication and media sociology and has been president of the Japan Society for Laughter and Humor Studies since its founding in 1994. He has published widely on many aspects of Japanese humor and laughter and is former director of the Osaka Prefectural Museum of Kamigata Comedy and Performing Arts, which he helped found in 1996. In July 2000 he was chair of the International Society of Humor Studies' twelfth Conference in Osaka and was a member of the society's Executive Board from 2001 to 2003. He is regularly interviewed on both Japanese and American media on the subject of humor in Japan.

MASASHI KOBAYASHI was a graduate of Kyoto University in Jurisprudence. His distinguished career with Mainichi Broadcasting System (formerly New Japan Broadcasting), which included time as Bureau Chief for North America in New York (1977–80), was followed by appointment as Professor in the Broadcasting Department of the Osaka University of Arts, where he completed his chapter for this volume. In retirement he continued to be active in the Japan Society for Laughter and Humor Studies. He made a particular study of the humor of *senryū*, with a view to promoting its appreciation internationally.

JESSICA MILNER DAVIS is a Visiting Fellow in the Faculty of Arts and Social Sciences at the University of New South Wales, Sydney. She is also pro-chancellor of the university. She served as president of the International Society for Humor Studies (ISHS) in 1996–97 and again in 2003–4. As joint chair of the 1996 ISHS eighth Conference in Sydney, she established the Australasian Network of Humour Scholars and its series of annual colloquia on humor. She is a member of the Editorial Boards of *Humor: The International Journal of Humor Research* and for other series in humor. Since the 1970s, she has published and taught on the history and theory of comedy and on styles of humor.

HEIYŌ NAGASHIMA is a graduate of Kyoto University's Department of Literature. In 1991 he retired after some thirty highly regarded years as director of television for NHK (Japan Broadcasting Corporation) and turned to theater production and pursuit of his interests in humor. Since 1998 he has served as executive secretary of the Japan Society for Laughter and Humor Studies. He also specializes in performance of *rakugo*, *manzai*, and *kōdan*.

SHŌKICHI ODA is well known in Japan as the distinguished author of many published studies over the last twenty years on humor, joking, laughter, and classical Japanese humorous literature. A graduate in law from Kobe University, he has had a long and successful career as a writer and program maker for television and radio comedy. He is vice president of the Japan Society for Laughter and Humor Studies. His interests in humor embrace comic writing as well as the history and philosophy of comic forms and laughter in Japan in general, and he has written many successful scripts and jokes for both *manzai* and *rakugo*.

KIMIE ŌSHIMA is a Lecturer in Sociolinguistics and Cross-Cultural Communications in the Department of Foreign Language

Studies at Bunkyo Gakuin University in Tokyo. She holds an M.A. in international communication and a Ph.D. in sociolinguistics and is a member of the Japan Society for Laughter and Humor Studies. Since 1997 she has also been producing *rakugo* performances in English, with successful tours in the United States, Singapore, Australia, Malaysia, the Philippines, and elsewhere, as well as in Japan itself. Her publications range from a study of communicative humor in Japanese and *rakugo* in English (*eigo rakugo*) to the social function of ethnic jokes in Hawaii.

JOEL F. STOCKER is Assistant Professor in the Department of Applied English at I-Shou University, Kaohsiung, Taiwan. He contributed his chapter in this volume as Foreign Research Fellow at the National Museum of Ethnology in Suita, Japan. His dissertation in anthropology at the University of Wisconsin, Madison, dealt with the production, marketing, and consumption of comedy and the portrayals of Osakan culture by Yoshimoto Kōgyō Inc.'s New Star Creation entertainment school. His recent research deals with the history of professional *manzai* and the role of Kansai-area media companies in developing entertainers, shows, and audiences.

MAKIKO TAKEKURO is a doctoral student at the University of California at Berkeley in the Department of Linguistics. She researches linguistic politeness, cross-cultural communication, and language and gender. In humor studies, she has collected conversational jokes in movies and advertising, and she plans to investigate further the roles of jokes and joking in spontaneous discourse and their reflection of the wider social framework of language.

ROKUO TANAKA is an independent scholar who is attached to the University of Hawaii at Manoa in the Department of East Asian Languages and Literatures. He has a particular interest in traditional satiric humor and parody in Japanese literature, and he aims to complete a comprehensive history of comic verse in the Edo period, examining its spirit, forms, and intertextuality, as well as its origins and traditions, so as to promote its accessibility to an international audience.

MARGUERITE A. WELLS is former Associate Professor in Japanese and Director of the Japanese Course at the University of Wollongong (in New South Wales). She has taught at both the Australian National University and Oxford University, and she held numerous visiting appointments in Japan, including a Japanese Government Postgraduate Research Scholarship (Tokyo University, 1972–74); Visiting Fellow at the Japanese National Institute for Educational Research in Tokyo with a Fellowship from the Japan Society for the Promotion of Science (1981); Japan Foundation Fellow at Kyoto University Institute for Research in the Humanities (1987–89); and Curtin University (Western Australia) Postdoctoral Fellowship to Kyoto University (1994). She has acted professionally and trained in the Ōkura school of *kyōgen*. She publishes on Japanese theater and humor and has coauthored teaching materials on Japanese language and culture.

BIBLIOGRAPHY

Abe Goh. "Political and Social Satirical Cartoons in Nepal." In *Bungakuronsō: A Collection of Treatises on Languages and Literature*, vol. 15. Kagawa: Tokushima Bunri University, 1998.

Abe Kōbō. *Bō ni Natta Otoko: The Man Who Turned into a Stick; Three Related Plays*. Translated by Donald Keene. Tokyo: University of Tokyo Press, 1975.

Aiba Akio. *Rakugo Nyūmon*. Tokyo: Kōbun Shuppan, 1991.

Akutagawa Ryūnosuke. *Kappa*. Translated by Geoffrey Bownas. Tokyo: Tuttle, 1971.

Andō Eriko. "Kyōgen, Shōgeki to Shite no Shiten Yori." *Engekigaku*, March 1977.

Anon. "Omata no Waraikō." In *Hōfu Shi Shi: Shiryō 1—Shizen, Minzoku, Chimei*, edited by Hōfu Shi Shi Hensan I'inkai. Hōfu: Hōfu City Authority and Ōmura Printing Company, 1994.

———. "Omata no Waraikō." In *Zoku Hōfu Shi Shi*, edited by Misonoo Ōsuke. Hōfu City: Zōten Hōfu Shi Shi Kankōkai and Ōmura Printing Company, 1960.

———. "Waraikō." In *Hōfu no Minzoku Geinō o Tazunete*, edited by Hashiguchi Teruo. Hōfu City: Hōfu no Bunka o Takameru Kai, 1989.

Apte, Mahadev L. *Humor and Laughter: An Anthropological Approach*. Ithaca, N.Y.: Cornell University Press, 1985.

Aston, William G. *A History of Japanese Literature*. Tokyo: Tuttle, 1972. First published 1899.

Bangasa. Osaka: Bangasa Senryū Honsha, 1913–.

Beat Takeshi [Kitano Takeshi]. *Asakusa Kid*. Tokyo: Ōta Publishing, 1988.

Benedict, Ruth. *The Chrysanthemum and the Sword: Patterns of Japanese Culture*. Boston: Houghton Mifflin, 1946.

Bensky, Xavier. "Manzai: Metamorphoses of a Japanese Comic Performance Genre." Master's thesis, McGill University, 1998.

Bentley, Eric. *The Life of the Drama*. London: Methuen, 1996.

Bermant, Chaim. *What's the Joke? A Study of Jewish Humour through the Ages*. London: Weidenfeld & Nicholson, 1986.

Blyth, R. H. *Edo Satirical Verse Anthologies*. Tokyo: Hokuseido Press, 1961.

———. *Haiku*, 4 vols. Tokyo: Hokuseido Press, 1981.

———. *Japanese Life and Character in Senryū*. Tokyo: Hokuseido Press, 1960.

———. *Oriental Humor*. Tokyo: Hokuseido Press, 1959.

Bowen, Barbara. *Les Caractéristiques Essentielles de la Farce Française et leur Survivance dans les Années, 1550–1620*. Urbana: University of Illinois Press, 1964.

Boxer, Diana. *Complaining and Commiserating: A Speech Act View of Solidarity in Spoken American English*. New York: Peter Lang, 1993.

———. "From Bonding to Biting: Conversational Joking and Identity Display." *Journal of Pragmatics* 27 (1997).

Bremmer, Jan, and Hermann Roodenburg, eds. *A Cultural History of Humour*. Cambridge, U.K.: Polity Press, 1997.

Brown, Penelope, and S. C. Levinson. *Politeness: Some Universals in Language Usage*. Cambridge: Cambridge University Press, 1987.

Chapman, Anthony J., and Hugh Foot. *Humour and Laughter: Theory, Research, and Applications*. London: Wiley, 1976.

Chun Shin-yong. "Introduction." In *Humour in Korean Literature*, edited by International Cultural Foundation. Seoul: International Cultural Foundation, 1982.

Clifford, James. *The Predicament of Culture: Twentieth-Century Ethnography: Literature and Art*. Cambridge, Mass.: Harvard University Press, 1998.

Cohn, Joel R. *Studies in the Comic Spirit in Modern Japanese Fiction*. Cambridge, Mass.: Harvard University Press, 1998.

Condren, Conal. "Between Social Constraint and the Public Sphere: On Misreading Political Satire in Early-Modern England." *Contemporary Political Theory* 1, no. 1 (2002).

———. *Satire, Lies, and Politics: The Case of Dr. Arbuthnot*. Basingstoke: Macmillan, 1997.

Cooper, E., and Marie Jahoda. "The Evasion of Propaganda: How Prejudiced People Respond to Antiprejudice Propaganda." *Journal of Psychology*, no. 23 (1947).

Davis, Jessica Milner. *Farce*. London: Methuen, 1978. Rev. ed., New Brunswick, N.J.: Transaction, 2003.

——— [Jessica R. Milner]. "The Mechanics of European Farce." 3 vols. Ph.D. thesis, University of New South Wales, 1971.

Deep, Dhurba. *The Nepal Festival*. Kathmandu: Variety Printers, 1992.

Dower, John. *Japan in War and Peace*. London: Fontana Press / Harper Collins, 1995.

————. *War without Mercy.* New York: Pantheon Books, 1986.

Earhart, Byron. *Japanese Religion: Unity and Diversity.* 3rd ed. Belmont, Calif.: Wadsworth, 1982.

Ebara Taizō. *Ebara Taizō: Chosakushū.* Vol. 2. Tokyo: Chūō Kōronsha, 1979.

Feinberg, Leonard. *The Satirist.* Ames: Iowa State University Press, 1963.

Fukumoto Ichirō. *Haiku to Senryū.* Tokyo: Kōdansha, 1999.

Furst, Dan. "Omoshiroi Mono ja: Kyōgen as Universal Comedy." *Kyōto Journal,* Winter 1987.

Furukawa Hisashi. "Kyōgen no Fūshi." In *Nōgaku Zensho.* Edited by Nogami Toyoichirō. Tokyo: Tōkyō Sōgensha, 1980.

————. *Kyōgen no Kenkyū.* Tokyo: Fukumura Shoten, 1948.

Furusato Daidō o Horiokosu Kai, ed. *Furusato Daidō.* Vol. 3. Yamaguchi: Kobunsha, 1982. Vol. 8. Yamaguchi: Colony, 1993.

Gruner, C[harles]. R. "Dogmatism and the Understanding/Appreciation of Satire." Paper presented at the Convention of the Speech Communication Association, Chicago, 1974.

————. "An Experimental Study of Satire as Persuasion." *Speech Monographs,* no. 32 (1965).

Gun Sam-lee. "Humour in Drama." *Koreana Quarterly* 12, no. 3 (1970).

Haga Hideo. "Matsuri no Naka no Warai." *Gengo Seikatsu* 325 (1979).

Hamada Giichirō. *Edo Senryū Jiten.* Tokyo: Tōkyōdō Shuppan, 1986.

Hashimoto Hiroyuki. "Warawanai Hito ga Arimasu ka—[Owarai Geinin] no Genzō." *Nihon no Bigaku* 20 (1993)

Hearn, Lafcadio. *Glimpses of Unfamiliar Japan.* Rutland, Vt.: Tuttle, 1986. First published 1894.

Hibbett, Howard. *The Chrysanthemum and the Fish: Japanese Humor since the Age of the Shoguns.* Tokyo: Kodansha International, 2002.

Highet, Gilbert. *The Anatomy of Satire.* Princeton, N.J.: Princeton University Press, 1962.

Hodgart, Matthew. *Satire.* London: Weidenfeld and Nicolson, 1969.

Horie Seiji. *Yoshimoto Kōgyō no Kenkyū.* Tokyo: Asahi Bunko, 1994.

Horiuchi Hideaki and Akiyama Ken. *Taketori Monogatari Ise Monogatari.* In *Shin Nihon Koten Bungaku Taikei,* vol. 17. Tokyo: Iwanami Shoten, 1997.

Humor: International Journal of Humor Research. Berlin: Mouton de Gruyter, 1988–.

Ibuse Masuji. "The Charcoal Bus." In *Modern Japanese Stories*. Translated by Ivan Morris. Tokyo: Tuttle, 1962.

Iijima Yoshiharu. *Warai to Ishō*. Tokyo: Kaimeisha, 1985.

Iizawa Tadasu. "Gehin na Kyōgen." In *Shibai: Miru Tsukuru*. Tokyo: Heibonsha, 1972.

Inokuchi Shōji. "Nihon no Warai Gyōji." *Gengo* 23, no. 12 (1994).

Inoue Hiroshi. *Warai no Ningen Kankei*. Tokyo: Kōdansha, 1984.

Inoue Hisashi. "Jiguchi Ochi ni Tsuite no Mono." In *Go*, Great Essays of Japan, no. 70. Tokyo: Sakuhinsha, 1988.

Izumi Motohide, ed. *Kyōgen: Traditional and Shakespearean of Izumi School* [sic]. Japan: Izumi Souke [sic], 1993.

Jump, John D. *Burlesque*. London: Methuen, 1972.

Kanda Bōjin. *Edo Senryū o Tanoshimu*. Tokyo: Asahi Shimbunsha, 1989.

Katsura Bunji, Jippensha Ikku, et al. *Ōyose Hanashi no Shiriuma*. Japan: n.p., Tempō era, 1830–1844.

Katsura Shijaku. *Rakugo de Shijaku*. Tokyo: Chikuma Shobō, 1993.

Kawaguchi Hisao, ed. *Wakan Rōeishū Ryōjin Hishō*. In *Nihon Koten Bungaku Taikei*, vol. 73. Tokyo: Iwanami Shoten, 1965.

Keene, Donald. *Dawn to the West*. New York: Henry Holt and Co., 1987.

———. *World within Walls: Japanese Literature of the Pre-modern Era, 1600–1867*. New York: Holt Rinehart and Winston, 1976; Tokyo: Tuttle, 1978.

Kenny, Don. *A Guide to Kyōgen*. Kyoto: Hinoki Shoten, 1968.

Kindaichi Haruhiko. *Nihongo*. Rev. ed., vol. 1. Tokyo: Iwanami, 1988.

Kizugawa Kei. *Kamigata no Warai: Manzai to Rakugo*. Tokyo: Kōdansha, 1984.

Kōjien. 2nd ed. Tokyo: Iwanami Shoten, 1955; 5th ed. Tokyo: Iwanami Shoten, 1998.

Kojiki, trans. Donald L. Philippi. Princeton and Tokyo: Princeton University Press and University of Tokyo Press, 1969.

Kokubungaku Kaishaku to Kanshō. *Bungei Yōgo no Kiso Chishiki*. Tokyo: Tōbundō, 1983.

Kokumin Bunko Kankōkai, ed. *Kyōka Kyōgen*. Tokyo: Kokumin Bunko Kankōkai, 1913.

Koyama Hiroshi, ed. "Nihon Koten Bungaku Taikei." In *Kyōgenshū*, 2 vols. Tokyo: Iwanami Shoten, 1960, 1961.

Kurahashi Ken. *Engeki Eiga Buyō Terebi Opera Hyakka*. Tokyo: Heibonsha, 1983.

Kyōgen Ōashū. In *Kyōka Kyōgen*. Tokyo: Kokumin Bunko Kankōkai, 1913.

Lebra, T. Sugiyama. *Japanese Patterns of Behavior.* Honolulu: University of Hawaii Press, 1976.

Lee Jae-son. "Laughter in the Literature of the Enlightenment Period." In *Humour in Korean Literature.* Edited by International Cultural Foundation. Seoul: International Cultural Foundation, 1982.

Maeda Isamu, ed. *Kamigata Engei Jiten.* Tokyo: Tōkyōdō Shuppan, 1966.

Man'yōshū. In *Nihon Koten Bungaku Zenshū,* edited by Kojima Noriyuki et al., vol. 5. Tokyo: Shōgakkan, 1992.

Manzai Kyōkashū. In *Kyōka Kyōgen,* edited by Kokumin Bunko Kankōkai. Tokyo: Kokumin Bunko Kankōkai, 1913.

Matsumoto Hitoshi. *Matsumoto Bōzu.* Tokyo: Rokkingu On, [January] 1999.

Matsumoto Shigeru. *Motoori Norinaga, 1730–1801.* Cambridge: Harvard University Press, 1970.

Matsushita Kōnosuke. *Shōbai Kokoroechō.* Tokyo: PHP Research Institute, 1973.

Maynard, Senko. "On Back-channel Behavior in Japanese and English Casual Conversation." *Linguistics* 24 (1986).

Mibu Kyōgen Dainembutsukō, eds. *Mibu Kyōgen Kaisetsu.* Kyoto: Ishihara Ōbundō, 1999.

Mikes, George. *Humour in Memoriam.* London: Routledge and Kegan Paul, 1970.

Miller, G. R., and P. Bacon. "Open- and Closed-mindedness and Recognition of Visual Humour." *Journal of Communication,* no. 21 (1971).

Minemura Fumito, ed. *Shin Kokin Wakashū.* In *Nihon Koten Bungaku Zenshū,* vol. 26. Tokyo: Shōgakkan, 1992.

Mita Jun'ichi. *Shōwa Kamigata Shōgeishi.* Tokyo: Gakugei Shorin, 1993.

Miyake Kazuko. "Nihonjin no Gengo Kōdō Patān—Uchi, Soto, Yoso Ishiki—." In *Tsukuba Daigaku Ryūgakusei Center Nihongo Kyōiku Ronshū,* vol. 9. Tokyo: Tsukuba University, 1994.

Morrison, Terry. *Kiss, Bow, or Shake Hands.* Tokyo: Macmillan Language House, 1999.

Murasaki Shikibu [the Lady Murasaki]. *The Tale of Genji.* Translated by Edward G. Seidensticker. Tokyo: Charles E. Tuttle & Co., 1978.

Nagashima Heiyō, ed. "Sha-re-, Dajare-gaku Koto Hajime." Report of a symposium between panelists Oda Shōkichi, Nomura Masaaki, W. Young, and Nagashima Heiyō, in *Waraigaku Kenkyū,* no. 6. Osaka: JSLHS, 1999.

Nakamura Akira, *Nihongo Rhetoric no Taikei.* Tokyo: Iwanami, 1991.

Nanba Toshizō. *Shōsetsu Yoshimoto Kōgyō.* Tokyo: Bungei Shunjū, 1991.

Natsume Sōseki. *Botchan.* Translated by Sasaki Umeji. Tokyo: Tuttle, 1968.

———. "Bungaku Hyōron." In *Sōseki Zenshū,* vol. 10. Tokyo: Iwanami Shoten, 1966.

———. *I Am a Cat.* Translated by Aiko Ito and Graeme Wilson. Tokyo: Tuttle, 1972.

Nelson, Andrew N. *Japanese-English Character Dictionary.* Tokyo: Tuttle, 1978.

Nihon Koten Bungaku Daijiten Henshū I'inkai, eds. *Nihon Koten Bungaku Daijiten,* vol. 4. Tokyo: Iwanami Shoten, 1984.

Nitobe, Inazo [Niitobe Inazō]. *Bushido: The Soul of Japan.* New York: Putnam, 1905.

Nomura Masaaki. *Rakugo no Rhetoric.* Select Books of Heibonsha, no. 165. Tokyo, 1996.

Oda Shōkichi. *Nihon no Yūmoa: Koten Setsuwahen.* 2nd ed. Tokyo: Chikuma Shobō, 1987.

———. *Nihon no Yūmoa.* Tokyo: Chikuma Shobō, 1986.

———. *Warai to Yūmoa.* Tokyo: Chikuma Shobō, 1979.

Okada Asatarō. *Kansei Kaikaku to Yanagidaru no Kaihan.* Tokyo: Isobe Kōyōdō, 1927.

Okada Hajime, ed. *Haifū Yanagidaru Zenshū.* 12 vols and index. Tokyo: Sanseidō, 1976–78, 1984.

Okitsu Kaname. *Edo no Warai.* In *Shōnen Shōjo Koten Bungakukan,* vol. 24. Tokyo: Kōdansha, 1992.

Ōmi Sajin and Fujiwara Seiken. *Senryū Nyūmon.* Osaka: Hoikusha, 1977.

O'Neill, P. G. *A Guide to Nō.* Kyoto: Hinoki Shoten, 1954.

Onoe Keisuke. *Ōsaka Kotobagaku.* Tokyo: Sōgensha, 1999.

Osada Chūichi [Osada Shūtō]. "Futsukoku Engeki Genjō." *Waseda Bungaku,* March 1894.

———. "Futsukoku Kigeki." *Waseda Bungaku,* May 1894.

Ōshima Kimie. "Rakugo: Sit-Down Comedy." *Humor and Health Journal* 8, no. 3 (1998).

Panday, Ram Kumar. "The Himalayan Heritage of Humour." Paper presented at the eighth ISHS Conference, University of New South Wales, Sydney, Australia, July 2000.

———. *Nepalese Humour.* Kathmandu: Muskan Prakashan, 2000.

Park, C. K. "Biting Satire on Conglomerates a Hit." *Korea Herald,* November 5, 1987.

Pollard, Arthur. *Satire.* London: Methuen, 1970.

Potts, L. J. *Comedy.* London: Hutchinson University Library, 1949.

Rutt, Richard. "Kim Sakkat, the Popular Humorist." In *Humour in Korean Literature,* edited by International Cultural Foundation. Seoul: International Cultural Foundation, 1982.

Sakanishi Shio. *Japanese Folk-Plays: The Ink-Smeared Lady and Other Kyōgen.* Tokyo: Tuttle, 1960.

Sakuramoto Tomio. *Sensō to Manga.* Tokyo: Sōdosha, 2000.

Sanryū Bitō, ed. *Senryū Sōgō Jiten.* Tokyo: Yūzankaku Publishing, 1984.

Sarariiman Senryū Kessakusen. Tokyo: Kōdansha, 2000.

Sasano Ken, ed. *Nō-kyōgen,* by Ōkura Toraaki. 3 vols. Tokyo: Iwanami Bunko, 1942, 1943, 1945.

———. *Warambegusa,* by Ōkura Toraaki. Tokyo: Iwanami Bunko, 1962.

Scollon, Ronald, and Suzanne W. Scollon. *Intercultural Communication.* Oxford: Blackwell, 1995.

Senryū. Osaka: Shinyōkan Publishing, 2001–.

Senryū Manga to Banzuke Iroiro: Shakai Hyakumensō. Tokyo: Dai Nihon Yūbenkai Kōdansha, 1931.

Shimizu Isao. *Taiheiyō Senki no Manga.* Tokyo: Bijutsu Dōjinsha, Tokyo, 1971.

Shimoyama Hiroshi. *Edo Ko-Senryū no Sekai.* Tokyo: Kōdansha, 1994.

Shin'engei. July 1918.

Shinmura Izuru, ed. *Kōjien.* 2nd ed. Tokyo: Iwanami Shoten, 1955.

Sugimoto Nagashige and Hamada Giichiro, eds. *Senryū Kyōshi.* In *Nihon Koten Bungaku Taikei,* vol. 57. Tokyo: Iwanami Shoten, 1958.

Sugiura Mimpei. "Gekokujōteki Shakai no Katami: Kyōgen." In *Bungaku,* vol. 32. Tokyo: Iwanami Shoten, 1964.

Suzuki Katsutada. *Senryū Zappai Edo Shomin no Sekai.* Tokyo: Miki Shobū, 1996.

Taho Akira. "Taishō Bunka no Shakaiteki Kōsei: Kindai 'Manzai' no Seiritsu o Jirei ni." In *Jinbu Ronsō,* vol. 28. Osaka: Osaka City University, 2000.

Takekuro Makiko. "Conversational Jokes as a Politeness Strategy: Observations from English and Japanese," Japan Women's University, Tokyo, *Journal of the Graduate School of Humanities* 4 (1997).

Tale of the Heike, The. Translated by Kitagawa Hiroshi and Bruce T. Tsuchida. Tokyo: University of Tokyo Press, 1975.

Tanabe Seiko. *Senryū Dendendaiko.* Tokyo: Kōdansha, 1988.

Tanaka Hatohei. "Kamigata Engei no Nagare." *Sōzō Suru Shimin* 40 (1994).

Tanaka Rokuo. "Ishikawa Masamochi and the Shokunin-zukushi Kyōka Awase." Master's thesis, University of Hawaii, August 1977.

Tanaka Yukinari. *Daidō Gei no Mukashi.* Hōfu City: Kōbunsha, 1980.

Teruoka Yasutaka and Gunji Masakatsu. *Edo Shimin Bungaku no Kaika (Nihon no Bungaku* series). Tokyo: Shibundō, 1967.

Test, George A. *Satire: Spirit and Art.* Tampa: University of South Florida Press, 1991.

Togazawa Hidetoshi and Takano Satoshi. "Warai no Kagaku." *Mainichi Shimbun,* January 3, 1997.

Tōi Jun. *Edo Senryū no Jōjō o Tanoshimu.* Osaka: Shinyokan Publishing, 2004.

Toku Wakago Manzaishū. In *Senryū Kyōshi,* edited by Sugimoto Nagashige and Hamada Giichiro, in *Nihon Koten Bungaku Taikei,* vol. 57. Tokyo: Iwanami Shoten, 1958.

Tsubouchi Shōyō. "Ikanaru Hito ga Mottomo Yoku." *Waseda Bungaku,* January 3, 1898.

Ueda Makoto. *Bashō and His Interpreters: Selected Hokku with Commentary.* Stanford, Calif.: Stanford University Press, 1991.

Umesao Tadao, Kindaichi Haruhiko, et al. *Nihongo Daijiten.* Tokyo: Kōdansha, 1989.

Utsuo Kiyoaki. *Edo Senryū: Haifū Yanagidaru.* Osaka: Yōbunkan Publishing, 1998.

Wagner, Roy. *The Invention of Culture.* Rev. ed. Chicago: University of Chicago Press, 1980.

Wells, Marguerite. "The Decline of the Japanese Laugh." Paper given at the Nissan Institute of Japanese Studies, Oxford University, January 23, 1987.

———. *Japanese Humour.* Basingstoke: Macmillan, 1997.

———. "The Search for a Word." Paper delivered at the conference of the European Association for Japanese Studies, Budapest, 1997.

Wetzel, Patricia. "Are 'Powerless' Communication Strategies the Japanese Norm?" *Language in Society* 17 (1988).

Yamada Haru. *American and Japanese Business Discourse: A Comparison of Interactional Styles.* Norwood, N.J.: Ablex, 1992.

Yamaji Kanko. *Kosenryū Meiku Sen.* Tokyo: Chikuma Shobō, 1968.

Yamasawa Hideo, ed. *Haifū Yanagidaru.* Vol. 1. Tokyo: Iwanami Bunko, Iwanami Shoten, 1995.

Yong Suk-kee. "Laughter in the Korean Traditional Drama." In *Humour in Korean Literature*, edited by International Cultural Foundation. Seoul: International Cultural Foundation, 1982.

Yoshida Seiichi and Hamada Giichirō, eds. *Senryūshū Kyōkashū*. In *Koten Nihon Bungaku Zenshū*, vol. 33. Tokyo: Chikuma Shobō, 1961.

Yoshikawa, Muneo Jay. "Popular Performing Arts: Manzai and Rakugo." In *Handbook of Japanese Popular Culture*, edited by Richard Gid Powers, Hidetoshi Kato, and Bruce Stronach. New York: Greenwood Press, 1989.

Yoshikoshi Emiko. "Warai no Kaishaku—Atsuta Jingū Suishōjinji o Rei to Shite." *Geinō* 33, no. 6 (1991).

Yoshimoto Kōgyō Ltd., ed. *Yoshimoto Hachijūnen no Ayumi*. Osaka: Yoshimoto Kōgyō Ltd., 1992.

INDEX

Abbott, Bud, and Lou Costello, 59
Abe Kōbō, 127
absurdism, 127, 128
Achako
    and *shabekuri manzai*, 57, 58,
      59–61, 62, 65
acting style in *kyōgen*, 5, 141–3,
    149
advertising. *See* Japanese television
aggression
    extended metaphor and, 208
    farce and, 149, 207–8, 208–9
    kyōgen and, 147, 208–9
    satire and, 207–8, 209, 210
aidoru (idols), 2, 68. *See also* "idol"
    manzai teams
Akera Kankō
    and *kyōka*, 114, 115, 116, 119
Akera-ren, 115, 119
Akita Minoru
    and scripted *manzai*, 59
Akutagawa Ryūnosuke, 208
Amaterasu Ōmikami (Sun Goddess)
    and laughter, 4, 13
ancient poetry
    humor in, 5–6, 111–12
anonymity
    humorous columns in news-
      papers and, 7, 182–83
    of place in satire, 208
    senryū and, 7, 159
Apte, Mahadev L.
    on humor and mass media, 70
Asahi Shimbun, 2. *See also* "Kata-
    ekubo" column (*Asahi Shim-
    bun*); "Tensei Jingo" column
    (*Asahi Shimbun*)
Asahina, 134, 143–44
Aston, William G.
    on *kyōka*, 113

audience for satire, 207
auspicious plays
    and *kyōgen*, 132, 133, 137
    See also under *manzai*
authority. *See* conventional autho-
    rity

Baika Shin'eki (pub. Akera Kankō),
    115
Bangasa, 171
bargaining, 30
The Battle of the Books (Jonathan
    Swift), 194
Beat Takeshi (Kitano Takeshi), 9, 66
Beaumarchais, Pierre-Augustin
    Caron de, 5
Benedict, Ruth
    on shame of being laughed at,
      16
Bensky, Xavier
    on changing audience for
      entertainment in *yose*, 57
Bentley, Eric
    on farce and aggression, 208
"blind man" *kyōgen*, 140
Blyth, R. H.
    on *kyōka*, 113
    on *senryū*, 166, 198–200
Bō Shibari (*Tied to a Staff*), 136,
    137, 139
boke (the fool)
    in "free talk" style shows, 68
    in humorous communication,
      105–6
    in *manzai*, 5, 29, 51, 57, 60,
      61, 62, 67
    See also *tsukkomi*
Botchan (Natsume Sōseki), 196
Buddhism
    and *rakugo*, 99

and obscene humor, 9
conventional authority, challenge to
and farce, 127, 128, 129, 145,
147, 149
and *kyōgen*, 139, 145–47 (see
also *gekokujō*)
and satire, 6, 145, 147, 210
See also comic rebellion
conversational comedy
and *rakugo*, 104–6
conversational jokes, 78, 85
definition, 86
in Japanese and English-language movies (and televi-
sion) and actual conversation, 2
in business environment,
94–95
examples, 91–93
frequency of and degree of
formality in relationship
between participants, 2,
89–90, 95
qualitative differences, 91–94
in relation to total utterances, 87–89
and rhetorical differences
between Japanese and
English, 94
and sociocultural norms,
94–96
method chosen for study of,
86–87
See also jokes and joking
creativity. *See* culture of originality
critical jests. *See* comic criticisms
culture of bargaining
negotiation and, 30–31
culture of originality
and flexibility, 31
culture of shame/guilt. *See* "guilt
cultures"; "shame cultures"

Daido-Omata District
and Warai-kō, 42, 46
Daikon no Hana (Radish Flower),
91

daily life in Osaka
and laughter, 29–30
daimyō (big landowner, feudal
lord), 146
daimyō kyōgen (great-name
kyōgen), 146
Davis, Jessica Milner
on farce, 128–29, 132, 149
Dazai Osamu, 10
deshi (rakugo apprentices), 100,
102. See also *rakugo*
dirty jokes, 148
discourtesy. *See* rudeness
*Dochi Hagure (Between East and
West)*, 145
DownTown. *See* Hamada
Masatoshi ("DownTown");
Matsumoto Hitoshi

Earhart, Byron
on *kami*, 41–2
Edo period
humor in, 112–13
kyōka in, 123
Edo *senryū*, 154
emotions
Japanese classification of, 17
Japanese control of, 16–17
Japanese expression of,
15–16
empathy
and farce, 130–31
See also romantic comedy;
sentimental comedy
English-language conversational
jokes, compared with Japanese.
See under conversational jokes
engo (intertextually associated
words), 122
equilibrium or quarrel farces, 129,
130, 139–40
kyōgen and, 135, 136, 137
Erewhon (Samuel Butler), 208
The Essence of the Novel
(Tsubouchi Shōyō), 212
excretion
and laughter, 17

Iizawa Tadasu
    on *kyōgen*, 146
Ikuji no Naishi
    and *kyōka*, 121
Ikutama Shrine (Osaka)
    manzai at, 52, 55
illustrations accompanying *senryū*
    and types of humor, 200, 201,
    202
Inoue Hiroshi
    on Japanese gods, 41
Inoue Hisashi, 9, 10
    on *sha-re*, 77–78
Inoue Kenkabō, 170
internalized standards
    and externalized standards,
    211–12
interpersonal relations
    jokes and humor in, 6–7, 105,
    106–7
    perceptions of and conversa-
    tional jokes in Japanese and
    American English, 2, 95–96
iromono (variety acts), 53
irony, 210
    and criticism, 187
    pen names, 121
    and *senryū*, 24, 161, 166–67,
    171, 200
Izumi school of *kyōgen*, 131, 136

Japan Society for Laughter and Hu-
    mor Studies (JSLHS), 34n10
Japanese conversational jokes,
    compared with English-language
    conversational jokes. *See under*
    conversational jokes
Japanese culture
    and externalized standards,
    212
    and European classifications,
    193
Japanese economy and politics
    and complacency and cyni-
    cism, 212–13
    humor and, 2
    See also political caricatures;

political criticism; political
    leaders; political oppression;
    political satire
Japanese entertainment industry
    and *manzai*, 51, 54, 57–66
    See also Yoshimoto Kōgyō
    Inc.
Japanese expression of emotions,
    15–16
Japanese festivals
    and ritual performances of
    laughter, 38, 41
    See also *warai* ([ritual perfor-
    mances of] laughter)
Japanese folk religion
    and *warai*, 41
Japanese humor, 1, 13
    in ancient poetry, 5–6,
    111–12
    in Edo period, 112–13
    and festivals, 37
    and *haikai-renga*, 21
    and *haiku*, 19, 20
    in interpersonal relations,
    105, 106
    Japanese words for, 8, 194 (see
    also *haikai; yūmoa*)
    literature on, 10
    negative aspects of, 148 (*see
    also* containment; expurga-
    tion)
    newspaper writers and, 190
    in newspapers, 1–2, 179–90
    and novels, 10–11
    and obscenity, 8–9
    performance forms of (see
    kyōgen; manzai; rakugo)
    and political criticism, 187
    (*see also* comic criticisms)
    and political leaders, 189
    scatological, 9
    and *senryū*, 20, 23–24 (see
    also under *senryū*)
    stereotypes in, 106
    study of, 11–12
    in television advertising, 75,
    80–82

238

jokes and joking (*continued*)
  and rhetorical differences
    between Japanese and
    English, 94
  and sociocultural norms,
    94–96
  narrative jokes, 78, 106 (see
    also *rakugo*)
  and *sha-re*, 78
  western style, 106
  See also dirty jokes; *neta*
    jokes; toilet jokes
jōruri (puppet theater), 112
jōryū no komedii, 130

ka-chō-fū-getsu (flowers, birds,
  wind, and moon)
  and *haiku*, 164
kabuki, 5, 9–10, 112
kadozuke manzai (door-to-door or
  gate *manzai*), 52, 68
kakeai (repartee), 68
kakekotoba (pivot words), 76. *See
  also* punning
kami ("gods"), 41–42
  warai (ritual performances of
    laughter) and, 42
Kamigata Manzai Ōkoku, 63, 64
Kamigata Manzai Taishō contest,
  63
Kanda Bōjin
  on *senryū*, 166
Kaneko Michi. *See* Chie no Naishi
Kappa (Akutagawa Ryūnosuke), 208
Karagoromo Kisshū, 115
Karai Senryū (Karai Hachiemon),
  22, 156, 158, 159
karukuchi (a comedy-patter genre),
  68, 69, 101
karumi (lightness)
  in *senryū*, 170
"Kataekubo" column (*Asahi
  Shimbun*), 179–80, 180–81, 182
Keene, Donald
  on humor, 10
Ki no Sadamaru, 114
kibyōshi, 112

Kichibei, 58
kigeki (comedy), 8, 30, 127, 194.
  See also comedy; *Shōchiku
  Shinkigeki*; *Yoshimoto
  Shinkigeki*
kigo (season words)
  in *haiku*, 23, 164, 170
  and *senryū*, 171
Kim Hyong-gon, 205
kireji (cutting words)
  in *haiku*, 164, 165
  and *senryū*, 171
kō (mutual aid society), 42, 48
Kobayashi Issa, 165
Kobe
  ban on *manzai* in, 54
kōdan recitation, 53
Kojiki, 4
kōkyū manzai (high-class *manzai*),
  54–57
Konishiki, 81
konto manzai (skit *manzai*), 61–62
Korea
  punning in, 193
  satire in, 204–5, 206, 207
kosenryū (old *senryū*), 154, 156
Kozue no Yuki (*Snow on the Treetops*), 119
kusuguri (tickle, or jab of laughter)
  in *rakugo*, 102, 103, 104–5
kyōgen, 5
  and aggression, 147, 208–9
  and auspicious plays, 132, 133
  and challenge to conventional
    authority, 139, 145–47 (see
    also *gekokujō*)
  classification of, 193–94
  and comedy, 131, 194
  and comic punishments,
    139–41
  complex plots, 136–39
  and empathy, 143, 144
  and equilibrium or quarrel
    farce, 135, 136, 137
  as farce, 5, 132–36, 146, 149,
    150, 206
  combination of types, 136,

"USO Hōsō" column
Yomo no Akara, 115
Yong Suk-kee
    on farce and aggression, 207–8
"Yoroku" column (*Mainichi
    Shimbun*), 189
yose (variety halls)
    changing audience for enter-
      tainment in, 57
    in Osaka, 53
    and *rakugo* performance, 53,
      99, 101
    Yoshimoto Kōgyō Inc. and
      low-priced admission to,
      58–59
Yoshimoto Comedy Theater
    (Osaka), 30
Yoshimoto Kōgyō Inc.
    and low-priced admission to

    yose, 58–59
    and *manzai*, 51, 54, 57–66, 70
    market consolidation of *yose*
      and entertainers by, 59
    and *shabekuri manzai*, 57–66
    See also New Star Creation
      (NSC) school
Yoshimoto Sei, 57, 58
Yoshimoto Shinkigeki, 30
You're Right, Mr. Chairman, 204–5
yūgen
    and expression of emotions,
      15–16
    and *haiku*, 20
yūmoa (humor), 8, 194. *See also*
    humor

Zeami
    on *nō* and *kyōgen*, 131